Putin's War in Syria

Putin's War in Syria

Russian Foreign Policy and the Price of America's Absence

Anna Borshchevskaya

I.B. TAURIS

LONDON • NEW YORK • OXFORD • NEW DELHI • SYDNEY

I.B. TAURIS
Bloomsbury Publishing Plc
50 Bedford Square, London, WC1B 3DP, UK
1385 Broadway, New York, NY 10018, USA
29 Earlsfort Terrace, Dublin 2, Ireland

BLOOMSBURY, I.B. TAURIS and the I.B. Tauris logo are trademarks of
Bloomsbury Publishing Plc

First published in Great Britain 2022

Cover design by www.paulsmithdesign.com
Cover image: President Vladimir Putin, 2018. (© LUDOVIC MARIN/AFP/Getty Images)

A catalogue record for this book is available from the British Library.

Names: Borshchevskaya, Anna, author.
Title: Putin's war in Syria : Russian foreign policy and the price of America's absence /
Anna Borshchevskaya.
Description: London ; New York : I.B. TAURIS, 2021. |
Includes bibliographical references and index.
Identifiers: LCCN 2021010173 (print) | LCCN 2021010174 (ebook) |
ISBN 978-0-7556-3463-7 (hardback) | ISBN 978-0-7556-3464-4 (epub) |
ISBN 978-0-7556-3465-1 (pdf) | ISBN 978-0-7556-3466-8 (ebook other)
Subjects: LCSH: Russia (Federation)—Foreign relations—Syria. | Syria—Foreign
relations—Russia (Federation) | Syria—History—Civil War, 2011—Participation,
Russian. | Russia (Federation)—Foreign relations—Middle East. |
Middle East—Foreign relations—Russia (Federation)
Classification: LCC DK68.7.S95 B67 2021 (print) | LCC DK68.7.S95 (ebook) |
DDC 956.9104/23347—dc23
LC record available at https://lccn.loc.gov/2021010173
LC ebook record available at https://lccn.loc.gov/2021010174

ISBN: HB: 978-0-7556-3463-7
         ePDF: 978-0-7556-3465-1
         eBook: 978-0-7556-3464-4

Typeset by RefineCatch Limited, Bungay, Suffolk
Printed and bound in Great Britain

To find out more about our authors and books visit www.bloomsbury.com
and sign up for our newsletters

Contents

Preface and Acknowledgments

From the moment I began studying the Middle East in the early 2000s, I saw many issues that overlapped with Russia. Later, in the summer of 2008, I spent three months in Syria as a graduate student studying Arabic; Syria, like no other country I had visited, felt Soviet to me, and I had experienced the Soviet Union firsthand as a child. You could feel the fear permeating the air in Syria when you walked down the street, while pictures of Bashar al-Assad looked down at the people; you could see the stagnation, dysfunction, corruption, and the growing dissatisfaction, especially among the youth. Syrians often expressed respect towards the Soviet Union if I mentioned that I was born in Russia; unsurprisigly, they did not do the same about the United States, at least not in public, when they learned I was American. Several years later, when protests broke out in Syria in March 2011, I could not say I was entirely surprised.

When I began writing about Russia's Middle East policy, it was an understudied topic. Since the fall of the Soviet Union, Russia's relationship with Europe (both Eastern and Western) has received primary attention; few focused in detail on Russia's relationship with the East. Putin's intervention in Syria took many by surprise and highlighted this gap. Increasingly, scholars and analysts are devoting their attention to it. I hope this book contributes to a better understanding not only of the intervention and Russia's overall Middle East policy, but also what it means more broadly about Russia, its relationship with the West, as well as with itself. As more information comes to light about the Syrian intervention in the coming the years, I hope research and discussion of Russia in the Middle East will conintue to improve.

I am especially grateful to professor Mark N. Katz, who has followed the Kremlin's Middle East policy for decades, and whose knowledge and experience, as well as his reading of earlier draft chapters has been invaluable in helping me write this book. I am also especially grateful to the Washington Institute for Near East Policy, which has provided me with the opportunity to research and write on Russia in the Middle East at a time when few were paying attention to this topic, and for continued support of my work. Parts of this book are drawn from my earlier analysis, and to that end I am grateful to the Institute's Executive Director, Rob Satloff, and Research Director, Patrick Clawson.

I am also grateful to my colleagues, including Andrew Tabler, whom I first met when I travelled to Syria, for his knowledge of the country, and for reviewing several draft chapters; to Bilal Wahab, Hanin Ghaddar, and Philip Smyth for conversations about the region and US policy as they pertained to this book.

I also would like to thank an anonymous US military source for reviewing another chapter, as well as Miriam Lanskoy and Stephen Blank for conversations about Russia and support of this project. I am also thankful to my publisher and editor, Tomasz Hoskins, for his insightful edits; Andrew Devine, whose copy edits further improved the manuscript, to project manager Merv Honeywood for his patience and flexibility during the production process, and to John Silvester for indexing the book.

I would also like to thank Professor Michael Mandelbaum and Anne Mandlebuam for years of mentorship and friendship, and my family for their support. Of course any mistakes are my own.

Introduction

The Assad family ruled Syria for decades in one of the world's most repressive dictatorships. Then the so-called "Arab spring" protest spread throughout the Arab world starting in early 2010. In Syria these initially peaceful protests broke out throughout the country in March 2011 demanding government reform. Bashar al-Assad responded with violence and repression. As events unfolded over the coming years, many have described it as Syria's civil war. But that description obfuscates an incredibly complex reality. The sheer multitude of actors that have become involved in Syria makes it impossible to find an analogue in the recent history of conflicts. Even the 1992–5 Bosnian war with its ethnic cleansing had fewer actors involved. On top of the backdrop of civil war, the Assad regime unleashed ethnic cleansing against his own Sunni population. Syria became a haven for terrorists and a source of massive refugee flows into Europe—a bleeding wound that Western officials could ill afford to ignore. But counter-intuitively, this situation increased hesitation about any major military involvement. Syria also turned into a cynical great-power playground—it has emerged as the great example of Iranian determination to dominate the region, a litmus test for Turkey's shifting priorities, and perhaps the most important space in which Russia's great-power ambitions compete with the West.

The focus of this book is the latter, on Russia's role in Syria, and how the Middle East fits into broader Russian foreign policy. It is about how the Russian intervention in Syria changed the tide of the war in the context of Western ambivalence, and the tragedy that American absence brought about. It is also about how Putin's Russia constructed its relationships in the Middle East and leveraged them to support its Syria intervention. Putin has learned certain key lessons from the recent past—including from the Soviet experience in Afghanistan to conduct a very different and much more successful campaign in Syria—a campaign which, from a military perspective, will likely serve as a guide for future Russian operations. This book is, thus, also about the Kremlin's lessons learned from Syria. Lastly, it is about how the West sees Russia, and what it gets wrong.

Another Afghanistan?

On September 30, 2015 the Russian military intervened in Syria to prop up Assad. Moscow had been supporting Assad in previous years in multiple ways, but Vladimir Putin raised the stakes to the next level by bringing in the military, a move that took the West by surprise. Why would Putin do this? After all, the Russian economy had been in a downward spiral for years. Moscow was already involved in a conflict of its own making in Ukraine after Putin illegally annexed Crimea. Moreover, Syria does not border Russia. Unlike Ukraine, Syria lies outside the former Soviet Union, that is, outside what Moscow still considers its "privileged sphere of influence." Why does Syria matter to the Kremlin so much that it risks fighting a two-front war it seems unable to sustain? Indeed, the last time Moscow undertook an explicit military intervention outside the (now former) Soviet Union was in Afghanistan in 1979, a costly intervention that, according to conventional wisdom, contributed to the Soviet Union's eventual unraveling.

And indeed the ghosts of Afghanistan appeared as soon as Putin's Syria intervention began, both in Russia and in the West. Many misjudged Russia's intervention. A number of Russian and Western analysts predicted that Russia's entry into the Syrian crisis would cause Russia to overreach, put the state into a situation of a quagmire, similar to the Soviet experience in Afghanistan. Three days after Moscow's 2015 Syria intervention, then-US president Barak Obama said, "An attempt by Russia and Iran to prop up Assad and try to pacify the population is just going to get them stuck in a quagmire and it won't work."[1] As the Russian military campaign began, the Pentagon claimed that the Russian strategy was "doomed to failure."[2] In March 2016, six months after the intervention, when Putin announced his first faux "withdrawal" from Syria, *The New York Times* reported that according to US officials Putin "had reached a turning point in his campaign, where the costs, domestically and internationally, of staying engaged outweighed the advantages."[3] Approximately two years later, President Trump's former national security advisor John Bolton also said that Russia was "stuck" in Syria.[4]

Yet at the time of writing, more than five long years after the intervention, Putin has been able to achieve many of his key objectives in Syria without incurring crippling costs—in what turned into the longest overt Russian military engagement abroad since the Afghan war. As far as Putin is concerned, an erosion of a US-led global order is a step closer with Assad's victory in Syria. Assad, who unleashed one of the worst humanitarian tragedies since World War II, remains in power, while what is left of the opposition is weak and demoralized. Assad faces many problems of his own but is increasingly looking at acceptance from Middle East leaders, while Western leaders are largely absent from the ongoing Syria tragedy. As a matter of perception, Putin officially returned Russia to the Middle East as a great power and as a mediator that can talk to all sides. When he brought the Russian military into the Syrian theater, he forced the West into dialogue on his terms. Syria now is the one arena where the West *has* to talk to Russia. In Russia itself, while Syria gave Putin a brief domestic popularity boost, the Russian public appears more focused on a myriad of pressing concerns closer to home, even as a slim majority, according to polls, would like to see Russia end its involvement in Syria. To be sure, Moscow also faces serious obstacles in Syria. But domestically, the costs have not yet outweighed the benefits.

A Failure of Imagination

The famous 9/11 Commission report, tasked with creating a "complete account of the circumstances surrounding the September 11, 2001 terrorist attacks" on the United States, had concluded that US officials misunderstood the true threat of al-Qaeda due to a "failure of imagination."[5] Over a decade after the report's release, that same failure of imagination continues to plague Western policymakers who could neither anticipate the Russian intervention in Syria, nor accurately assess its true significance. Statecraft and military affairs are an art, not a science, and quantitative data such as the state of a country's economy cannot always account for deeper motivation of human behavior. Far from severely crippling the country, Russia's Syria intervention put on full display, for all to see, that it had developed the confidence and ability to push back against the West and its way of war, while the West remained oblivious to this reality, consumed with other priorities.

How has Putin, to date, avoided a situation where the costs of being in Syria outweigh the benefits the Kremlin derives from it? To answer this question, this book reviews Putin's apparent determination to avoid another Afghanistan in Syria. More than anything, Russians themselves (whether pro- or anti-Putin) talked about Afghanistan in the context of the Syria intervention—either a fear of getting sucked into a quagmire, or of the need to avoid it. The book describes and assesses Putin's Syria campaign from political/diplomatic, military, economic, and domestic political angles. It traces what steps the Russian government took in Syria from each of these angles, what costs and benefits the Kremlin reaped, to the extent that it is possible to calculate these costs, and reviews Moscow's relationship with Iran. It also discusses the role of the West and other actors in Syria in terms of how it relates to how Putin's intervention fared. But first, the book places Syria into the broader context of Russian foreign policy, and Middle East policy in particular.

Western studies of Russia have been traditionally skewed towards its interests in Europe, but the Russian state historically worried to the same degree, if not more, about its southern frontiers—Central Asia, the Caucasus, and the Middle East. The new Biden administration appears set to continue on the path of its two predecessors—pivoting away from the Middle East. This approach is guided by the belief that great-power competition is first and foremost with China, so the Middle East is a distraction and a drain on resources. Such a belief is misguided. It is wrong to dismiss Russia as a mere declining power that cannot thwart Western interests. Competition with China, for its part, need not be at the expense of ignoring other key strategic challenges. As for the Middle East, it is, and always has been, a central arena for any great-power competition. Thus the West cannot truly compete with Russia (and China) if it ignores the Middle East.

Certain aspects of Putin's approach to Syria and the Middle East are transactional, tactical, and unique to his reign, but others have enduring, historic resonance to Russian policymakers. These aspects are connected with perceptions of geostrategic threats and vulnerabilities and Russia's place in the world, as well as deeper unresolved identity issues. They began centuries before Putin, and will continue after Putin is gone—in the Middle East and beyond.

Part One

Russia and the Middle East

1

Tsarist Russia's History in the Middle East and North Africa

Far from an arbitrary whim of the latest Russian authoritarian, Putin's Syria intervention highlighted longstanding Russian interests, fears, and ambitions. Thus, a brief discussion of Russian history insofar as it relates to the Middle East and the Muslim world is crucial to understanding Putin's Russia and its intervention in Syria.

Russia's Identity, Fears, and Early Links to the Middle East

Internal debate over centuries about where Russia belongs—in the East or the West—has shaped, and continues to shape, Russia's foreign policy. Nikolai Berdyaev famously wrote that within "the Russian soul," East and West are in a continuous state of conflict.[1] This unresolved identity crisis has been a constant theme throughout Russia's history. Russia's early development resembled the Ottoman Empire, a growing nation that absorbed lands on its periphery. By contrast, Western European empires such as the British Empire conquered and held colonies separated geographically from the countries themselves. Thus, at least partly due to geographical separation, these countries developed their own identities, separate from their colonies. Russia did not. As prominent Russia historian Geoffrey Hosking argued, in Russia imperialism dominated the idea of nationhood.[2] Harvard historian Serghii Plokhy argued in the same vein, "Russia today has enormous difficulty in reconciling the mental maps of Russian ethnicity, culture, and identity with the political map of the Russian Federation. In other words, it has a major problem in responding to the key demand of modern nationalism[.]"[3]

Westerners tend to associate expansion with wealth and power, but in Russia expansion had been associated with poverty and insecurity. Indeed, Russia's constant militarization and expansion created a debate that continues to this day about whether it is offensive or defensive, though from the Russian perspective there is simply less separation between two than in the West. In this vein, historically, Russian rulers were convinced that Russia's more immediate threats came from the West and the South, including the so-called "soft underbelly" that encompasses modern-day Caucasus and the Middle East.

Russia's links with the region we call today the Middle East and North Africa originated prior to the genesis of the Russian state. Geostrategic, economic, cultural, and religious considerations have driven Russian rulers to compete for domination there for centuries. Pursuit of great-power status, recognition as an equal by the West and access to crucial waterways—that is to say commercial as well as cultural and religious interests—have guided Russia in all its iterations, and continue to guide Putin's Russia to this day.

It is important to remember that an independent Russian state emerged only in the 1470s. This process took centuries, and the Middle East and Islam played an important role. In the late 900s, Constantinople's Orthodox Christian church began a major mission to Kyivan Rus, the first Eastern Slavic state established by the Rurik dynasty. The Grand Prince of Kyiv, Volodymir, received his baptism in 988 in Chersonesos, the ancient Greek colonial city off the coast of Crimea— itself an important, complex, and multifaceted place that straddled Christianity and Islam. Upon his baptism, Volodymir married Byzantine imperial princess Anna, the sister of Byzantine emperor Basil II—a feat that many had previously considered impossible for a pagan "barbarian." From the moment of Volodymir's baptism, the religious connection with Constantinople became critical to the Rus people as Eastern Orthodox Christianity began to spread over the coming decades, while trade with the Middle East emerged as one of Volodymir's main achievements.[4]

Repeated Mongol invasions eventually weakened Kyivan Rus, and it broke into several principalities. By the early 1200s, the Golden Horde forced these lands to submit to its rule, held "under the Tatar yoke," described thus because the Mongols attacked together with steppe tribes called the Tatars. Among the Horde's key allies and trading partners was Mamluk-ruled Egypt on the Mediterranean—another important early Russian connection to the Middle East. The Mongols ultimately could not hold all their lands, but for an extended period of time subjugated the earth from which the Russian state would later emerge, the eastern Rus lands.

In 1261, Prince Daniel, a junior Rurik prince of the Great Vladimir-Suzdal principality (Suzdalskoye Knyazhestvo), or the Grand Duchy of Vladimir, inherited the land of Muskovy (now Moscow) upon the death of his father, Great

Prince Alexander Nevsky. Under Prince Daniel it absorbed Vladimir-Suzdal and eventually emerged as the Grand Duchy of Muscovy, *Velikoye Knyazhestvo Moskovskoye*—the most powerful house in northeastern Rus, which continued to rise steadily in the coming decades and centuries, in large part due to Muskovy princes' alliances with the Mongol khans.[5]

By 1453 Constantinople had fallen to the Ottoman Empire, but the Orthodox Church leadership remained. In 1472 Muscovy ruler Grand Prince Ivan III married Princess Sophia, niece of the last Byzantine emperor, Thomas Palaelogus. Symbolically, the marriage signaled that Byzantium would continue. Historians note Ivan functioned as both a khan and a basileus (Byzantine emperor). His claim to power was dual—both religious and secular. Furthermore, the title of Grand Prince also created an association with Kyivan Rus.[6] In 1521, The Grand Duchy of Muscovy began official relations with Persia (as Iran was called until 1935).

Muscovy princes dreamt of overthrowing the "Tatar yoke," but also of subduing other Rus lands, most notably Novgorod, a rival allied with the Grand Duchy of Lithuania. Unlike Muscovy, the Novgorod principality was a republic, ruled by an elected assembly. For Muscovy's rulers, power and economic drivers centered on land. Novgorod chose instead to focus on trade as its vehicle for growth and development. Perhaps for this reason Novgorod enjoyed a relatively high degree of individual freedom for its day, while Muscovy became set on an authoritarian path.

By the 1470s, the Mongol Khanate, now called the Great Horde, ruled by Khan Ahmed, was weakened by persistent internal divisions. Ivan III of Muscovy saw an opportunity to challenge their rule, but first he attacked Novgorod in an alliance with the Tatars, whose support played an important role in a decisive battle that brutally crushed Novgorod in 1471. Ivan was now strong enough to assert full independence. He refused to continue paying tribute to the Horde and stove off the invasion Ahmed launched in response to the refusal. In 1478 Novgorod and the Horde each challenged Ivan III separately and for different reasons, but he crushed Novgorod's resistance. Khan Ahmed for his part ultimately could not muster enough military power to fight Ivan and, in the fall of 1480, withdrew his military which he had originally intended to use to attack Muscovy. According to historians, the retreat marked the first clear assertion of Muscovite sovereignty. As Plokhy writes, "Muscovy, which got to keep Novgorod, began its history as a fully independent state by crushing a democratic rival."[7]

Vasili III succeeded Ivan III and continued Moscow's expansion by military force. His son, Ivan IV—Ivan the Terrible—was crowned in 1547. He proclaimed

Russia a Tsardom (*Tsarstvo Russkoye*) and took on the title tsar, derived from the word Caesar—a result of Moscow's vision at the time of Russia as the "Third Rome," the last and final heir to Constantinople with a messianic mission to protect and spread the Orthodox faith. Indeed, nearly thirty years prior to Ivan the Terrible' s coronation, the monk Filofey allegedly wrote him a famous letter, "[T]ake care and take heed, pious tsar; all the empires of Christendom are united in thine, the two Romes have fallen and the third exists and there will not be a fourth."[8] Thus Muskovy simultaneously claimed several sources of legitimacy: the Golden Horde, Christian Byzantium, and Kyivan Rus.[9] Muskovy also acutely cared about its international prestige, "as a latecomer to the international scene."[10] Demand for Western recognition as an equal emerged at the very birth of the Russian state. That demand is still at the heart of how Russia sees itself. Meanwhile, the religious pillar of the Russian identity, its powerful Orthodox church, also continuously played out in Russia's relations with the Muslim world and the Middle East. Historian Orlando Figes asserts, "Russia's imperial identity was practically defined by the conflict between Christian settlers and [Muslim] Tatar nomads on the Eurasian steppe."[11] Whether or not one agrees with that, certainly it is difficult to deny that the church historically played a crucial role in the Russian consciousness, national identity, statecraft, and warfare, and continues to play this role in Putin's Russia.

Driven by insecurity about its borders and desire for status, the new Russian state pursued relentless expansion south, east, and west, "at an average rate of 50 square miles per day for hundreds of years, eventually covering one-sixth of the earth's landmass."[12] In the West it is common to discuss Russia in terms of only the East–West dynamic, but this perception is inaccurately skewed towards Europe. Over the coming centuries, the Russian state defined its chief threats as vacillating between both the South and the West—a constant dichotomy that remains in place to this day.

Tsarist Russia, Muslims, and the Middle East

The new Russian state soon clashed with the Ottoman Empire and went to war in 1568, in what became the first of over a dozen major and minor wars between the Ottomans and the Russians, including World War I. Russia remained a tsardom until 1721 when Peter the Great proclaimed Russia an empire, and chose the term "emperor" over "tsar," in practice, Russians used both terms interchangeably.

Imperial Russia pushed east into Siberia and west to the Polish-Lithuanian Commonwealth. Peter the Great famously "opened the window" into Europe for Russia—a policy of Westernization illustrative of both Russia's internal identity disagreements and geopolitical aspirations, underpinned by an understanding that Russia lagged behind the West technologically and needed to catch up. When Peter toured Europe, he focused on its superior technology, more so than on the "culture and refinements" of European life,[13] and in this context, he laid the foundation for Russia's entry into Europe as a great power.

At the start of Peter's reign, Russia had no access to the sea, or any navy to speak of. Sea access, including access to the strategically vital Mediterranean, along with construction of a large Russian navy, became a chief priority of his foreign policy ultimately aimed at recognition as a great power. To gain this recognition, Peter and subsequent Russian rulers believed it was necessary to demonstrate command of the high seas. Peter studied shipbuilding extensively, and with great passion, from the Dutch and the British, including working as a ship's carpenter.[14] He also founded the famous Russian Navy School. The Mediterranean offered opportunities to compete with European great powers, establish control and gain access to strategic commercial routes. Russia is a historic land power, and the Mediterranean ironically offers advantages to a such power because, to gain influence in the surrounding region, it is enough to control the coast. The coast matters the most strategically, and a country with limited means, such as Russia, can meaningfully compete for these specific nodes, rather than for the vast entirety of the region. Thus, it is difficult to overstate the longstanding historic importance of the high seas overall, and the Mediterranean in particular to the Russian state. Indeed, the search for warm water ports has emerged as a crucial constant in Russian foreign policy.

In the coming decades Moscow pushed south and southeast, into what are now Central Asia and the Caucasus. Russian rulers who followed Peter the Great, but perhaps especially Catherine the Great, believed that for Russia to be a great power that competed with European powers, it had to push south and develop a naval presence on the Black Sea that would then gain it entry into the Mediterranean. The push southwards again highlighted the perception of threat coming from the South and the Ottoman Empire. Catherine the Great in particular stressed this threat. Meanwhile, with its expansion into Central Asia and the Caucasus, Russia's interests clashed with Persia's. In 1796, Catherine the Great sent troops into the Iranian North Caucasus, and arguably only her death that year prevented a Russian invasion of Iran. Soon afterwards Iran became part of the Great Game as an area of competition between Moscow and Great

Britain—the greatest geopolitical competition of the nineteenth century—and a perception emerged in Russia that the West, and Great Britain in particular, was always out to weaken the country.

The Kremlin looked to the Middle East with an eye towards securing naval access in the Black Sea and in the Mediterranean to develop Russia's trade and make Russia a great power, but also to obtain buffer zones. Catherine the Great famously said, "I have no better way to defend my borders than to extend them," a phrase that perhaps most succinctly shows the connection between offensive and defensive action in official Russian thinking. Great-power aspirations that included a search for sea access, and insecurity have been constant primary drivers of Russian interests. Religious interests have been another. According to Figes, Catherine the Great wanted to see the Russian Empire "as a Black Sea power linked through trade and religion to the Orthodox world of the eastern Mediterranean, including Jerusalem." To that end, religious issues of appeal to Christian communities also continued to matter, especially under Catherine the Great. According to Figes, she "even dreamed of re-creating the Byzantine Empire where the Ottoman Empire stood."[15]

Moscow's 2015 Syria intervention seemed unprecedented to many, but it was Catherine the Great who first brought Russia into the Levant, during a war with the Ottoman Empire in 1768–74. During the war, in July 1770s, the Russian fleet, though inexperienced and in poor condition, defeated the Turkish navy on the Mediterranean, off the island of Chios—the Ottoman navy turned out to be in even worse shape than Russia's. Russian forces then proceeded to capture and briefly occupied what is now Beirut, at the time a fortress on the coast of Ottoman Syria, during two separate Russian Mediterranean fleet expeditions—the first in June 1772 and then again from late 1773 to early 1774. This episode underscored Russia's deeper interests in the Levant, and shows us that even today Russia's identity is more nuanced than to be focused solely on the Western threat.

Russia's main goal at the time was to assist Egyptian Arab despot Ali Bey al-Kabir (originally born in Abkhazia to a Georgian priest), who rebelled against the Ottoman Empire.[16] As Paul du Quenoy wrote, the occupation was not a fleeting moment but "complemented a well-documented Russian desire to play an expanded role in the Levant," and establish "forward positions on the Mediterranean."[17] Russian occupiers created the first modern maps and other detailed notes on the region that for du Quenoy "suggested a desire to return."[18] Moreover, he observes that the way Russian officials behaved during the occupation bore a striking similarity to the already-established Russian practice of engaging and controlling the peoples of the steppe on Russia's southern periphery. This practice, described in detail by Michael Khodorkovsky, included establishing Russia's superior status through an alliance agreement, one that incorporates an explicit recognition of Russian greatness, and paying tribute to the Russian state.[19] Russia's brief occupation of Beirut went largely forgotten, but this episode shows how the Russian state viewed this region as an extension of its push south, and Russian behavior in this episode foreshadowed the Russian Empire's future engagement with the Middle East and North Africa.

Russia won this eighteenth-century war and the two sides signed the Treaty of Kuchuk Kainardja. The sultan ceded territory on the Black Sea to Russia and renounced overlordship of the important Crimean Khanate. But in addition, St Petersburg (Russia's then capital) claimed the treaty gave it the right to represent Orthodox Christians in the Ottoman Empire, though in reality the language was "ambiguous and distorted by translations."[20] The treaty also served to "broaden Russia's commercial and diplomatic positions on the Mediterranean" through freedom of navigation, trade, consulates, and the freedom to intervene on behalf of pilgrims.[21] This was an important and often missed consequence of the war, and represented a loss for the Ottoman Empire. At the war's end, the so-called "Eastern question" (political and territorial issues surrounding the disintegration of the Ottoman Empire) that stood at the heart of the upcoming Crimean War had already surfaced. Over the coming years and centuries, Russian overtures to later Egyptian rulers continued.

Less than a decade later, in 1783, Russia annexed the Crimean Khanate. Soon afterwards Napoleon invaded Russia, and Russia won a key battle in 1812 that ultimately led to the defeat of the French. As a result, Russia emerged as a major player in European politics.[22] The larger context for Russia's position in Europe was the emphasis on state militarization that far exceeded anything in Western Europe, along with the availability of massive military manpower. This enabled Russia to put together a large army, even though soldiers in this army were treated far worse than their Western European counterparts. A major military victory helped formally secure Russia's position.

Then, in 1829, Russia secured another victory, this time against Turkey. As a result, Moscow obtained additional influence as a protector of Armenian and Greek Orthodox communities in the Ottoman Empire under the Treaty of Adrianople. The treaty had a number of other provisions. Among others, it granted Russia access to the Danube and opened the Dardanelles Straits to all commercial vessels, though a number of questions remained opened in this regard that the Turks and the Russians would ultimately resolve four years later, with the Treaty of Hünkâr İskelesi.

Catherine the Great also understood the importance of the Kurds, one among the many nomadic tribes on Russia's southern borders, many of which eventually became incorporated into the Russian Empire as a result of Russian territorial conquests. In 1787, she commissioned the publication of a Kurdish grammar in Russia, and, starting from 1804, Kurds increasingly played an important role in helping Russia fight against Persia and the Ottoman Empire.[23] Putin too would return to this theme in his Syria intervention. Because many Muslims inhabited the Russian Empire, Russia also had a large international infrastructure for those making the Hajj. While other scholars argued that the state built this infrastructure to control and limit the pilgrimage, Eileen Kane wrote that the state also used it to extract benefits—to capture revenue and create additional justification for expansion.[24] These themes also played out in Putin's Syria intervention.

Russia also clashed with Iran during its push into the Caucasus and Central Asia. In the nineteenth century, the two countries fought two wars in 1804–13 and 1826–8. Iran lost both and ceded to Russia lands that are now parts of modern-day Azerbaijan, Georgia, Armenia, and Turkmenistan. These wars took a serious toll on Iran's treasury. Anti-Russian sentiment rose high in Iran, both on religious grounds and out of resentment for the ruinous financing of losing war efforts. It was in this context that an angry mob murdered Russia's ambassador Alexander Griboyedov along with his staff in Tehran, in February 1829. Griboyedov had helped to negotiate the Treaty of Turkmenchay that ended the war with Russia in 1828 on humiliating terms, from the Iranian perspective. Not until December 2016 would a Russian envoy be murdered again by foreign nationals in a foreign country.[25]

Jerusalem has always mattered to the Russian Orthodox Church. But in the nineteenth century it emerged as especially important, and Russia sent more pilgrims there at the beginning of the century "than any other branch of the Christian faith."[26] The Church exercised influence over Greek, Armenian and Arab Orthodox communities in the Ottoman Empire, and it funded schools, churches and hostels in Palestine and Syria.[27] Moscow also aspired to reclaim Constantinople's Hagia Sophia as the Mother Church, and Constantinople as the capital connecting Moscow to Jerusalem. One Russian theologian wrote in 1840 that Jerusalem "is our native land, in which we do not recognize ourselves as foreigners."[28] Archimandrite Uspensky, who led the ecclesiastical mission to Jerusalem in 1847 underscored Russia's complex identity when he wrote, "Russia from eternity has been ordained to illuminate Asia and to unite the Slavs. There will be a union of all Slav races with Armenia, Syria, Arabia and Ethiopia, and they will praise God in Saint Sophia."[29]

Prior to 1853, Russia's geopolitical influence was on an upswing, but in that year came the Crimean War, or the Eastern War, as it is referred to in Russia—a crucial juncture for Russia, but also Europe and the Middle East—a war that did not simply affect the Crimean Peninsula, but also spanned areas from Jerusalem to Constantinople, the South Caucasus and the Balkans, and the Black, Baltic, and White Seas, and even touched the Far East. Moscow bore the greatest responsibility for starting the war, specifically Tsar Nicholas I. The disintegration of the Ottoman Empire came to define the war, with the Eastern question being on the lips of many Europeans at the time. Officially, Nicholas I claimed to represent Orthodox Christians within the Ottoman Empire and to prevent an Islamic revolution in Constantinople. The war ended in 1856, and Russia lost disastrously. The consequences were varied and profound. Among others repercussions, Russia lost its prominent position in the Middle East, which it did not regain until the Cold War. Importantly, upon this defeat, Russia built "a patriotic myth, a national narrative of the people's selfless heroism, resilience and sacrifice."[30]

Russia's defeat in the war checked its southward expansion and shifted its ambitions. Russia and Iran began to work together, as Russia sought to pull Iran into its sphere of influence. The Iranian shah for his part needed money and began borrowing from Russia either at outrageous rates or with political strings attached, while the Iranian public bore the costs. This situation added to the rift between the Iranian government and the public's positions towards Russia—one that remains to this day, and one that is not reciprocated in Russia, where no such strong rift exists between the government and the public on this issue.

World War I broke out soon after and Ottoman Turkey fought alongside Germany and Austria-Hungary against the Russians, British, and French. In March 1915, Russia and Britain signed a secret pact, the Constantinople Agreement—Russia would annex Constantinople and retain control of the Dardanelles Strait that connected the Black Sea with the Mediterranean and the Gallipoli Peninsula. In exchange, Russia agreed to British claims to other parts of the Ottoman Empire and central Persia.[31] The agreement highlighted that Russian state priorities remained unchanged.

Just over a year later, in May 1916, Britain and France, with Russian agreement, secretly signed the Sykes-Picot agreement, which stipulated the division of the Ottoman Empire into spheres of influence. The next year, however, in October 1917, the radical Bolshevik revolution overthrew the government and the Bolsheviks leaked the agreement to the world in their official publication, *Pravda*. The Bolsheviks also supported the secession of the socialist "Gilan Soviet" in northwestern Iran.[32] Originally an extremist minority group, the Bolsheviks would emerge as dominant through effective propaganda and unprecedentedly ruthless repressions and violence. They also employed effective propaganda that the state first used domestically and then turned outward to the rest of the world. In the coming decades Russia plunged into the horrors of Bolshevik and then Soviet rule, which officially emerged in December 1922.

The "Third World," for its part, mattered to the Soviet Union from the very beginning, in some aspects more so than Europe, as part of Soviet revolutionary plans for a global socialist state.[33] Lenin perceived the Third World—to which the Middle East belonged—as the "weakest link" of world capitalism. "Let us turn our faces towards Asia," he famously proclaimed when the communist revolution failed to erupt in Europe, "The East will help us conquer the West."[34] Indeed, Bolshevik forces even prepared to invade British India through Afghanistan[35]—a brief and largely forgotten episode that did not materialize, likely due to lack of resources, but is nonetheless significant because it shows the direction of Bolshevik thinking.

2

The Soviet Union in the Middle East and the Afghanistan Intervention

Although the world changed fundamentally, the Middle East remained front and center of Kremlin interests and global ambitions, as the "Third World" assumed special importance in the battle of Cold War ideologies. Indeed, the first serious crisis of the Cold War emerged the Middle East. It is no accident that of all Arab states, the Kremlin would in time forge a special relationship with Syria. And, as the years went by, Soviet policy in the Third World came full circle with the invasion of Afghanistan, the most ambitious and extensive Kremlin involvement in the Third World. This experience, and more precisely, its many failures, provided key lessons for Vladimir Putin, which led him to a very different intervention in Syria.

The Soviet Union's Approach the Middle East

For all the radical departures of the Soviet Union, it did not divorce itself entirely from tsarist traditions. The Marxist-Leninist ideology of world revolution replaced messianic ideas of Eastern Orthodoxy and pan-Slavism, but in a sense, both were aggressive and expansionist. The tsarist legacy of offensive policies towards Turkey and Iran, as well as pursuit of access to geo-strategically crucial waterways continued to underpin Soviet activities. Moreover, even as the Soviet Union suppressed religion internally, it initially attempted to use it externally for political ends. Eileen Kane documented that in the 1920s and 1930s, building on the tsarist legacy, the Kremlin briefly helped non-Soviet Muslims (mainly from Persia, Afghanistan, and China) make the hajj to Mecca through Soviet lands, in an effort to help spread the socialist revolution and generate currency to fund Stalin's industrialization campaign. The Kremlin also competed with the Persians and the British for control of, and profit arising from, the global hajj traffic.[1]

During World War II, both Great Britain and the Soviet Union invaded and occupied Iran to secure access to the country's oilfields and ensure access to supply lines vital during the war effort. At the end of the war, during the July 1945 Potsdam conference, Stalin demanded among other things that Turkey give some of its eastern territories to the Soviet Union, and claimed—unsuccessfully— the right to a trusteeship over Tripolitania, a Libyan province, as reparations for war damages.[2] These events show continuity of interests in the Mediterranean and the MENA region that persisted despite a profound change in the Kremlin leadership and its governing ideology.

More broadly, the world views of the Soviet Union and the West were heading for a confrontation. On July 21, 1945, US President Harry Truman spoke at the symbolic raising of the US flag in Berlin. The pervious world order, based on a balance of power, had brought poverty and the devastation of two horrific world wars. Truman articulated a better alternative:[3]

> We have conclusively proved that a free people can successfully look after the affairs of the world ... We are not fighting for conquest. There is not one piece of territory or one thing of a monetary nature that we want out of this war. We want peace and prosperity for the world as a whole ... If we can put this tremendous machine of ours which had made this victory possible to work for peace, we could look forward to the greatest age in the history of mankind. This is what we propose to do.

The United States wanted to see new order built on international institutions, to usher in an era of peace and prosperity, and to be sure led the creation of this order. But Joseph Stalin and the revolutionary communist ideology could not share this vision.[4] On February 9, 1946, Stalin delivered an electoral speech in which he blamed capitalism for the start of two world wars and proclaimed a Soviet victory. "Our victory signifies, first of all, that our Soviet social system was victorious ... our Soviet state system was victorious ... Now, everybody, friends and enemies alike, admit that the Red Army proved equal to its tremendous task."[5] Stalin could foresee no peace for as long as capitalism existed. The Communist Party, he said, "intends to organize another powerful upswing of our national economy that will enable us to raise our industry to a level, say, three times as high as that of prewar industry ... Only when we succeed in doing that can we be sure that our Motherland will be insured against all contingencies[.]"

Thus began the official pronouncements of the Cold War. Indeed, an influential American liberal Supreme Court Justice William Douglas interpreted Stalin's speech as a "declaration of World War III."[6]

One of the first major crises of the Cold War was soon to erupt—and it involved the Middle East, which shows the continued importance of this region in great-power rivalries. In early 1946, Stalin refused to withdraw from Iran, despite earlier promises to do so. Great Britain by contrast kept its promise. Stalin, for his part, rather than withdraw, provided training and military support to separatist movements in Iranian Azerbaijan (the Azerbaijan people's government) and Kurdistan (separatist republic of Mahabad). Stalin eventually withdrew, in no small part due to US pressure, but not until approximately 2,000 had people died as a result of Azeri and Kurdish separatists' clashes with Iranian forces. To this day, Iranians talk resentfully of the Soviet occupation.

Stalin saw all states, including those in the Middle East, as either communist or non-communist. He initially supported the creation of the state of Israel, likely in an effort to dislodge British influence in the region,[7] but very soon broke off relations with the Jewish state entirely when he understood that Israel would choose the West. As Robert O. Freedman writes, from World War II until Stalin's death in 1979, the Soviet Union pursued two separate policies toward the so-called Northern Tier (Iran and Turkey)—countries with greater geographical proximity to and history with Russia and its imperialism, who tended to ally with the West—and Southern Tier (the rest of the Middle Eastern states), which by contrast had more experience with Western imperialism and less contact with Russia. They were therefore more welcoming of Russian influence than Turkey and Iran.[8]

After Stalin's death Nikita Khrushchev soon emerged as the new Soviet leader, following a brief stint by Georgy Malenkov. Khrushchev "saw the world as being divided into three main zones or blocs—the socialist bloc, the capitalism bloc, and the Third World, which he hoped to win over to communism through political support and large doses of economic and military aid."[9] By the end of Khrushchev's stay in power until October 1964, Moscow regained a relatively stronger position in the Middle East than under Stalin. Still, Khrushchev's foreign policy priorities lay outside the Middle East. But it was under Khrushchev that the Soviet Union emerged as a global power.[10] And it was only when Leonid Brezhnev and Alexei Kosygin emerged in Khrushchev's place that Soviet priorities shifted to the Middle East, as the Soviet Union remained a global power.[11]

In 1964, under Brezhnev, the Soviet Navy created the 5th Eskadra (squadron) in the Mediterranean. Its purpose was to serve as a symbolic display of state power (*"derzhavnost"* in Russian); as diplomatic support for Soviet allies; and last, but perhaps most importantly, as maritime forward defense. Until approximately the mid-1980s the 5th Eskadra gave the West a run for its money on the Eastern Mediterranean. Building on the tsarist traditions, Soviet strategic planners believed it was especially important to cover the southern flank of the eastern Mediterranean as part of its vulnerable "soft underbelly" mentioned earlier. For the Soviet Union in particular, it meant establishing a counterweight against NATO operations.[12] Thus, the Soviet Union made a push for an expanded navy (something that Putin would also later do). The Soviets also routinely deployed military personnel to support allies in the region, both officially and unofficially.

The Soviet Union was working hard to challenge the US navy, which had emerged as a global force after World War II. While the Soviet army had superiority in land power, it could not alter the balance of power in Europe without countering or limiting the global nature of the US navy; any conflict they would engage with the United States or the West would be waged on multiple fronts, leaving Russia exposed. Thus, Soviet Admiral Gorshkov attempted to create a blue-water navy as a peer to the United States and gain global base and port access for the Soviet Union. In February 1968, Gorshkov made the cover of *Time* magazine when he declared, "The flag of the Soviet navy now proudly flies over the oceans of the world . . . [s]ooner or later, the US will have to understand that it no longer has mastery of the seas."[13]

In fact, the Soviet navy never managed to supersede America's and at best ranked as second behind the United States. But Gorshkov's threat was taken seriously. Moreover, despite failure to outcompete the United States, Gorshkov transformed the Soviet navy from a submarine-dominated sea denial force that had coastal and defensive orientation. It was still submarine-centric but he began to expand strategic strike capability with an eye towards global power projection, to challenge in the Indian Ocean and the Mediterranean. Indeed, with regard to the latter, the 1973 Yom Kippur war was a watershed event because Soviet maneuvers showed the US navy had to wake up and rise to the challenge—which it did.

The Soviet Union meanwhile expended massive resources in its bid for influence in the Middle East at the expense of the United States. Once again the Russian state vied for influence in this region as part of the greatest geopolitical competition of the new century—this time with the United States. Arms sales, energy, aid, and the provision of training and advisors became a crucial tactic used in the region by the Kremlin. But others included disinformation, and elements of soft power projection. To that end Moscow also played on the Western colonial legacy in the region to portray itself as a better alternative, and provided scholarships for students from the region to study in the Soviet Union, primarily in Moscow. In the early years of the Cold War, as many observers had noted over the years, including George Kennan in his famous long telegram, deception and paranoia were deeply engrained in Russian culture—a society Marquis de Custine described in the late 1800s as "protected by lies," where "speaking the truth is to subvert the state."[14] US intelligence "walked in baby shoes" as one arrested Soviet spy told American interrogators in 1957—a view that KGB leadership shared.[15] Importantly, the Soviet leadership was playing the long game. To this day, democratic societies continue to struggle with the issue of how to fight back against authoritarian regimes without becoming like them, and miss warning signs—as they did with Putin in Syria.

Terrorist tactics also became an important element of Moscow's toolkit in the Middle East. The KGB funded, trained, advised, and equipped anti-Western terrorist groups in the region. Soviet General Alexander Sakharovsky, who led the KGB's First Chief Directorate, bragged in 1971 to Lt. Gen. Ion Mihai Pacepa, then head of Romania's industrial espionage department and later the highest-ranking Soviet intelligence officer to defect to the West, "airplane hijacking is my own invention."[16] Vaclav Havel, Soviet-era Czech dissident who became the first president of the Czech Republic, revealed in March 1990 that communist Czechoslovakia provided a thousand tons of Semtex explosives to the Libyan government, which then sent it to terrorist groups.[17] The Soviet Union also continuously utilized disinformation in the Middle East to undermine the US position in the region.[18]

While the Soviet Union was involved in all key issues in the Middle East, Syria in particular emerged as its closest ally in the Arab world. To be sure, Moscow never saw allies as equals but more as subjects, and Syria was more of a client state, but regardless, Damascus had planted itself in Moscow's orbit. Syria's geostrategic location was critical to ensuring the Soviet position in the region, which was consistent with historic Russian state interests. The radical and anti-Israel Syrian government professed both socialism and close cooperation with the Soviet Union, while the Soviet Union provided Syria with support in its struggle against Israel. Many Soviet citizens moved to Syria and, in turn, many Syrian elites studied at top Soviet schools such as Moscow State University and the Peoples' Friendship University. Intermarriage occurred in both countries. The Soviet leadership, for its part, sought to groom top students from allied countries whom it could later rely on for support. Soviet public broadcasts and statements referred to Syrians as "allies" and "friends." When Hafez al-Assad seized control of the country in November 1970, the Syrian dictatorship soon emerged as one of the most repressive in the world. According to Pulitzer Prize nominee Sam Dagher, the infamous Communist East German secret police, the Stasi, helped Hafez al-Assad to create his own secret police, the Mukhabarat.[19]

The Invasion of Afghanistan

The Soviet invasion of Afghanistan began in December 1979. It marked the pinnacle of Soviet involvement in the Third World—the first Soviet invasion outside the Warsaw Pact. Militarily, Afghanistan put up little resistance, and from this standpoint it was more of an orchestrated coup than an invasion; still, politically, the term "invasion" applied.[20] This pivotal invasion lasted a decade, cost thousands of lives and billions of dollars, and ultimately failed to achieve its desired goals. As a result of the Afghan experience, the Soviet leadership re-evaluated interventions as a future tool of foreign policy.[21] This element of the experience is important in evaluating Putin's Syria intervention. These lessons helped guide Kremlin assessments for future interventions, including Syria in particular. Avoiding another Afghanistan in Syria mattered to the Kremlin, and later chapters will discuss this in more detail. In this context, it is important to discuss several key elements of the Afghanistan invasion.

On December 24, 1979, the 103rd Guards Airborne Division of Soviet Airborne Troops landed in Kabul, Afghanistan.[22] Two days later, an explosion knocked out the telephone system in Kabul, and Soviet troops launched an attack on the country's Interior Ministry, Darulaman administrative complex and the Tajbeg palace. A radio station that described itself as Radio Kabul broadcast a pre-recorded message that announced, "the bloody apparatus of [Afghan leader] Hafizullah Amin ... had been broken," while the real radio Kabul fell soon after.[23] By the next morning, Soviet troops had taken control of the city.[24]

The Soviets officially claimed they came to Afghanistan upon a legitimate invitation of the country's government, which invoked the Treaty of Friendship, Good Neighborliness, and Cooperation, ratified in May 1979.[25] But in reality, the Kremlin engineered the invasion months earlier.[26] Then, as late as early 1984, the Soviets were still trying to find written proof of their "legitimate" presence. The Carter administration for its part had also begun a small covert operation aiding the mujahedeen months before the invasion. On July 3, 1979, then "President Carter signed the first directive for secret aid to the opponents of the pro-Soviet regime in Kabul." Russian hardliners had later interpreted it as an

American plan to draw the USSR into "its own Vietnam."[27] In reality, no such plans existed until after the Soviet invasion began.[28]

When the Soviet military invaded Afghanistan, it either first killed Hafizolla Amin, leader of the existing hardline communist government and of the People's Democratic Party of Afghanistan (PDPA), or Amin was already dead prior to the invasion.[29] Despite Moscow's official claim at the time that Amin did not die at Soviet hands, as Raymond L. Garthoff writes, "The direct Soviet military role in deposing Amin was clear."[30] The famous Metrokhin archives confirm just how much Moscow wanted and planned to get rid of Amin in the months prior to the invasion of Afghanistan.[31] After the invasion, the Kremlin also killed some of Amin's family members and installed as a puppet head of government the former deputy prime minister Babrak Karmal, whom Moscow had flown in from Eastern Europe, where he had previously remained in virtual exile.[32] On the very same day, on December 27, Karmal was named the Presidium of the Revolutionary Council in Kabul, and the next day Kabul radio announced that he would head the Afghan state. Karmal also appointed a new Cabinet.

The immediate trigger for the Kremlin's invasion of Afghanistan was the country's faltering communist regime. The Brezhnev doctrine stated that the Soviet Union had the right to interfere in a foreign country militarily, if necessary to protect its Communist Party from losing power because otherwise the international socialist struggle would weaken. The invasion, therefore, was about the Soviet Union's global image, and in particularly an image it cultivated in the Third World that featured so prominently in its ideological ambitions.

The Politburo met in March 1979 to discuss the situation. "'We cannot lose Afghanistan in any case' was the leitmotif of the discussion on March 17," wrote Alexey Vasiliev, one of Russia's prominent Arabists involved in the formation and implementation of Moscow's Middle East policy.[33] Soviet Premier Alexei Kosygin, KGB chairman Yuri Andropov, and Foreign Minister Andrei Gromyko all expressed this same sentiment prior to the invasion. Their broader considerations included a fear "that an Islamic government might inflame 40 million Muslims living in the Soviet Union"[34] On a broader plane, other issues were also at play, such as Brezhnev's growing domestic weakness.

Within days after December 27, 1979, Soviet military forces spread out across Afghanistan and further occupied critical areas such as airbases and strategic lines of communications. Communist Party mouthpiece *Pravda* claimed on December 30 that the intervention entailed a limited military contingent" which would be "fully recalled" upon completion of the mission,[35] but Soviet involvement instead only continued to build up. By January 1, 1980, the Soviet

Union sent to Afghanistan at least 50,000 troops, 200 aircraft, along with armored vehicles, heavy artillery, and other weaponry.[36] Over the years Soviet military involvement and expenditure grew steadily. By 1987, the number of Soviet troops reached 120,000.

The invasion was ruthless—a continued testament to the historic Russian approach to counterinsurgency that was also to play out in Syria under Putin. At the time, Afghanistan was one of the poorest countries in the world. The Soviet military laid millions of landmines throughout the country; sometimes it disguised bombs as children's toys. The Soviet air force carpet-bombed whole cities, utilizing scorched earth tactics and killing everyone. For example, the Soviet invasion wiped out 90 percent of Kandahar's population. Anthropologist Louis Dupree described Soviet actions as "migratory genocide."[37] Out of a total population of approximately 13 million in 1979,[38] over the next decade, 1.5 million Afghans died, approximately 5 million fled to Iran and Pakistan, and millions more became internally displaced.

Soviet treatment of Afghanistan varied somewhat by region. Their presence in Afghanistan also necessitated some construction, primarily for their own use. The Soviet Union for instance built roads and apartment complexes in major cities such as Kabul that the city's residents coveted because the buildings had built-in amenities that did not exist elsewhere, such as heating systems and hot water in winter. I know this from my personal experience living in Afghanistan while working for a US military contractor in Kabul in 2010–11. Akhmad Khalid Majidyar, a scholar on Afghanistan and the broader region, and currently a senior program officer at the National Endowment for Democracy, recalls his personal experience during the time he lived in Kabul until 1992, "We lived in Macroryan [a neighborhood in Kabul] in late 1980s and early 1990s before the civil war broke out. We enjoyed many amenities that did not exist anywhere else in Kabul, including heating system and hot water in winter. Many cabinet ministers and high-ranking officials lived in the neighborhood because of these amenities as well as better security."[39] Thus, a deeper look at the Soviet experience reveals a degree of nuance. This is not to say that the Afghans in Kabul had fond feelings towards the Russians. To the contrary, children in Kabul for instance grew up learning to crush red ants with their feet to symbolize resistance to the Soviet Union.

The Soviet Union faced worldwide condemnation for its actions, even from its traditional supporters at the UN General Assembly. Only Moscow's client states, plus a few others refrained from criticizing the Afghanistan invasion. Notably, Hafez al-Assad was one the few who supported the invasion, for which the Kremlin gave Assad weapons. The Afghans fiercely resisted the Soviets. The United States organized a campaign to support the Afghan insurgency and it received wide support—from the Europeans, China, Saudi Arabia, Iran, and others. The United States also imposed a grain embargo against the Soviet Union and denied certain key technologies that mattered in oil and gas, as well as computer industries.[40] Many countries including the US boycotted the 1980 Moscow Olympics, which dealt a major blow to Soviet prestige domestically and internationally. In June 1979, the United States and the USSR had signed a strategic arms limitations treaty, SALT II. But because of the Afghanistan intervention, President Carter withdrew the treaty from the Senate in January 1980 and it remained unratified and thus never formally went into effect.

The Kremlin spent a long time planning the groundwork for this operation. What surprised analysts and government officials at the time was the speed of the intervention, its size and scope, along with the ruthlessness with which the Kremlin eliminated the Amin regime. Analysts and policy makers were similarly surprised by Putin's Syria intervention, as well as its speed and audacity. Many intelligence analysts saw warning signs during the run-up to the Afghanistan invasion, but assumed the Kremlin would calculate the political and economic costs of invasion as being too high. This conclusion was proven wrong.[41] As MacEaching wrote, "This was *not* because of an absence of intelligence information on Soviet preparations for the move. It was that the operation being prepared was contrary to what intelligence analysts had *expected* Moscow would be willing to do."[42]

The Soviet invasion of Afghanistan sparked a debate in the West about whether the Kremlin's actions were offensive or defensive.[43] This was later to be echoed in the attempts of more recent analysts to explain Putin's Syria intervention: whether it was part of a strategy or a tactical response, and what it was that Putin ultimately wanted in Syria and out of the Syrian experience. Again, the debate highlighted the difference between how the West and the Kremlin viewed distinctions between offensive and defensive actions.

The Costs and Ultimate Withdrawal

The Soviet Union paid a high price for its invasion. The vast majority of Soviet soldiers who went into Afghanistan were conscripts with relatively little training, and for many even less desire to be in Afghanistan. They lacked the proper resources to fight a counterinsurgency on Afghan terrain, which was very different from what the Soviets were used to in Europe. Controlling rural Afghanistan, for instance, mattered more than its centers but Moscow was not used to such an approach. Nor did the Afghan government provide adequate support to the Soviet military.

Over the years no matter how hard the Soviet government tried to conceal its true activities in Afghanistan from Soviet citizens, it could not hide the thousands of body bags coming home, along with wounded soldiers, crippled physically and emotionally. Many citizens came to see Afghanistan as a place where young men, essentially boys, were simply sent to die by the cruel Soviet government. The Soviet Union never released complete figures, but available estimates suggest at least 15,000 died and far more were wounded. Throughout the entire decade of the intervention, the Soviet Union rotated roughly half a million troops in Afghanistan. The psychological damage to those who returned is even harder to quantify but it also played a major role. Indeed, the trauma was seared into the memory of the country's citizens, even if they did not experience it personally.

Yet these costs, while tragic, were hardly crippling. The Soviet army was 5 million strong during the invasion of Afghanistan. The Soviet economy was performing poorly, the military had problems in the medical services, and also had other difficulties. Even so, tens of thousands of casualties can hardly have dealt a serious blow to the military in terms of defense capabilities. Indeed, some of the costs the military incurred in Afghanistan would also have been incurred elsewhere, because the Soviet Union did not increase the total size of its army. For instance, troops had to be supported whether they were in Turkmenistan, or Belarus, or Afghanistan.

According to declassified CIA estimates, from 1979–86 the war cost the USSR 15 billion rubles, and from 1980–86 an average of $7 billion a year.[44] Specifically in terms of military aid, the Soviet Union provided Afghanistan with $330 million between 1973 and 1977, $650 million between 1978 and 1982, and $4 billion between 1983 and 1987.[45] The war went on for a further two years, but overall in sheer dollar terms the CIA admitted that these were not crippling costs. They had been rising faster than overall defense spending, as the CIA noted. However, it is hard to see these numbers as crippling, in the context of overall Soviet GDP.

These figures have been the subject of much debate and, ultimately, the true numbers are not known, but it is possible to get a general sense based on available information for simple comparison.[46] According to official Soviet data, total Soviet Gross National Product rose from 770 billion rubles in 1985 to 924 billion in 1989, based on actual prices.[47] Even with the caveat that these numbers should be taken with a large pinch of salt, they still show that the monetary price tag alone, should not have been crippling, even as the Soviet losses in Afghanistan were substantial and ever-growing. But the more significant costs were about more than sheer numbers alone.

The Soviet Union clearly also cared about domestic public opinion. The government periodically proclaimed a faux "withdrawal," not entirely dissimilar to what it would do several times in Syria, only to then increase the buildup. For example, in July 1986, Gorbachev announced a "first withdrawal" of troops without a time frame, but diminished the announcement by adding that Moscow still would not quit the war until "outside interference" in Afghanistan had ended.[48] In December 1987, on the eve of an upcoming summit between Ronald Reagan and Mikhail Gorbachev, a *Wall Street Journal* editorial began "How many times can the Soviets announce their withdrawal from Afghanistan without actually leaving?"[49] Recall also that *Pravda*, as mentioned at the start of this chapter, first claimed the intervention would be brief and limited, when the reality, as immediately became clear, was the exact opposite.

The worldwide condemnation of Soviet actions, sanctions and other costs also clearly mattered. The Soviet Union to some extent bore a political cost of deteriorating relations with China. India historically had been a major recipient of Soviet military aid, and the Afghanistan intervention became a problem; the Soviets could still play on the India–China rivalry, but this became harder. According to a recently declassified CIA assessment, the Soviet invasion put India in a difficult position. On one hand, New Delhi was reluctant to openly oppose the Soviet intervention due to its dependence on Soviet arms, as well as political and economic connections to Moscow. On the other, members of the Non-Aligned Movement—a bloc of states which sought during the Cold War to avoid a formal alliance with either the United States or the Soviet Union— condemned the Soviet invasion, and the Indian government was sensitive to "the harm to India's non-aligned image in seeming to condone the Soviet presence in Afghanistan."[50]

The invasion also became a major problem in Moscow's relations with Iran. Though the Islamic Revolutionary leaders would have proclaimed "Neither East nor West!" no matter what, the Kremlin arguably had a better chance of improving relations with Tehran without the Afghanistan intervention. The overthrow of a pro-American regime in Iran theoretically at least opened up opportunities for Moscow, but the Afghanistan intervention became an obstacle in capitalizing on these in any way. The intervention became a major contributing factor—along with the internal exiling of Soviet dissident and Nobel Prize winner Dr. Andrei Sakharov—to the growing belief in the West that détente with the Soviet Union could not continue. As Leon Aron writes, the Soviet costs of the "moral position" that Gorbachev had talked about—a feeling that permeated the entire Soviet society—perhaps played a greater role than dollar values and even loss of life.[51] Still, even the social costs alone did not prove sufficient.

In the end, the decision to withdraw came as a result of a different factor. The Soviet leadership came to accept that it simply could not stabilize Afghanistan, regardless of how much cost and effort it expended. This conclusion took years to form and was the chief reason out of many why the Soviet Union took so long to withdraw in the first place.[52] Vladimir Putin's Kremlin took this lesson to heart and remembered when it intervened in Syria. Gorbachev, for his part, sought to improve relations with the West. On April 14, 1988, the Soviet leadership signed a package of agreements that collectively came to be known as the Geneva Peace Accords on ending the war and Soviet withdrawal of troops from Afghanistan.[53] Even so, the Soviet involvement did not end entirely. Soviet military aid of $300 million a month to the Kabul government continued after the troops left, until Boris Yeltsin abruptly ended it when he took over from Gorbachev in December 1991.[54] The Soviet failure in Afghanistan left a lasting impression on both the Kremlin and Soviet (and then Russian) citizens. Putin's Russia would be different in the Middle East. It would be far more aware of the costs involved in foreign adventures, far more cautious in its involvement. It would not aim to fundamentally change the existing regime, nor put itself into international isolation, but to the contrary, it would enlist supporters and portray itself as part of a solution (even as it was also part of the problem). It would aim to keep domestic public opinion if not on its side then at least apathetic enough that it did not present a real danger. In short, avoiding another Afghanistan in the Middle East emerged, de facto, as a chief if unspoken aim. But first it is important to talk about how Putin emerged on the political scene and Moscow's relationship with the Middle East in those transition years.

3

Russia in the 1990s

The Soviet Union was about to heave its last breath. The signs were there even if many chose to ignore them. Sweeping change was on its way, both in Russia and in world politics. Russia was about to experience what were perhaps unique years in its history. Even so, certain constants remained. Preoccupation with the West, a desire for recognition as an equal, and ultimate failure to fully break away from the past laid seeds that would blossom in Vladimir Putin's Russia, which chose the Middle East as an arena of competition with the West.

With the coming of the 1990s, there was increasing disarray in Soviet internal politics, and this confusion spilled into foreign policy. Saddam Hussein invaded Kuwait in August 1990. In an unprecedented act, the Soviet Union joined the United States in a public condemnation of the invasion. George H. W. Bush assembled and led a joint coalition to liberate Kuwait, in what came to be known as the Gulf War, while the UN Security Council, where the USSR was one of five permanent members, authorized the use of force.

But the Kremlin's thinking on the war was confusing and contradictory. "Above all, the Gulf War emerged as the single most formative crisis to date in the gradual reformulation of the principles and interests of Soviet foreign policy," wrote Graham E. Fuller, former vice chairman of the National Intelligence Council at the CIA.[1] Gorbachev was losing his grip on power and more than anything sought to carve out a position for himself as a regional mediator to boost his domestic and international standing. The US buildup in Saudi Arabia as a result of the Gulf War raised concerns in Moscow, while right-leaning domestic forces, the Defense Ministry in particular worried about the loss of arms sales to Iraq. Even liberal forces in Moscow were uncomfortable with the use of force. One of Gorbachev's advisors was Yevgeniy Primakov, a skilled and experienced Arabist suspicious of the West, a man one Middle East official described to me years ago as "the fox of the Middle East." During the Persian Gulf War, Gorbachev had sent Primakov to try to broker a deal with Saddam Hussein. Thus, while Moscow generally complied with the UN resolution and coordinated with the West, Fuller writes, "Gorbachev sought repeatedly to weaken the thrust of American war tactics and bring an early end to the fighting. He was even willing to risk compromising the settlement terms specified by the Security Council itself."[2]

After the Gulf War, in June 1991, Soviet citizens elected Boris Yeltsin, a man who had radically broken away from the Communist Party the year before, as president of the Russian Soviet Federative Socialist Republic (RSFSR), as the Russian republic was known when it was part of the Soviet Union. In August 1991, Yeltsin publicly denounced the putsch (coup), led by communist hardliners against Mikhail Gorbachev' reforms. Yeltsin's popularity grew as a result. In August that year, during the failed communist putsch, protestors tore down the statue of Felix Dzerzhinsky in the square that bore his name. Dzerzhinsky, "Iron Felix," was the founder of the Cheka, the communist secret police which evolved later into the KGB, and symbolized Soviet power. The statue's fall was historic. Across the street stood Lubyanka, the notorious KGB headquarters; its security police watched from the windows, loaded weapons in hand. People on the street could easily see them from the square. The KGB could have shot at the protestors, but the truth was that the people no longer feared them. The Soviet Union was finished and they knew it. For many KBG officers, including one named Vladimir Putin, the coup failure, the siege, and statue's fall, were humiliating. It was a betrayal, and a betrayal required retribution. KGB general, Alexei Kondaurov thought, "I will prove to you that your victory will be short-lived."[3] And about a decade later, Putin would lead that path to victory and retribution.

Meanwhile, the new unfolding circumstances in the Middle East offered brief opportunities for the West. Washington began planning for a new peace initiative in the Middle East between Arabs and Israelis. As American point man for the peace process Dennis Ross wrote, "Radicals would be discredited, [Yasser] Arafat would be weak, regional moderates would be ascendant, our standing and authority in the region would be unprecedented, and the Soviets would be on our side."[4] From October 30 to November 1, 1991 Spain hosted a conference, co-sponsored by the United States and the Soviet Union in what became known as the Madrid peace conference. It aimed to launch a process and break the taboo of Arab states talking to the Jewish state.[5] The conference served as the first step in the Middle East peace process.[6]

Moscow's role in the Madrid peace initiative, for its part, officially remained indispensable—the United States and the USSR had for years funded opposing sides of the conflict. Thus, both had to be present if a real peace process were to take shape. Both officially acted as conveners. But in practice, the decay of Soviet institutions and the decline of Gorbachev's influence were on full display (against the backdrop of Yeltsin's growing popularity), and the event turned into an attempt to include the Soviet Union in a diplomatic effort that essentially ignored them. "Like the old aristocrats who had lost all their possessions to the nouveaux riches but would not give up their extravagant lifestyle, the Soviet leaders came to Madrid for their last ball. Everyone appreciated their presence but the conference itself was considered an exclusively American success," wrote Serhii Plokhy, adding "In the dozens of congratulatory letters received afterwards by its main organizer and promoter, James Baker, there was no mention whatever of the Soviet Union."[7] It comes as no surprise then that in later years, Yevgeniy Primakov spoke out against American domination of the peace process.[8] The rejection of Washington as the sole convener of chief international events colored the Kremlin's assumptions about Russian–American partnership in the Middle East and was echoed in diplomacy over Syria between John Kerry and Sergei Lavrov on Syria, which are discussed in the later chapters.

Less than two months after the Madrid conference, the Soviet Union ceased to exist. "We're now living in a new world," Gorbachev said famously as he announced the dissolution of the Soviet Union and his own resignation on December 25, 1991. Boris Yeltsin found himself the president of an independent state, rather than head of its largest constituent republic. As for Afghanistan, Yeltsin's government did not believe Najibullah could hold power. Former British ambassador to Moscow Rodric Braithwaite reported that Yeltsin, as the head of the Russian socialist republic, opened secret channels to the mujahedeen prior to the Soviet Union's collapse.[9] After the USSR's fall, Yeltsin's government aimed to move closer to the West and Yeltsin publicly opposed continued support for Najibullah. Kalinovsky writes, "For Russian politicians, Afghanistan primarily represented a POW issue; they felt no sense of obligation to the Afghan regime, nor were they concerned about preserving their own superpower status."[10] Hardliners in Russia never forgave Yeltsin—or Gorbachev, for that matter—for their decisions to cooperate with the West and to leave Afghanistan; they saw both as a betrayal, fed by belief that the CIA sought to weaken Russia in those early years by creating instability in Afghanistan and Central Asia and weaken Russia through undermining its vulnerable southern frontier.[11] Again, the perception of vulnerability of Russia's southern periphery played a role.

These narratives later bubbled up to the surface in Putin's Russia, where pro-Kremlin Russian analysts over the years blamed Americans for what they claimed was a direct and intentional increase of the flow of narcotrafficking out of Afghanistan and making deals with the Taliban to weaken Russia and boost the US position through military bases in the region. Some also claimed that Americans had been trying to do the same in Syria, and in fact linked US policies between the two countries as pursuing similar aims.[12]

With the fall of Communism, many Russians genuinely welcomed the West and the idea of democracy—something they had never experienced, but yearned for. For many behind the Iron Curtain, the West served as a model—an ideal to which they aspired. A 1991 poll found that 51 percent of Russian citizens preferred "a democratic solution to their country's daunting problems," while 39 percent "favored a strong hand at the helm."[13] The corrosive moral and economic degradation had taken its toll. The country's citizens lost confidence in the communist system and this played a critical role in bringing about the Soviet Union's downfall. In June 1992, Yeltsin addressed the US Congress not only as Russia's first democratically elected president but "as a citizen of the great country which has made its choice in favor of liberty and democracy," promising, "[t]here will be no more lies—ever."[14] This promise was an important public recognition of a central problem.

The United States, and the West more broadly, debated how to define new priorities in what George H. W. Bush defined as the "New World Order," Western leaders no longer saw the Kremlin as a threat and turned to what they perceived as more urgent priorities. A narrative took hold in the 1990s that Russia now walked a path towards democracy. The reality however was far more nuanced. The country indeed experienced unprecedented freedom in many areas of life, but Yeltsin, despite making many plausible statements, did not dismantle the old system entirely. Liberal reforms – including crucial economic reforms – were not implemented as envisioned by true liberals. Russia's identity crisis resurfaced in the 1990s, when the country and its elites struggled to define a unifying national idea after the fall of communism. In the end, Russian elites failed in this endeavor. Rather than transform Russia into a Western-style democracy, Yeltsin's Russia ultimately resulted in a system based on personal power, and it is from these seeds that Putin's Russia soon grew.[15]

The Middle East and Primakov's Multipolar World

Under Gorbachev, Moscow's Middle East policy was already undergoing a massive transformation. In addition to condemning Hussein's invasion of Kuwait, Gorbachev restored full diplomatic relations with Israel in October 1991, joined the US in co-sponsoring a UN resolution that reversed the November 1975

"Zionism is Racism" resolution, and allowed hundreds of thousands of Soviet Jews to emigrate to Israel. Changes under Yeltsin continued in the same vein, but were more profound and in other cases represented a full departure.

Yeltsin did not appear to pursue a coherent policy in the region. He appeared to have little interest in the Middle East,[16] and his priorities lay more with domestic issues, the post-Soviet space, the United States, Europe, and China. In his early years, Yeltsin often sided with the United States on Middle East issues although that began to change towards the end of his presidency. Russia's retreat from the region under Yeltsin was the exception, rather than the rule for the Kremlin. In this sense, Yeltsin's policies fundamentally shifted from the Soviet Union's. Still, the retreat was only partial, and excluded Turkey and Iran, which continued to matter to Yeltsin's Russia in much the same vein. Professor Robert O. Freedman wrote, "Concerned about its 'soft underbelly' in Transcaucasia and Central Asia, regions that were threatened by radical Islam, Moscow focused its Middle East efforts on Turkey and Iran, both of which had a considerable amount of influence in the two regions."[17] To that end, Moscow continued to cultivate its Kurdish card to hold against Turkey. The PKK maintained a presence in Moscow, while some with close ties to the PKK appeared at international public forums. To push back, Ankara maintained ties with Chechen separatists, providing them with aid, sending fighters into Chechnya when fighting began in 1994, and hosting some expelled Chechen fighters. Indeed, Robert Colson, a scholar on Kurdish issues wrote, "by early 1994, the Kurdish question began to play a prominent role in the Russian–Turkish relations as it impacted directly Russia's war in Chechnya."[18] This back and forth resulted in a 1995 bilateral agreement to "prevent terrorism," where both countries agreed to share intelligence on terrorism, Turkey promised to end support for the Chechen cause, and Moscow promised that the PKK "would no longer be a legal organization in Russia". Among other things, as Olson notes, the agreement also seemed to imply that Turkey would take a step back from Moscow's growing assertiveness in the entire South Caucasus region. This shows Moscow's continuing perceptions of vulnerability from the entire southern region that stretched far and wide, from the North Caucasus into the Middle East. Indeed, Olson quotes one Russian analyst who, at around that time, asserted that to prevent Turkey from harming Russian interests, Russia needed an alliance with Armenia and Iran, and in the future possibly with Georgia, Iraq, and even a potential independent Kurdish state.[19] Even after signing the agreement, mistrust remained on both sides, and Moscow was not about to give up its Kurdish card. Indeed, three years later, Moscow briefly gave Abdullah Ocalan, founder of the Kurdistan Workers Party

(PKK), refuge in Russia after Syria expelled him. At its founding in the early 1970s, the PKK had subscribed to a largely Marxist-Leninist ideology and used violence to further its goals of a Kurdish state. The PKK was a useful tool for the Kremlin against Turkey during the Cold War. As for the Caucasus, over the years, Turkey would lose leverage there to Russia, which had important implications for the Russian–Turkish relationship in Syria after the Russian intervention.

The Gulf was also an important market for Russian weaponry and a source of loans that the Russian economy sorely needed. Russia's concern about its "soft underbelly" highlighted its longstanding core interest in the region, which mattered regardless of who was in charge in the Kremlin. Interests in weaponry also fit with broader longstanding commercial interests.

With regard to Iran, the two countries continued to grow closer than they had under the Soviet leadership, though a thaw had already begun with Ayatollah Khomeini's death in 1989. Improved ties with Iran did not start with Yeltsin, but rather built on the last years of the Soviet experience, and Putin took that trend even further. Yeltsin's Russia sold conventional arms to Iran and turned to nuclear cooperation. Tehran also sided with Moscow during Chechnya's separatist struggle in the early 1990s, and Moscow's first war with Chechnya in 1994–6. Iran also helped Moscow end Tajikistan's civil war in 1992–7, and the Russia–Iran relationship was on the upward trajectory before Putin arrived in office. Moscow's relationship with Ankara was rockier than with Tehran and went through ups and downs during the Yeltsin era. Still, by and large, it was clear this relationship mattered to Moscow. Similarly, Moscow under Gorbachev had begun to expand economic ties with Turkey, and the Kremlin built on this experience in the 1990s. Although Moscow and Ankara had their differences and concerns (such as fears of Ankara fanning pan-Turkic sentiment in the South Caucasus and Central Asia), they had proven inflated, and more to the point, bilateral trade had expanded in the 1990s. Erdogan himself said that the 1990s marked the beginning of a period when economic and trade relations became "the driver" of Russian–Turkish relations.[20]

That said, the shift in Russia's policy towards the region was visible. In April 1993, Yeltsin and Clinton had the following exchange as part of a two-hour meeting:

The President   I would like to get your support for a firm position enforcing UN resolutions on Iraq and Libya.

President Yeltsin   We have no real influence on Iraq. It is true they owe us $2.5 billion.[21] They say to us if we stop supporting the US, they will give us $4 billion. So this is a "cheap" policy for us. We will not be selling weapons to them nor any spare parts.

…

The President   Just one more question, about the Middle East. We have invested quite a lot in trying to get the peace talks back on track. I'd like to ask you to discuss where you are, and how you can influence the Palestinians to agree to a date.

President Yeltsin   We have cut back our contacts with the Palestinians. That was during the Soviet period—the Central Committee maintained contacts. Now we have no contacts, delegations, or anything. Although the Syrians are trying to deal with the details of the political situation, it is such a difficult thing to do. Our cooperation with the Syrians is cut way back. That's our position. Now, with regard to debt: Syria owes us a lot, and so we need $120 billion. We would like to sell the debt, but we cannot do so because of sanctions against Cuba. Shokhin jokes that maybe you can buy the Cuban debt.

The President   One final question: You know we have a big dispute—Libya. They are harboring two people who had a big role in destruction of the Pan Am 103 flight. We have had mixed signals. Sometimes they like to cooperate— other times they say no; the answer is that Khaddafi's whole government would fall if those two people were let out. Khaddafi will not even discuss the trial of these two people.

President Yeltsin   Our position regarding this is that there is no cooperation now. If you want strengthened sanctions, we will not oppose them.[22]

Building on Gorbachev's earlier steps, Moscow continued to develop multifaceted ties with Israel. In addition, it attempted to pursue a neutral role in the Arab-Israeli conflict. Thus, even though Yeltsin claimed the Kremlin had cut back substantially on contacts with the Palestinians, it did not abandon them entirely. Russia remained a co-sponsor of the Middle East peace process, although unlike the Soviet Union, for Yeltsin's Russia the Arab–Israeli conflict was not the nucleus of its Middle East policy.

A key aspect to the early Yeltsin years is the internal struggle between pro-Western senior officials such as Andrei Kozyrev and those advocating a tougher and anti-Western posture such as Yevgeniy Primakov. Yeltsin himself contributed to the problem because, while he did a lot to bring down communism, he also helped preserve key aspects of the Soviet regime, including, critically, the KGB. As much as the West wanted to see Yeltsin as a democrat, in reality, he straddled two worlds—Russia's Soviet past and a nascent and fragile democratic present; it did not end well. "By the end of 1993 I knew that the chance to radically transform Russia into a modern democracy with an open-market economy could well have been missed . . . a half-reformed Russia would be tortured by its double identity," wrote Kozyrev.[23] Again, Russia's identity ran as an important undercurrent.

Despite reduced ties with Syria, Moscow continued to sell conventional arms to Damascus and was also willing to help transfer weapons from North Korea to Syria.[24] Furthermore, some reports suggested that Moscow's involvement in the Syrian chemical weapons arsenal—built earlier primarily with Soviet assistance in the first place—continued during the 1990s. In September 2013, as the West was discussing a deal with Putin on Russia's removal of Assad's chemical weapons arsenal, the *Moscow Times* reported:

> In the 1990s, a frequent visitor to Damascus was General Anatoly Kuntsevich, ironically an adviser to then-President Boris Yeltsin on eliminating chemical weapons. *Der Spiegel* wrote last year of Kuntsevich's missions: "The chemical weapons expert allegedly established connections with leading members of the Syrian regime, received large amounts of money from them and, in exchange, provided them with details on how to manufacture VX, a powerful chemical agent. He reportedly also shipped 800 liters of chemicals to Syria that were required to produce the poison gas. Kuntsevich's activity stopped in 2003 when he died unexpectedly on a flight from Damascus to Moscow.[25]

By 1996 things also began to change significantly both in Russia's Middle East policy, and broader US–Russia relations. Internally, the hardliners won, and after a long and complicated political process, in January 1996, Yeltsin appointed Primakov, who had no aspirations to become president, as foreign affairs minister. The same year, Vladimir Putin, an unknown former KGB officer at the time, had entered Boris Yeltsin's government, starting as his first deputy manager and rising through the ranks in the coming years to become director of the Federal Security Service (successor to the KGB), and secretary on the Russian Security Council.

Primakov had clashed with the West on Iraq, Bosnia, and NATO enlargement.[26] (Russians themselves over the years typically used the term NATO "expansion" rather than "enlargement," which highlights the different interpretations of these events.) Primakov provided a clear foreign policy vision—one of a multipolar world, a vision he outlined publicly at least as early as 1996, once he became prime minister. "After the end of the Cold War we saw an emergence and evolution of a tendency in which the old bipolar confrontational world began to be transformed into a multipolar one," he declared.[27] But more than simply a description of a view of international relations taking shape on its own, Primakov believed that a multipolar world would be better than one dominated by the United States and worked towards the implementation of his vision over the coming years. His vision took hold. As foreign minister, he came to New Delhi in April 1996, and proposed a trilateral partnership with India and China to promote multipolarity.[28] He then came to New Delhi again in December 1998 as prime minister to make the same proposal, even if at the time the Chinese leadership was less receptive to the idea than India's leaders.[29] Primakov also presented Russia to the Middle East as a partner that was culturally closer to the region than Western countries. Primakov wrote:

> [M]illions of Muslims live in Russia; unlike in many Western countries, they are not immigrants but form part of the indigenous population. There is perhaps no other state with a Christian majority and a Muslim minority that can serve, in the way Russia does, as an example of peaceful cohabitation, of sharing and adapting each other's cultures and creating a very special kind of community. On top of this Russia enjoys a unique position as a bridge between Europe and Asia.[30]

The view of Russia as a unique country that did not colonize the Middle East, could understand the region like no other, and yet is distant enough from the area that, unlike Iran, it could play the role of a neutral mediator, is another key feature of what would become Putin's approach to the Middle East.

One meeting in April 1996 between Bill Clinton and Boris Yeltsin is illustrative with regard to the Middle East and Russia's need for great-power status even in the 1990s. Yeltsin came in angry because Primakov convinced him that the United States was trying to marginalize Russia in the region. Clinton used the term "equal partnership," which appeared to pacify Yeltsin and said Russia could play an important role through its existing influence with Syria and Hezbollah.[31] The following excerpts are from this discussion:

> **BNY** [Boris Yeltsin] I don't understand the American approach in Lebanon. You seem bent on going it alone. That's what Primakov is telling me—the Americans are running a separate operation. Christopher is trying to repeat what he did in '93. This won't be a success if you persist in trying to sideline Russia and France.

> **WJC** [Bill Clinton] That's not correct. No one's sidelining anybody. We've got to work together. Primakov can play a helpful role, particularly with the Syrians. But our concern is that the parties not be able to play these foreign ministers off against each other. I'm particularly worried about Assad in that

regard. The other factor is the Israelis. They don't want the French or the EU to represent them. The US and Russia continue to work together as cosponsors of the peace process, and we're making every effort to coordinate our efforts.[32]

BNY This is not very convincing. I think that since these four ministers have gone there with a joint plan of action, they should work together, not separately. Obviously they have their own instructions . . .

WJC Look, you're just not seeing it correctly. It would be a big mistake for all of them to go to see Assad all together and deal with him as a committee . . . As for Primakov, his going to Syria obviously makes sense because of your relationship with the Syrians. But there are two sides to this, and we need to bring the Israelis along too. Chris and I felt that four-on-one with Assad would invite him to exploit differences among us . . .

As for Syria and Hezbollah, there too you've got influence. Use it well. Hezbollah doesn't want the peace process to succeed. They want Peres to lose the election. But Hezbollah and Syria also want to maintain some sort of relationship with Russia, so please use that leverage to get them to accept the ceasefire . . . None of us has any intention of sidelining Russia, in the Middle East or anywhere else. You've had a relationship with Syria for a long time, and there are important things you can do with the Syrians . . . I want historians fifty years from now to look back on this period and say you and I took full advantage of the opportunity we had. We made maximum use of the extraordinary moment that came with the end of the Cold War.

BNY The key word you just used was "equal" partnership. This will restore trust and confidence.

Based on the experts cited earlier, it is hard to say that both sides took full advantage of opportunities they had. This exchange also shows that while some may look fondly on the Yeltsin era, Moscow was not easy to work with then, and perceptions of the West treating Russia unfairly, along with great-power ambitions even if unmatched by abilities and resources, remained and were beginning to emerge in approximately 1996.

Moscow would soon clash with the United States over Iraq. Kozyrev often said that Russia's support for the UN policy towards Iraq was "the litmus test of Russia's stand on the civilized, democratic side of the barricade."[33] In those initial years, as one Russian analyst described it, "various economic actors within Russia sought cooperation with Iraq in pursuit of their own economic gain . . . However . . . there was more or less a consensus on the need to engage Iraq. This could only be done through diplomacy."[34] The Kremlin tried to get the West to lift sanctions against Saddam Hussein.[35] Baghdad owed a hefty debt to Russia. Although

Yeltsin mentioned a $2.5 billion figure to Bill Clinton, other sources cited higher figures in subsequent years—anywhere between approximately $4 and $7 billion.[36] And, in 2005, Russian reports indicated a debt of over $10 billion.[37] Likely, debt interest kept accumulating as the years went by, which could account for some of the discrepancies, although this does not explain them all. Regardless, even if the exact debt total is somewhat opaque, it is clear that Baghdad owed Russia a lot of money in the 1990s and Moscow was eager to benefit economically from the relationship, especially as the struggling Russian economy needed funds. Moscow also attempted to mediate between Iraq and the United Nations. Yeltsin strongly and vocally opposed the use of force in Iraq.

Russian analyst Helena Belopolsky wrote what seems to be in line with the Kremlin's thinking:

> An initially reactive Russian policy, impeded by the desire to rejoin the West, gave way to an adaptation in Russian policy in response to negative American policy decisions. Iraq became an instrument with which to address deleterious American actions ... The important shift in policy in the mid-1990s brought about a shift in the value of Iraq in Russian foreign policy ... by late 1994, Russia began to use its relationship with Iraq to challenge the United States on issues ranging from economic sanctions to military intervention.[38]

Primakov headed Moscow's diplomatic campaign in Iraq, which appeared to be an effort to return Russia as a major power player in the region, and moreover, restore Russia's status as a global leader.[39] Indeed, Russian analyst Dmitry Trenin of Moscow Carnegie Center and former colonel in Soviet and then Russian military intelligence wrote, "Our interests in Iraq were political, to keep Iraq as opposition to American hegemony."[40]

Although Moscow's efforts appeared ineffective at getting Hussein to allow UN inspectors to monitor the country's so-called "presidential sites," the Kremlin continued to insist that these efforts bore fruit in February 1998.[41] That year, Russia–US relations took a significant turn for the worse as Russia insisted that there could be a diplomatic solution, but after waiting for Russian diplomacy to work, the United States saw that it produced no results. Defense Minister Igor Sergeyev publicly denounced the American position as destabilizing, "rigid and uncompromising."[42] US defense secretary William Cohen said that Moscow's "so-called compromises" could not resolve problems with Saddam Hussein and cited reports that "Russia had offered to sell Iraq machinery that could be used to produce bioweapons and that Russians working as UN inspectors had been passing secrets to the Iraqis. (The first Russian to join a UN inspection team was a former KGB station chief.)"[43] The following year Moscow would also clash with the United States over Kosovo—a clash that Putin's Kremlin has not forgotten to this day. When Primakov learned en route to Washington in March 1999 about the bombing of Belgrade—on the day of the Orthodox Easter—he turned his plane around and went back to Moscow, and the next month reports surfaced that between 80 and 100 Russian mercenaries, sponsored by ultranationalist All-Russian Spiritual Heritage Movement, had appeared in Yugoslavia.[44] Vladimir Putin's later utilization of so-called private military companies (PMCs) in Syria, chiefly the Wagner group, was not nearly as unprecedented or surprising as it may have seemed to casual observers. On the contrary, it was an extension of a longstanding tradition. Putin was not going to be a revolutionary.

4

Putin Returns Russia to the Middle East

As Russia failed to fully break away with its past, the past slowly took over the present. In July 1999, Vladimir Putin, as the head of the FSB, placed a wreath of flowers to mark the death of former KGB chairman Yuri Andropov. This act foreshadowed a great deal about Putin and the direction in which he would take Russia. It would have been unimaginable for a former SS officer to become chancellor of the Federal Republic of Germany (West Germany) after World War II, but a former KGB officer took the highest position of power in post-Soviet Russia. In August 1999, Yeltsin named Putin as prime minister. Yeltsin resigned in December that year, leaving Putin as acting president. That month, Putin unveiled a memorial plaque to Andropov at the infamous Lubyanka.[1]

Putin chose Andropov, a man involved in the decision to intervene in Afghanistan, and instrumental in empowering the KGB domestically after a relative decline that followed Stalin's death in a period of thaw (ottepel). For all the many individuals that analysts have suggested Putin has followed over the years, and the different narratives he has utilized, Andropov has been his constant role model, even if he may not have fully understood him. Andropov is perhaps best known for his particular focus on suppressing domestic dissent (bor'ba s inokomyshliyem) and expanding the KGB's foreign intelligence activities.

The Second Chechen War

The coming second Chechen War ushered Vladimir Putin out of obscurity into the full driver's seat of Russian state power. Shortly becoming president, Putin told a group his former FSB colleagues, only half in jest, "A group of FSB operatives, dispatched under cover to work in the government of the Russian federation, is successfully fulfilling its task," as The Economist reported on the incident.[2] Between September 4 and 16, 1999, four apartment bombings shook the cities of Moscow, Volgodonsk, and Buynaksk. These left approximately 300 dead and hundreds wounded, and spread terror throughout the country.[3] Putin, then prime minister in Yeltsin's Kremlin, immediately accused Chechens and declared a second war on Chechnya. He presented himself as someone who would stop at nothing to get the terrorists. He would follow them everywhere and "wipe them out in the outhouse" (*mochit' v sortire*), as he said famously on September 24, 1999.[4]

The Kremlin used the bombings to turn the political domestic message to war with the Chechens—who, it is important to remember, remained Russian citizens. Russia was again struggling with itself. And the media also played a crucial role in Putin's assent to power.[5] The message of fear and war, together with images of Putin, came to dominate television—what the Russians call "*zombiyashchik*" (literally a "zombie box," a tool to turn people into "zombies"). Famous Russian war correspondent and former Chechen War soldier Arkady Babchenko used this reference years later when he described state messaging after the bombings and how state propaganda turned the public mood away from reconciliation with Chechnya, towards hatred and killing.[6] After Putin's tough public stance against terrorism, his approval ratings skyrocketed in the fall of 2000 from 2 percent to 45 percent,[7] but doubts remain to this day about FSB's culpability for the bombings, rather than Chechen separatists.[8] The possibility that a man in charge of one of the world's major nuclear arsenals could have started his political career with a major act of terrorism against his own people speaks volumes about Putin's Russia. It also frames the persistent and profound confusion in the West in dealing with Putin on key foreign policy issues—simultaneously casting him as part of a problem and part of the solution, including in the Middle East. And as Russia began fighting with itself, in the later years, it took the fight outside its borders.

After Putin oversaw the razing Chechnya's capital, Grozny, to the ground, Moscow remained as an occupying force until 2009. Military and political aspects of the Chechnya campaign resurfaced in Syria and for this reason it is important to mention them here. Moscow continuously learned from every military experience, and by the second Chechen War it had incorporated a number of lessons from the first war. In January 1995, the Russians were surprised and embarrassed by the degree to which the Chechens had utilized communication tools such as cell phones and the internet, and swore never again to lose the "information war,"[9] a promise they were able to keep, at least internally. By the second Chechen War, the press in Russia no longer enjoyed the degree of freedom it had under Yeltsin, and Moscow had been able to control the domestic narrative as well as introducing better telecommunication equipment in the military theater in Chechnya.

In addition, Moscow engaged in what military experts Les Grau and Timothy Tomas called a "Russian version of 'remote' war as exercised by NATO forces against Kosovo," even though the Russian version had executed these efforts crudely and imprecisely, unlike NATO.[10] This approach showed both learning from Western military campaigns (Russia has a very long and under-appreciated history of such learning), and a desire to fight a war remotely, with fewer casualties, a goal that came out especially clearly in Syria. Indeed, a 2020 Russian military journal article on prospects for future combat methods featured a map that appears designed, based on the layout of the artillery and how the forces are dispersed, for intermediary conflict, based on lessons learned from local warfare, from Chechnya to ISIS in Syria.[11]

The Russian military also did not permit moratoriums or ceasefires, which could have allowed the Chechen forces to regroup and introduced better communications equipment for their forces. A few other lessons stand out. In the first war, Moscow had also under-estimated the effect of cultural knowledge and winning "hearts and minds," and underscored the importance of training in the combat zone—something that the Russian military would have several opportunities to do in the coming years. This is not to say that the Russians intervened in Syria to gain live combat training, but that the intervention provided such an opportunity that the Kremlin used to its full advantage.

On the diplomatic track, a number of parallels with Syria also stand out. In the mid-2000s, the Parliamentary Assembly of the Council of Europe (PACE) wanted formal peace talks with Chechen leaders. Moscow engineered this process and pushed faux opposition members it had first installed in Chechnya. Analysts dubbed Moscow's approach in Chechnya back then as "Chechenization"—this process involved a charade where Moscow pretended to talk to what it called genuine Chechen opposition leaders, but in reality only allowed those it handpicked to participate.

Here is how this process worked. Moscow insisted that "separatists" could participate in the political process if they rejected terrorism and extremism. Theoretically, this sounded more than reasonable to a Western ear—those who reject violence should be given a chance to participate in a political system. But there were two problems in the Russian context. First, in reality, anyone who identified publicly as a separatist in Chechnya would "issue a death warrant to himself."[12] Second, and more to the point, Russian federal law forbade as "extremist" any activity that infringed upon the territorial integrity of the Russian Federation. The law deemed any kind of separatist conviction as extremist, regardless of the methods a person used to pursue separatist aims[13] In this circular logic, anyone could engage in opposition activity within the political system, as long as they did not represent genuine opposition; to be a genuine opponent meant to subscribe to extremist views. Thus, at the time, it became "quite obvious that voluntarily or not Europe actually agreed to organize a negotiation ground with participation of only one side to the conflict."[14] Simultaneously, in order to crush the Chechen independence struggle, Putin ignored and marginalized moderate and secular Chechens, such as the legitimately elected president at the time, Aslan Maskhadov.[15]

Putin's Foreign Policy

If Russia struggled with defining its key unifying national idea in the 1990s, Putin's regime provided an answer—and he defined it in terms of security, as a reaction against democratization of the 1990s and perceived chaos that came with it.[16] More broadly, Russia once against defined itself in relation to the West—Putin blamed the West for Russia's problems during that decade. Contrary to many assestions that Putin's regime has no ideology, Putin created one–state paternalism and patriotism based on appeals to glorious past and rejection of liberalism. On December 30, 1999, the day before he officially became acting president, a famous, oft-cited document attributed to Putin appeared on the government's website, "Russia at the Turn of the Millennium."[17] One of the document's central points was that Russia is a country with unique values in danger of losing its unity—which, in and of itself, is a historic Russian fear. This again points to the fundamental issue of Russia's identity issues—and how the state had manipulated these to drive anti-Western security narratives with the aim of eroding the US-led global order, in a worldview that blurs the lines between offensive and defensive actions. Moreover, a look at Russia's distribution of forces over the years under Putin has been heavily weighted towards the south, another indicator of the Kremlin's threat perceptions.[18]

On January 10, 2000, while still interim president, Putin approved Russia's National Security Concept. The document highlights "attempts to create an international relations structure based on domination by developed Western countries in the international community, under US leadership, and designed for unilateral solutions (primarily by the use of military force) to key issues in world politics in circumvention of the foundational rules of international law … A number of states are stepping up efforts to weaken Russia politically, economically, militarily, and in other ways."

The Security Concept defines NATO enlargement (as mentioned earlier, Russians call it expansion) as one among major threats "in the international sphere," and references a "multipolar" world and Russia's role as "one of the influential centers," echoing Primakov. In addition, threats to Russia's national security, according to the National Security Concept, were "manifested in attempts by other states to counteract its strengthening as one of the centers of influence in a multipolar world, to hinder realization of its national interests and to weaken its position in Europe, the Middle East, Transcaucasia, Central Asia and the Asia-Pacific Region." This new approach also entailed demanding recognition of Russia's legitimate privileged interests in its so-called near-abroad, loosely defined as *Russkiy mir* (Russian world) throughout the countries of the former Soviet Union. Thus, from the very beginning, the Kremlin under Putin viewed the West with distrust and hostility. Indeed, the Kremlin aimed to position Russia in opposition to the West, and emphasized the importance of respect for state sovereignty. It is in this context that Putin famously bemoaned the loss of greatness as he famously proclaimed that the break-up of the Soviet Union was the greatest geopolitical tragedy of the twentieth century.[19] Above all else, Putin wanted an image of greatness, stability, and respect—and true democratization had no place in this vision. Soon afterwards he reinstated the music of the Soviet national anthem, and in more ways than one, Putin's Russia has been singing different words to the same music ever since. Moscow never declared open war on the West, but in line with traditional Russian thinking, war is more of a spectrum than a clear separation between war and peace, offensive and defensive, and Putin's Kremlin over the years has consistently stuck to the line that it was the West that started being hostile to Russia first, and that Russia is only defending itself. Western officials for years failed to see that, whether they realized it or not, Moscow was at war with them—just not the kind of war to which they were accustomed.

Fear and historic insecurity motivated the Kremlin under Putin, just as it had motivated so many of his predecessors. In early 2000, discussing Russia's policy in the North Caucasus, Putin explained that the fear of Russia's collapse drove his decisions. "What's the situation in the North Caucasus and in Chechnya today? It's a continuation of the collapse of the USSR," he said, "This is what I thought of the situation in August [1999], when the bandits attacked Dagestan: If we don't put an immediate end to this, Russia will cease to exist. It was a question of preventing the collapse of the country."[20]

This fear of collapse was linked with ascribing nefarious motivations to the West, especially the United States, after the collapse of the Soviet Union, both in the Middle East and the post-Soviet space. Putin was relatively cautious on foreign policy in his early years, but the Kremlin vocally opposed the US invasion of Iraq in 2003 and in early 2004 his international posture noticeably turned more aggressive after the massacre of Beslan in North Ossetia in September 2004, when a group of armed Chechen and Ingush terrorists seized a school in Beslan, North Ossetia. This domestic incident affected foreign policy.

The Kremlin responded with force that led to the deaths of 380 of the hostages, 186 of them children.[21] Ilyas Akhmadov, former Chechen foreign minister, recalled in his book that when he spoke to the organizers of the terrorist act, the ultimate responsibility lay with Shamil Basayev who planned the operation with the aim of using children as hostages, but nonetheless Shamil did not expect Putin to shoot at children.[22] Many inside Russia, especially relatives of the hostages, hold the Russian government responsible for this tragedy and criticized its botched rescue.[23] Putin used Beslan as a justification for deepening Russia's democratic backslide and stressed that Russia had to project strength. He indirectly blamed the West for this incident:[24]

> We showed ourselves [to be] weak. And the weak get beaten. Some would like to tear from us a "juicy piece of pie." Others help them. They help, reasoning that Russia still remains one of the world's major nuclear power[s], and as such still represents a threat to them. And so they reason that this threat should be removed. Terrorism, of course, is an instrument to achieve these aims ... I am convinced that in reality we have no choice at all ... What we are dealing with are not isolated acts intended to frighten us, not isolated terrorist attacks. What we are facing is direct intervention of international terror directed against Russia.[25]

The narrative that the West sponsors terrorism inside Russia, as part of a concerted effort to weaken if not destroy the country is a theme that Putin continued to echo over the coming years. This narrative is crucial for understanding Russia's position in Syria. By 2004 Putin had taken a noticeably anti-Western posture. This was the year that saw the rise of "color revolutions"— peaceful protest against authoritarians and unfree elections that swept the post-Soviet space. To be sure, these uprisings began earlier, with the Bulldozer revolution in Serbia in October 2000, and continued with the Rose revolution in Georgia in November 2003, already on the cusp of 2004. Yet it was Ukraine's orange revolution of November 2004–January 2005 that impacted Putin especially deeply, in part because Ukraine matters so much with regard to Russia's struggle with its identity. And as former Putin advisor Gleb Pavlovky said, he saw the protests as a US ploy to invade the Russian border, in a "neurotic reaction of a weak country."[26] Other color revolutions followed and touched the Middle East, with Lebanon's 2005 Cedar Revolution, a point that did not receive as much attention in the former Soviet Union, but showed that the Middle East mattered in the Kremlin's assessment of perceived threats and the role of the West in them. In this context, two years later, in Munich in February 2007, Putin famously accused the United States of destabilizing activities worldwide.[27] Meanwhile, the FSB had emerged as immensely powerful by this time. By January 2008, the internal debate on securitization increasingly shifted towards those who favored a view that the US preeminence in international affairs and its perceived proclivity in favor of the use of military force, presented the main (even if not the only) threat to Russia.[28] Thus, in January 2008, Makhmut A. Gareev, president of Russia's Defense Academy argued that the NATO-led campaign in Yugoslavia "ushered in, in essence, a new epoch not only in the military, but also in the universal history, the epoch of open military-force diktat."[29] Gareev defined separatism and terrorism as most dangerous threats to Russia—only in this view, they were all created externally, outside of Russia.[30] In August that year Moscow invaded Georgia.

In 2011, Putin's foreign policy reached another stage of aggression in the context of NATO's Libya campaign and protests in Syria, where Putin took a firm position in support of Syria's president Bashar al-Assad. With regard to Libya, as then officially prime minister, Putin compared the NATO campaign to "medieval crusades."[31] Late 2011–early 2012 saw massive anti-Putin uprisings throughout the country—the largest since the fall of the Soviet Union, against what many perceived as a fraudulent Duma election. Even the protest organizers themselves were surprised at such a massive turnout, and the Kremlin certainly was. Russia experts Fiona Hill and Cliff Gaddy wrote that Putin's core identities which were the source of his strength here became a weakness and prevented him from foreseeing the protests.[32] Putin became enraged and accused the United States, specifically State Secretary Hillary Clinton of "giving the signal" for protestors to come out. He could not believe that the protests could have erupted on their own.

Yet his regime showed itself to be resilient. Putin managed to crush the protest movement and win the 2012 presidential election. Putin wept as he delivered his speech. He stressed several times that this was a "fair election," and noted that "no one can impose anything on us," that the Russian people can identify "provocations which have only one goal—to destroy the Russian statehood and seize power."[33]

Thus began the next stage of Putin's foreign policy, with an even greater emphasis on external powers trying to "destroy Russia's statehood." In the winter of 2012, Putin penned five articles in the Russian press. While they touched on his traditional themes and talked about his political and economic vision to address a myriad of problems plaguing the country, he referred to what was for him a new theme—he proclaimed Russia as a unique "state civilization." Leon Aaron described this new rhetoric as one that "harks back to Russia's two most reactionary rulers: the nineteenth-century tsars Nicholas I and his grandson, Alexander III," who made Russia's secret political police a key state institution and formed Russia's allegedly distinctive identity in official state ideology of "Orthodoxy, Autocracy and Nationality." Aaron concluded, "[w]ith minor linguistic adjustments, this slogan of Nicholas I and Alexander III seems now to have been adopted by Mr. Putin."[34] In the context of this newly adopted slogan, the illegal annexation of Crimea followed two years later. Indeed, when Putin explained why he annexed Crimea, he framed it as a defensive response to centuries, not years, of Western hostilities towards Russia. "[W]e have every reason to assume that the infamous policy of containment, led in the 18th, 19th and 20th centuries, continues today. They are constantly trying to sweep us into a corner because we have an independent position,"[35] he said. Intervention in Syria came the following year.

Return to the Middle East: A Pragmatic Approach

As mentioned earlier, Moscow's foreign policy, and its approach to the Middle East in particular, grew out a vision that Primakov had articulated in the late 1990s. In the context of restoring Russia as a great power with a vision towards a multipolar world, in the Middle East, Putin sought to gain political influence in the region and put a higher emphasis on Russia's business interests: arms and energy (oil and gas) sales, as well as high-tech goods such as nuclear reactors.[36] But anti-Americanism stood in the backdrop of these interests. Indeed, the January 2000 Foreign Policy Concept defined Moscow's priorities in the Middle East as "to restore and strengthen [Russia's] positions, particularly economic ones," and highlighted the importance of continuing to develop ties with Iran.[37] The same document also highlighted "attempts to create an international relations structure based on domination by developed Western countries in the international community, under US leadership." The most recent version of this document from November 2016 also highlights the importance of the Middle East in Russian foreign policy and names "external interference" (a euphemism for the United States), as a major cause of instability in the region.[38] Together, these documents show continuity in the Kremlin's thinking about Russia's role in the region, and that of the West as a threatening, adversarial power.

Primakov believed that the US invasion of Iraq in 2003 contributed to the spread of terrorism,[39] and that secular dictatorships in the Middle East provided stability. "When US troops invaded, Iraq was a secular state, and while I do not wish in any way to condone Saddam Hussein's regime, with the many errors and crimes it committed, it cannot be accused of failing to establish stability on the religious front," wrote Primakov; and he added "After the US occupation, Iraq became a faith-based state, governed according to the Islamic model."[40] This claim is inaccurate and especially illustrative of the distortions in Russian interpretations of US actions in the Middle East. While religious and sectarian parties obtained some prominence in the post-invasion government, Iraqi legal codes and legislation have been fundamentally secular since the US invasion. The new Iraqi state also did not use the word "Islamic" as part of its name, another important indicator of state secularism. Moreover, it was Saddam Hussein who had inscribed in his own handwriting the word "Allahu Akbar" into the Iraqi flag in the beginning of the 1990s as part of his "Faith campaign" to use religion in Iraq for political purposes. By contrast, during internal Iraqi discussions about it after the invasion, the phrase came close to being removed— another indicator of the more secular direction the Iraqi state had taken after the invasion. In the end the font was changed to Kufi. These misrepresentations concerning Iraq and the 2003 invasion underscore the false choice Primakov laid out between "secular" but "stable" dictators and radical Islamists. Under Putin, Moscow had pursued similar equivocation and inaccurate narratives with regard to Syria and Assad, and radical Islamists. Specifically, Putin's Kremlin presented it as a choice between a "secular" dictator and radical Islamists who are worse, in even more black and white terms than Primakov—the Kremlin had not openly admitted that the Assad regime committed any crimes, let alone promoted Assad's encouragement of Islamic radicalization.

If the Soviet Union followed a communist ideology in the region, Putin's return to the Middle East entailed cooperation with everyone there—both traditional allies and adversaries. Rather than a communist ideology, Putin presented a vision of a multipolar world, where Russia had to advance its influence in the region at the expense of the West, and in this zero-sum context, Putin pursued other interests, chiefly economic gain, primarily through arms and energy trade. To give a few examples, in December 2002, then Russian foreign minister Igor Ivanov said in an interview, "It appears this is the year when we finalized a multi-vector policy, one in which different geographical directions and priorities supplement, rather than contradict, each other."[41] Once again countering a perceived negative picture of Russia in the West, he said, "I think the image of an either impoverished or money-spinning mafia-like Russia, an image spontaneously or sometimes purposely created in the West in the 90s, is gradually receding into the past."[42] In December 2003, Alexander Yakovenko, director of the Foreign Affairs Ministry's information and press department, wrote in government official *Rossiysakaya Gazeta*: "Today not one significant international problem is being solved without Russia."[43] There was also a crucial cultural element to Putin's outreach to the region. Putin presented Russia as a unique civilization that straddles East and West that can serve as a bridge and mediator.[44] As well as stressing its large Muslim minority, deep history of relations with the Muslim world, and geographical proximity to it, Putin simultaneously invoked Russia's "uniqueness" to justify a democratic backslide domestically and support of authoritarian leaders abroad, including in the Middle East.[45]

The arms sales element of Moscow's approach is important because historically the region had been a top destination for Russian weaponry, and Putin aimed to further this process. However, for Moscow arms sales have always been a foreign policy tool, rather than a more narrow commercial interest. While this can be said in part of many countries, including the United States, the US simply will not sell weapons to certain actors and states. US arms sales also go through rigorous and lengthy approval to ensure transparency and compliance with regulations, such as prohibitions of secondary arms sales. In other words, responsible states go to great lengths to put safeguards in place to prevent weapons from falling into the wrong hands or being used to prolong a conflict. For example, the US held a ban on arms sales to both Armenia and Azerbaijan from 1993 to 2002.[46] That is, the ban was officially lifted after September 11, 2001 when American foreign policy shifted towards counterterrorism. Even so, US arms did not simply start flowing into the region after the ban was lifted. Rather, in more recent years, the United States provided limited security assistance to Azerbaijan specifically for counter-terrorism efforts to support the US or its coalition partners, and worked to ensure full compliance with counter-terrorism law.[47]

Russia on the other hand had been selling arms to both Armenia and Azerbaijan. In 2016, then prime minister Dmitry Medvedev defended these sales in the following terms: "They would buy weapons in other countries, and the degree of their deadliness wouldn't change. But at the same time, this could to a certain degree destroy the balance [of forces in the region]."[48] It is difficult to imagine a senior Western official defending arms sales to two conflicting parties essentially by saying "if we don't do it someone else will, and they will make things even worse." More to the point, Medvedev essentially implied that Moscow was content with the existing status quo of a frozen conflict; and the only other alternative is even worse—he could not even imagine a better scenario, where the conflict was resolved.

One can certainly quibble or outright disagree with specific cases of US arms sales and broader security assistance—or indeed failure to provide either one—when getting into the detail of specific cases. Such a conversation is more than warranted. Later chapters will discuss this in more detail in the context of Syria, specifically the meager assistance given to the Syrian rebels. But to do this broader conversation justice would be beyond the scope of this discussion and would be to stray from the main point here—that Russia, unlike the West, simply does not have a transparent and responsible process in place when it comes to arms sales and has no qualms about using arms to perpetuate a conflict if it servers a larger foreign policy objective. Those who know they will not get US arms often turn to Moscow. Russian arms sales also get approved quickly and come with few strings attached; and prohibition of secondary arms sales is not a concern when dealing with Russia, unlike with the United States. Thus, In July 2012, at a meeting of the Commission for Military Technology Cooperation with Foreign States, Putin said, "We see active military technical cooperation as an effective instrument for advancing our national interests, both political and economic."[49] And in December 2013, deputy prime minister Dmitry Rogozin, went as far as to say that the Federal Service for Military Technical Cooperation—the agency leading arms sales abroad—was "the country's second foreign policy agency" and that its objective in selling arms was so that Russia could "gain or increase [its] influence" in other countries. Rogozin also said that Russia's arms sales are the most important element of its relations with other countries.[50] One would be hard pressed to find a similar statement from a senior Western official. Western states tend to view building relationships through a prism of different values, where arms sales can certainly be a key element, but not a foundation on which a relationship is built.

Putin's pragmatic approach to the Middle East has shown itself to be more successful than the Soviet Union's focus on ideology.[51] Putin's Russia is more of the view that, ultimately, it is difficult to construct anything permanent in the Middle East, unlike with other regions or countries. In this spirit, Putin balanced good relations with Sunni and Shia powers, as well as Israel, even as in reality he favored the anti-American Shia forces in the region. Indeed, by 2010, just prior to the outbreak of the Arab Spring, Putin had built in the Middle East "good relations with every government and most major opposition movements."[52] Ostensibly balancing good relations with everyone while still favoring anti-American forces remains Putin's approach to this day—and it is one that, crucially, helps guard against getting "stuck" in the region. Certainly, fear of getting "stuck" has not been absent from the Kremlin's thinking. Prominent pro-Kremlin academic Sergei Karaganov once said in an interview that it is in fact the United States that is always trying to push Russia into getting stuck in the Middle East and Russia must guard against that. "Our geopolitical opponents still dream of drawing us [into the Middle East] so that we get stuck there. They sometimes talk about it."[53] Other less prominent Russian pro-Kremlin analysts had expressed a similar sentiment with regard to Russia in Syria.[54] With regard to Russian security, Putin faced the same problem that the Soviet Union did—in a conflict with the United States, the US global navy still has a maritime strike capability that Russia, as a land power, cannot match. Putin placed a special emphasis on the Russian navy, especially when he officially returned to a third presidential term in 2012; and by the next year, he had resurrected the Russian Mediterranean squadron. For Putin, just as for his predecessors, the Mediterranean remained a crucial strategic choke point. Moreover Russia had no alternatives to Syria for naval support on the Eastern Mediterranean, and throughout 2013 the Kremlin attempted to diversify by asking (unsuccessfully) for Russia's own naval bases in Cyprus and Montenegro in late 2013, though Cyprus allowed the Russian military to use the Cypriot airbase and seaport in Limassol.[55] These efforts show how much emphasis Moscow placed, and continues to place, on maritime access in this region.

5

The Russia-Iran-Syria Triangle

Russia's relationship with Syria is important in its own right, but it also stands within an anti-Western Russia-Iran-Syria triad in the Middle East. It must be viewed through this prism because these are the states most committed to driving American, and more broadly, Western forces out of the region as opposed to Sunni governments and Israel—forces traditionally aligned more with the West. Indeed, Russia's relationship with Syria was always about more than simply Syria itself. Thus, this chapter examines the Russia-Iran-Syria triangle.

Iran

Pragmatic Cooperation

Putin sought closer ties with Iran from the beginning of his tenure, building on the last years of the Yeltsin era, when some of the more hawkish members of the Russian parliament had also advocated for closer ties with Iran. Indeed, by the end of the 1990s Moscow became Iran's main supplier of conventional arms.[1] Given the complicated history between the two countries, it comes as no surprise that from 1999 to 2013, Russia–Iran relations vacillated "between antagonism and friendship."[2]

In October 2000, while in his first year in office, Putin publicly and unilaterally abrogated the 1995 Gore-Chernomyrdin pact, which allowed Russia to complete existing arms agreements with Iran on conventional arms, but required that it abstain from all other future deals; in exchange, the United States agreed not to sanction Russia for selling advanced weaponry to a US-designated state sponsor of terrorism. Some had argued that in practice the agreement's limitations on Russia's arms sales to Iran were illusory. The pact essentially gave Russia "a free pass" to sell conventional arms to Iran until 1999[3] and after that deadline passed, others observed, Moscow simply did not hold up its end of the bargain and continued to sell Iran weapons.[4] Still, Putin's public cancellation of the pact sent a message that Moscow wanted closer cooperation with the Islamic Republic and the following year, in March, Mohammad Khatami came to Russia. The visit was historic, and paved the way for further improvement in bilateral ties. No Iranian president had come to Moscow since the 1979 Islamic Revolution.

Geopolitical considerations appeared to be the primary reason for Putin's push for closer cooperation with Tehran. Tehran had looked the other way on Russia's actions in Chechnya. Iran also wielded some influence in the South Caucasus and Central Asia, where the Kremlin traditionally felt vulnerable. Still, there was also a bigger game at play. As typical for Moscow, it involved the West, and chiefly the United States. Professor Mark N. Katz wrote that Putin worried that then-Iranian President Mohammad Khatami's "dialogue of civilizations" would bring Iran closer to the United States.[5] And over a decade after Khatami's visit, in the context of the growing stand-off between Russia and the West, senior Russian Middle East expert Georgiy Mirsky wrote:

> Several years ago, I heard from the lips of one MID [Ministry of Foreign Affairs] employee such reasoning: "For us, a pro-American Iran is worse than a nuclear Iran." Wow, I thought, if many people in Smolenskaya Square think way, this doesn't bode well for Russian diplomacy ... it once again demonstrates the strikingly narrow political horizon of people in whose brains there is nothing but hatred of America, and hatred that is largely contrived, artificial and hypocritical. It doesn't matter what will happen with Iran and in general with the Middle East—the main thing is that Washington wins nothing.[6]

Though the Kremlin prioritized political considerations, economic reasons were another factor. Moscow continued to increase arms trade and nuclear cooperation with the Islamic Republic.[7] Tehran also made no secret of its interest in purchasing the S-300 system—a surface-to-air missile system usually referred to in the West as SAM—from Russia. That said, geopolitical motivations still took precedence. Both Russian and Iranian officials over the years have been fond of describing the SAM system as exclusively defensive, and while this is partly correct, SAMs also help to contest and control airspace, and thus augment regional balance of power from a military perspective.

Both Russia and Iran also held the world's largest natural gas deposits, and while they emerged as competitors in the energy field, they simultaneously cooperated in this field and saw no contradiction in this regard. As oil prices rose, there was all the more reason to expand bilateral ties. One Russian analyst also observed in December 2006, that although Russia and Iran were not friends, "[t]he material interests that drive Russian relations with Iran are strong and go beyond narrow interests of particular power groups. Iran is, in fact, an important trading partner for Russia, and one of the few larger markets for Russia's industrial and technological output, which has been painfully insignificant in comparison with its fuel exports."[8] Overall Russia–Iran trade was never the primary driver of the relationship, and in numbers had typically been quite insignificant. None the less, it has grown in recent years. By 2005, Russia was among the top ten exporters to Iran according to International Monetary Fund statistics.[9] In 2008, bilateral trade reached $3.7 billion.[10] In 2018, according to official Iranian statistics, Iran exported $533 million worth of commodities to Russia in 2018—a 36 percent growth as compared to 2017.[11]

Moscow and Tehran also shared opposition to Sunni Islamism—at least broadly speaking, for neither shied away from working with them when it suited their geostrategic agenda. This shared opposition has led to a double standard on Sunni-versus-Shia terrorism for the Kremlin. In February 2003, the Russian Supreme Court designated the Sunni Muslim Brotherhood a terrorist organization, while the Shia Hezbollah received no such designation. In practice, over the years Putin has ended up working with Sunni Islamists (while Moscow and Tehran have worked, when necessary, with the Taliban, which was traditionally anti-Shia and anti-Russian). Under Putin, Moscow leaned closer to the anti-Sunni forces in the region.

There are several examples of Putin working with Islamists. In Chechnya, Putin preferred to install a former mujahid and a warlord who would remain loyal to the Kremlin and lead Chechnya's Islamization, as Chechnya's secular and moderate opposition became sidelined. As the fighting in Iraq continued after the 2003 invasion, Assad supported the anti-US Sunni jihadist insurgency and Putin looked the other way. In Egypt, despite the fact that the Muslim Brotherhood was officially labeled a terrorist organization in Russia, Putin reached out to Egypt's Morsi after he took over Egypt's presidency in June 2012 and was just as willing to work with him as we was with his predecessor. In Afghanistan, Moscow began communication with the Taliban as early as 2007, and while Moscow's official reasons for talking to the Taliban has been that the Taliban were fighting ISIS, ISIS did not even exist in 2007, while the Taliban's relationship with ISIS is not clear-cut. At a more fundamental level, Bashar al-Assad, who presented himself as a secularist who protected minorities and fought Sunni extremism, in reality was simply the flip side of the same coin. As mentioned in other chapters, Assad himself not only encouraged radicalization, but his repression of his citizens remained the main recruitment tool for Sunni terrorists. Putin, who framed issues in a similar dichotomous manner—either authoritarian order or chaos and terrorism—had much in common with Assad in this sense.

Iran's Nuclear Program and Moscow's Interests

In the early to mid-2000s, Iran's nuclear aspirations grew into a major multilateral issue. Yet debate about it in the West differed from discussion in Russia. Moscow clearly would have preferred that Iran would not develop a nuclear weapon. However, it did not worry about this issue to the same degree as did the West. Soviet and then Russian diplomat on arms control and non-proliferation issues, Victor Mizin, wrote in October 2000 that Russia's political scientists "pay lip service to the politically correct notion that proliferation is dangerous," but Moscow does not share the Western notion of "rogue states." Deployed ballistic missiles would not threaten Russian troops stationed abroad as they do American troops, he wrote, and unlike in the West, Russia has no domestic lobbies to pressure the government on such issues. Russian analysts, he wrote, used "very politically correct words ... about concerns that Iran is developing missile capabilities." However, "No one in the Russian political elite is seriously considering the threat of this development."[12] His comment highlights Moscow's geopolitical and perhaps economic preferences that trumped what Western governments would consider chief security considerations. Western governments were concerned about Iran's nuclear program not in and of itself, but because Tehran's sponsored terrorist activities aimed at Western interests, citizens, and allies. The US State Department does not worry, for example, about the French nuclear program because it is peaceful. This line of reasoning, taken further, suggests that Moscow did not consider Iranian activities to be as destabilizing and dangerous as the West did, or at the very least did not think the Western approach to limiting Iran's nuclear program was useful.

In 2002, Russian defense minister Sergei Ivanov outlined Moscow's policy toward nuclear proliferation, "The key criteria of Russian policy in this sphere are our own national security, the strengthening of our country's international positions and the preservation of its great power status."[13] This is a fairly vague statement, open to interpretation in terms of Moscow's actual concerns for Iran's nuclear proliferation. It leaves no ambiguities, however, with regard to Moscow's ultimate self-interest and desire for great-power status.

Over the years that have followed, Russian officials have periodically reiterated that Western concerns about Iran's nuclear program are overblown.[14] In 2006,

Lavrov said sanctions would turn Iran into a second North Korea.[15] Putin, Sergei Lavrov, and other senior Russian officials argued that Iran deserves to be an "equal partner" in resolving Middle East issues, and that sanctions hurt Russia–Iran trade.[16] In a June 2003 interview with the BBC, Putin said, "We will strongly oppose the attempts to oust Russian companies from the Iranian market with the pretext of Iran's possible production of nuclear weapons."[17] To give another example, in April 2009, Lavrov said, "To date, neither the IAEA data nor expert assessments provide grounds for confidently asserting that Tehran is developing a military nuclear program. This, incidentally, was reflected in the report of the US intelligence community, published in 2007."[18] And later, in February 2017, Lavrov said Iran should be a full-fledged member of a wider anti-terrorism coalition.[19]

The Kremlin, on the one hand, often reiterated that it supported the IAEA and stood firmly by international legal principles. It also said that it was unacceptable for Iran to develop a nuclear weapon. Yet simultaneously, the Kremlin shielded Tehran from Western pressure and defended its nuclear program as peaceful, even in the face of International Atomic Energy Agency (IAEA) evidence to the contrary.[20] In a 2010 interview, Lavrov, as reported by MGIMO, "called for clarification of all points of Iran's nuclear program. He added that the problems were caused by the imperfection of the existing nuclear non-proliferation regime."[21] Thus, implicitly, Lavrov blamed the very international legal system it professed to support in the face of perceived US unilateral action. Moreover, fourteen years after Putin's BBC interview, a joint report by two Kremlin-funded think tanks listed sanctions as one among key obstacles in development of Russia–Iran trade.[22] This finding shows continuity and consistency in terms of the Kremlin's thinking and priorities. And in the winter of 2006, two authors observed in the Middle East Policy journal:

> While the US administration tries to produce international opposition to Russia's moves, Moscow continuously argues that this issue is manipulated and over-politicized ... A cyclical pattern emerged: Russia first makes an offer to bring Iran to the terms of the international community; Iran inclines toward the Russian position; after some time, Iran says it will take its own independent position, and the process comes back to the point where it started. The early months of 2006 witnessed this pattern once again ... Although Russia will not be happy if Iran gains nuclear weapons, it is still, in Russian strategic thinking, vital to pursue the Iranian nuclear program as a facilitator of regional geopolitical considerations and a prerequisite for securing a place in the global power-production market.[23]

The 2003 Iraq War gave Russia and Iran another reason for increased cooperation as part of Moscow's relations with the West. The war exposed Tehran's and Moscow's shared sense of perceived Western encroachment and aversion to what it perceived as active Western efforts to spread liberal democracy by sponsoring protests and toppling authoritarian regimes. Over the coming years, it was the West, especially NATO, and color revolutions, that Moscow came to perceive as its chief threat, which it prioritized over Iran's nuclear proliferation. This priority was clearly stated in Moscow's 2010 and 2015 military doctrines. Moscow does not want another nuclear rival in the region, but sees such a prospect as less threatening than does the West.[24]

Difficulties in the Russia–Iran relationship persisted, however. When Mahmoud Ahmadinejad assumed the Iranian presidency in August 2005, Putin had hoped for greater cooperation between Moscow and Tehran, and enticed Tehran with offers to enrich its uranium to commercial grade. He also offered to serve as a mediator between Iran and the West to alleviate any security concerns that they may have about Iran's nuclear program. As Mark N. Katz wrote, Tehran instead appeared set on a more independent course, and did not want Russia's help in enriching uranium. Still, bilateral cooperation continued. Thus, in December 2005 the two countries signed a billion-dollar arms deal that included twenty-nine Tor-M1 missile-defense systems to protect the Bushehr nuclear power plant. The following year, Moscow also invested $750 million in energy projects in Iran.[25]

Moscow's arms sales to Iran increasingly raised concerns in Washington. The trade complicated the imposition of sanctions on the Iranian regime over its nuclear program, and reports suggested that Tehran—along with Damascus—may have been transferring light arms and missiles to Hezbollah and Hamas. Iran also began boosting its naval presence. A Congressional Research Service report warned in September 2006, that Russian arms sales to Iran could pose a major security threat to the United States.[26] Other experts felt at the time that Iran was still too weak to pose a serious security challenge. Still, there were reasons to worry about Russia's arms trade with Iran. For one thing, between 1995 and 2005, over 70 percent of Iranian arms imports came from Russia.[27] China and India remained Moscow's top arms customers, but Iran came third, and thus deals with Iran were not irrelevant. In August 2006, the United States sanctioned Rosoboronexport and Sukhoi, Russia's two key defense production entities, designating them in violation of the Iran Nonproliferation Act of 2000.[28] More specifically, the sanctions applied "to the specific entities and their successors, sub-units or subsidiaries and not to their respective countries or governments,"[29] which included not only Russian but also North Korea and Cuba. Thus, the sanctions prevented US firms from working with certain companies, including Rosoboronexport and Sukhoi.[30] Russia's foreign ministry condemned the sanctions as "clearly illegitimate."[31]

In the context of growing Western concern over the Iranian nuclear program, Moscow endorsed the P5+1 format in June 2006 to negotiate limiting Iran's nuclear program.[32] For the Kremlin, once again, arms sales were not simply a source of financial gain, but of something more important—political leverage. Putin saw the negotiation platform as an opportunity to try to pull Iran closer into its orbit and use the track in other ways to serve the Kremlin's interests. Thus, it sought to dilute or delay sanctions against Iran in a carrot-and-stick approach—signaling that it could protect Tehran if it moved closer to Russia, but always keeping the option of siding with the West if it did not. The negotiation format was helpful to Russia in this regard. In October 2007, Putin visited Tehran—the first visit by a Russian or Soviet head of state since Stalin's visit in 1943 when northern Iran was under Soviet occupation. The visit overlapped with the Iraq surge and it is in this context that Putin once again highlighted his geopolitical priorities when he said, "We should not even think of making use of force in this region."[33]

The nuclear negotiations track also offered opportunities for Moscow to extract critical concessions from the West—and here Moscow made more inroads than it did with Iran. Putin used Russia's association with Tehran as a bargaining chip in his resistance to a missile-defense shield in Eastern Europe oriented toward Iran, Georgia moving closer to the West, and other points of disagreement with the West, as well as to maintain Russia's increased influence in the Middle East. Moscow's actions show that its interests in Tehran were strictly pragmatic and calculated based on realpolitik and within its continued perception of the West as a threat to Russia. "An opinion became prevalent in Moscow," wrote Talal Nizameddin, "that persistent US threats to launch a military campaign against Iran belied a greater ambition by Washington and its allies to weaken and isolate Russia."[34]

In May 2010, the Kremlin extracted an unprecedented concession from the West as part of the negotiations. Moscow would support some sanctions on Iran in exchange for the United States lifting sanctions against the Russian military complex enacted in 2006, and allow Moscow to sell anti-aircraft batteries to Tehran.[35] The concessions drew bipartisan criticism from American Congressmen and national security experts outside the Obama administration, including those who worked closely on Russia, for being overly naïve about Putin.[36]

When it came to what Moscow gained from Iran from the negotiations, the results at the time appeared mixed. Tehran would have preferred Russia not to support sanctions at all. It also felt snubbed when in 2010, under pressure from the United States and Israel, Moscow froze the sale of S-300 air defense missiles to Iran—a weapon system it had been trying to get from Moscow for years. Still, because Moscow never gave a firm commitment that it would never sell this weapon, the Kremlin retained a degree of flexibility.

In October 2011, shortly after anti-Assad protests broke out in Syria, a Hezbollah delegation paid its first official visit to Moscow—a visit that, according to the BBC Russian Service was "shrouded in mystery."[37] Approximately two months later, massive anti-Putin protests broke out throughout Russia. Putin blamed the West, and in particular the US State Department for "giving the signal"[38] for protestors to come out. Fear that protest could break out anywhere at any time increasingly began to guide Putin after the protests. And because, in his view, the West was out to unseat him (along with Middle Eastern authoritarians), he had added reason to move closer to anti-American actors such as Iran. Indeed, protests in Russia coincided with the Arab Spring, which Moscow became convinced was a US government operation, in the same way as he had viewed the color revolutions. In August 2017, Lavrov said, "Anywhere, in any country—in Eastern Europe, in Central Europe—there are a lot of facts about when the US embassy[39] literally runs the [political] processes, including the actions of the opposition ... I think they [Americans] themselves don't consider it an intervention because, first, they [think they] can do anything, and second, it's in their blood."[40]

The Syria Factor

By 2013, Russian–Iranian cooperation rose to unprecedented heights. Nikolai Bobkin, chief editor of the Russian magazine *Delovoy Iran* (Business Iran), described in 2013 the "unusual for official circles candor" with which Iranian diplomats talk about Russia as its closest ally.[41]

A number of convergent interests brought Moscow and Tehran to this point,[42] but Syria was key. On the nuclear front, the state-run Russian firm Atomstroy helped the Iranians complete the Bushehr nuclear power plant and officially handed the Iranians control of the facility in September 2013. The following year, Russia's state-run nuclear corporation Rosatom announced an agreement to build two new reactor units in Iran, possibly to be followed by six more. In light of Putin's standoff with the West over Russian aggression in Ukraine, bilateral cooperation has intensified and expanded to other sectors.

In 2013, Moscow began insisting that Iran be included in Syria peace talks.[43] In spring 2013, according to Russian sources, Russian and Iranian officials discussed the idea of Tehran joining the Moscow-led Eurasian Customs Union at a seminar in Tehran titled "Iran and Regional Cooperation in Eurasia."[44] Iranian Foreign Minister Ali Akbar Salehi attended the event and reportedly spoke of Iran's usefulness to the development and expansion of Eurasianism. The Customs Union in particular, and the Eurasian Economic Union that followed it in 2014, are part of Putin's effort to counterbalance the European Union. Putin never offered to allow any Arab country to join the Customs Union. Iran was never part of the Soviet Union, as were the other member countries. That said, Sean McMeekin argues in a recent book that tsarist Russia was in the process of absorbing northern Iran into the Russian Empire at the end of the nineteenth and start of the twentieth centuries—a process that only the Bolshevik revolution interrupted.[45] McMeekin's novel argument lends further support to the Kremlin's historical interests in the Middle East—interests that preceded the Soviet Union, and adds a layer of complexity to the already difficult Russia–Iran relationship. It also further justifies Iran's historic distrust of Russia.

In the context of the Customs Union discussion, Rouhani made his first trip to Armenia (a Customs Union member) as president in December 2016—ostensibly to improve ties, and signed a number of agreements upon the conclusion of the visit.[46] Over the coming years, the two countries continued improving ties. The discussion with the Customs Union ultimately led to action. In May 2018, Iran signed an interim free trade zone agreement with the Customs Union.[47] The agreement sets up a three-year period to work out the necessary details before signing a full-fledged agreement. Some may wonder how much the Customs Union really matters. Indeed, when it first started out, Western analysts did not necessarily take it seriously, either politically or economically. Yet a 2017 official German study observed that the Customs Union is a "midweight" in the global economy.[48] More to the point, the political optics of the organization likely outweigh economic ones. Armenia's current president Nikol Pashinyan for his part met with Rouhani in Tehran in February 2019, as the two countries increased economic cooperation.

In the months prior to Russia's Syria intervention, in January 2015, Russian Defense Minister Sergei Shoigu visited Iran and as mentioned earlier, in July that year, Qassem Soleimani, commander of the Iranian elite Quds force, came to Moscow. Soon after the start of the Russian intervention, in November, Putin visited Tehran. These were the first visits of officials on this level in at least a decade. After they met, Supreme Leader Ali Khamenei praised Putin for "neutralizing Washington's plots."[49] Putin discussed Iranian cooperation with the Customs Union, offered a $5 billion line of credit, and discussed expansion of bilateral trade. He also described Iran as a "trustworthy and reliable ally."[50] His comments again reveal his true priority of pulling Iran into his sphere of influence and undermining the US-led global order. Subsequent high-level meetings followed and soon became routine. Moreover, Hezbollah leader, Hassan Nasrallah, typically referred to Russia as an ally in his speeches.

When it came to the Iran nuclear negotiations, the Kremlin publicly highlighted Russia's indispensable role. When the Joint Comprehensive Plan of Action (JCPOA), more commonly known as the Iranian nuclear accord, was reached in July 2015, Putin issued an official statement not only praising the deal but also emphasizing Russia's participation in the process as an invaluable intermediary. "The Russian negotiating team and nuclear specialists made a considerable expert contribution to the preparation of a comprehensive agreement, which made it possible to reduce different, often diametrically opposed, positions to a common denominator," he said.[51] The Russian Ministry of Foreign Affairs tweeted that the accord was "based on the approach articulated by President Vladimir Putin."[52]

Almost immediately upon the conclusion of the agreement, Putin lifted the freeze on the S-300 deal. Although at this point the S-300 was not the newest weapon—Moscow had the S-400 and was already in the process of developing an S-500—the transfer was still important.

The Syria factor also mattered when it came to the JCPOA. Nikolai Bobkin wrote in September 2015, "After Moscow made possible the agreement with Iran on the nuclear issue, the West is simply obligated to recognize Iran's influence on Assad," and to "cease to ignore [Iran's] role in resolving the Syrian crisis." He added, "Today, no one will deny that there has never been any 'moderate' democratic opposition in Syria about which they loved to talk so much about in the White House."[53]

The Kremlin was especially supportive of the completed Iran deal, and Putin even took credit for its approach.[54] Putin indirectly expressed his anti-Western priorities once more when he said that the deal meant that "bilateral relations with Iran will receive a new impetus and will no longer be influenced by external factors."[55] And shortly after Moscow's Syria intervention, Russian officials announced plans to open a $5 billion credit line to Iran.[56] In September 2016, Putin said that it would be "just" if Iran reached pre-sanctions level of oil production.[57] In November, he began discussing a $10 billion arms deal.

The Iran Factor in the Russia–Syria Relationship

Putin and Assad came to power at approximately the same time. Though the two men are quite different, they share certain key similarities. Both presented themselves to the West as secular leaders who wanted to work with it on combating Sunni extremism, but both in reality were always guided by different priorities. Both agreed on their joint opposition to the US role in global affairs and what they perceived it to mean for their own stay in power. Both opposed the 2003 Iraq War. As the fighting in Iraq continued, Assad allowed Sunni extremist fighters from around the region to cross into Iraq via Syrian territory, and while Syria supported the anti-US insurgency, Moscow looked the other way. Between 2004 and 2007, Syria emerged as the main transit point for Arab foreign fighters going into Iraq to join terrorist groups such as al-Qaeda.[58] Sam Dagher wrote, "[a]bout 75 percent of suicide bombings in Iraq during a one-year period starting in August 2006 were carried out by foreigners coming through Syria."[59]

Although Moscow long a had a special relationship with Syria and Putin worked to further improve ties with Damascus, a significant breakthrough came in January 2005, when Assad came to Moscow and met with Putin. The two countries discussed a number of issues, including on energy, and signed a "friendship" treaty. But perhaps the most significant development was that Moscow announced it would write off most of Syria's debt and sell arms to Damascus in return for Syria's permission to establish permanent Russian naval facilities in Tartus and Latakia. In the end Putin wrote off over $9.6 billion of the $13.4 billion debt—the largest single debt forgiveness of Putin's tenure at the time.[60] (In 2014, though, Putin forgave the bulk of Cuba's $32 billion debt to Russia.)[61]

Syria's relationship with Iran also began to change under Bashar. Under Hafez al-Assad, Syria retained autonomy from Iran, but Assad allowed Iran and Hezbollah unprecedented influence. Manaf Tlas, a Syrian general, who defected to the West in July 2012, said that in the mid-2000s after Iran and Hezbollah increasingly took control in Lebanon after 2005, these forces also took a firmer hold on Syria: "Syria itself began changing, Bashar submitted to the Iranians and Hezbollah, he gave them most of his cards, he became their hostage," though Assad did not see it that way.[62]

In February 2005, former Lebanese Prime Minister Rafiq Hariri was assassinated. Many Western governments suspected that Assad was responsible for the murder. Moscow, however, continuously diluted UN Security Council resolutions calling for Syria to cooperate fully with the investigation because, in

Moscow's view, the international tribunal violated state sovereignty and "unilaterally imposed a decision on Lebanon." These comments again exposed the Kremlin's priorities with regard to the US role in world affairs.

In August 2008, Assad joined a very small group of world leaders who "completely" supported Russia's invasion of Georgia. According to Russian press reports, Assad used the opportunity to request Iskander missiles and other weapons from then president Medvedev, because, according to Assad, Israel had provided training and weapons to the Georgians. The Syrian government, for its part, denied that Assad had expressed readiness to host these weapons. Previously, the Kremlin had disallowed Assad from having the weapons over fears they would harm Israel.[63] Upon conclusion of a 2008 meeting, however, Lavrov told journalists that Russia would supply primarily defensive weapons to Syria, which "will not disturb the strategic balance in the region," although Russia would still review Syria's requests for new weapons. Furthermore, several days later, Russia's charge d'affaires, Igor Belyaev, announced to Damascus that Russia would increase its naval presence off Syria's Mediterranean coast.[64]

The *Moscow Times* reported that Russian companies had invested $19.4 billion in Syria by 2009.[65] But perhaps more importantly, in the coming years, Russia emerged as Syria's primary weapons supplier. From 2007 through 2010, Russian arms sales to Syria reached $4.7 billion, more than twice the figure for the previous four years, according to the Congressional Research Service.[66] According to the Stockholm International Peace Research Institute (SIPRI), Russia accounted for 78 percent of Syria's weapons purchases between 2007 and 2012.[67] According to SIPRI, from 1993 to 2018, in total, Iran and Syria came out as Russia's top two arms recipients in the Middle East (excluding North Africa, see the Appendix). In Syria's case, sales especially spiked in 2006, and although they ebbed significantly between 2014 and 2017, the figure for 2018 shows a major spike. Between 2014 and 2017, the trade fell from 2 to 25 million trend indicator values (TIVs, the system SIPRI uses to measure arms transfers), but in 2018 it went up to 181 million (see appendix).[68]

Once the Syrian uprising began in March 2011, the Kremlin continued to support Assad unequivocally, no matter what Putin and Russian officials said about not being wedded to Assad. And not being wedded to Assad was not the only message coming out of the Kremlin. "Assad is not going anywhere," Lavrov said as early as December 2012. He even suggested that the West secretly wanted a Russian and Chinese veto on the Security Council. "No one has any appetite for intervention. Behind the scenes, I have a feeling they are praying that Russia and China are blocking the intervention."[69]

Before the military intervention, the Kremlin armed Assad and shielded him at the UN Security Council in multiple ways. The chapter on Russian diplomacy goes into detail on this topic. Yet one comment from Lavrov is perhaps most illustrative. In December 2016, when Lavrov met with his French counterpart to discuss Assad's use of chemical weapons, he said, "You have made your arguments and I made mine. We could continue like this for a while, but Laurent, do you see that glass of fruit juice in front of you on the table? You see it orange [it was], but you know what, I see it blue. You can give me all the arguments in the world but I will continue to say it's blue."[70]

Moscow helped Assad in numerous ways. It agreed to take Syria's crude oil in exchange for refined oil products to sustain the country's military and economy, and provided loans to stave off Syrian bankruptcy. Russian ships have been involved in several Syria-related incidents in international waters. In summer 2009, even before the Syrian uprising, the cargo ship *Arctic Sea* carrying timber was reportedly hijacked off the coast of Sweden—the first Baltic Sea piracy incident in hundreds of years.[71] Russia deployed its navy to locate the vessel, which was owned by a Finnish company and manned by a Russian crew. In the absence of information, intense speculation ensued, including the claim that the ship was carrying weaponry to Syria or Iran and that the hijackers were working for Israeli authorities.[72] According to Tarmo Kouts, an EU rapporteur on piracy, "Only the presence of cruise missiles on board the ship can explain Russia's strange behavior in this whole story." Kouts noted further that Russia's emergency response was much stronger than its response when it "engaged in a recent Somali piracy crisis."[73] A senior Spanish prosecutor described the incident as "a clear example" of arms trafficking.[74] Other incidents include the following. In January 2012, Cyprus customs officials intercepted a Syria-bound Russian ammunition ship.[75] In June 2012, a cargo ship traveling from Russia to Syria with weaponry, including Mi-25 attack helicopters, was forced to return to port after its British insurers withdrew cover. The Russian Foreign Ministry confirmed that the weapons were indeed Syria-bound.[76] In February 2013, Finnish customs officials investigated weapons smuggling allegations after discovering tank parts in a container aboard a ship traveling from Russia to Syria in violation of EU sanctions.[77] Other reports claimed that Russia was shipping weapons from its Black Sea naval ports to the port of Tartus.[78]

The Kremlin has also provided Assad with loans. According to flight manifests obtained by ProPublica, Moscow flew more than two hundred tons of "banknotes" to the Syrian regime in summer 2011, during periods when the fighting had escalated and the Syrian economy had begun to decline.[79] Such shipments helped prevent Assad's bankruptcy and allowed him to pay his forces even as Syria's foreign reserves dwindled. Between 2012 and 2018, Syria was also typically a top recipient of Russian aid. Between 2012 and 2016 it took the fifth or sixth place, and in 2017 it was fourth.[80] It is doubtful that Putin ever respected Assad, especially as Assad began losing his grip on power and Syria plunged into conflict. Putin respects those who can quell protest, rather than let it get out of hand. But he needed Assad because for him Syria was always about more than the country itself.

Part Two

Putin's Syria Intervention

6

The Military Campaign

When the uprising against Assad began in March 2011, Moscow supported him in multiple ways. Putin showed every indication that he was planning on sticking with Assad until the bitter end. Yet the year 2015 marked a qualitative change in Putin's support for the Syrian dictator. In 2015, the Syrian regime was losing ground, which reportedly alarmed both the Russian and the Iranian leadership. In July that year, Qassem Soleimani, commander of the Iranian elite Quds force, came to Moscow. A senior regional official reportedly said, "Soleimani put the map of Syria on the table. The Russians were very alarmed, and felt matters were in steep decline and that there were real dangers to the [Syrian] regime. The Iranians assured them there is still the possibility to reclaim the initiative." The official note, "At that time, Soleimani played a role in assuring them that we haven't lost all the cards."[1] Some suggest the trip was unconfirmed, though additional sources reported on this visit.[2] Regardless, Moscow's own fears of Assad's fall appeared real. In September 2015, during Russia's largest annual military exercises, Tsentr 2015, Moscow rehearsed its Syria operation. As early as November 2015, Lieutenant-General Ivan Buvaltsev, chief of main combat training directorate of Russia's armed forces said, "the task was set to simulate a military-political situation that would allow, so to speak, to immerse troops (forces) in the very situation that is now taking shape, in particular, in the Near and Middle East. And [the situation] frankly, is extremely alarming ... I am referring to the situation ... above all in Syria."[3]

Reports of Soleimani's trip were not made in isolation, but after a number of earlier and confirmed high-level Russian-Iranian contacts. By the time Soleimani arrived to Moscow in July, both governments had already agreed to boost support for Assad.[4] After Soleimani's visit, Moscow stepped up its military buildup in Syria, especially in late August and September. The Kremlin intensified Russia's naval presence in the Mediterranean, sent additional deliveries of advanced weaponry to the Assad regime, deployed a military advance team, and delivered prefabricated housing units to an airfield near Latakia.[5] The buildup, especially the presence of troops, already suggested a qualitative change in Russia's involvement.

On September 28, 2015, Putin addressed the UN General Assembly for the first time in a decade. He covered his traditional themes, such as complaints about post-Cold War US unilateralism and NATO expansion, accused the West of provoking revolutions and protests throughout the world, and suggested Washington was responsible for problems in the Middle East. He then proceeded to propose an idea he had been promoting prior to the speech: leading an anti-ISIS coalition with the West in Syria.[6]

The Kremlin does not usually announce its plans in advance in the way democratic governments do. However, by observing and listening it is possible to glean its intentions; the Kremlin does communicate, but too often analysts cannot see the forest for the trees, and fail to make vital connections. The UN speech, taken together with Soleimani's visit to Moscow and the military buildup, all provided clues. It is unlikely that Putin genuinely expected to see his coalition plans with the United States in particular come to fruition. If it may have been possible to make such an argument in the early 2000s, by 2015, after Georgia and Crimea, it is doubtful that he would have expected Washington to work with him. It is also possible that he did expect the Europeans, rather than the Americans, to work with him. He was willing to make an offer the Europeans could not refuse—in other words use coercion. Thus the speech signaled a change of intent with regard to Syria, it was a signal in and of itself, but fell mostly on deaf ears.

Two days after the speech, on September 30, the Kremlin gave the United States a one-hour warning before launching airstrikes in Syria. It was unclear at that point how long Moscow intended to stay, and some had suggested that initially, Moscow was thinking of a brief, several-months long military campaign. Still, Moscow's next military actions indicated a long-term intention to stay—an ambitious undertaking, especially since this intervention was Russia's first expeditionary push outside the former Soviet Union in three decades. Appetite, as the Russian saying goes, comes with eating.

If Moscow only wanted to ensure it had access to the Eastern Mediterranean, it did not need to continue backing Assad. As Russia's longtime Middle East expert and Putin critic, Alexander Shumilin, pointed out, the Syrian opposition was willing to work with Moscow.[7] It could have given basing and other access to Russia in exchange for support against Assad. Given Moscow's longtime and extensive connections in the country there was every reason to expect a place for Russia in a post-Assad Syria under such circumstances. Therefore, Putin's choice suggested additional priorities. Backing Assad to such an extent also went outside Putin's more flexible approach to the region, where he was willing to work with everyone to one degree or another. In Syria, like nowhere else in the region, Putin had clearly chosen a side, but the West misunderstood this point, in no small part due to Moscow's mixed signaling.

Putin's intervention was first and foremost, a statement of challenge to the US-led global order, made knowing that this move would go unopposed—the Kremlin felt confident it would be able to carry out its intervention. This challenge was simultaneously offensive and defensive—in line with Russia's historical approach to strategic thinking. As veteran expert on the Russian military Stephen R. Covington notes, "There is no Western equivalent to Russian strategic culture."[8] What is more, Covington continues, the current Russian approach "is also far more difficult for the West to discern" than that of the Soviet Union.[9] Perhaps because it has been so difficult to discern, and because the Kremlin is good at taking advantage of opportunities, the idea that Moscow had no ability to think strategically has been an easy, if a lazy conclusion. For Putin's Russia the fundamental security dilemma remained the same as for the Soviet Union—nuclear weapons aside, the single greatest threat to Russia's land power is the maritime strike capability the US navy brings to the table, and Putin's Russia had searched for a way to overcome this challenge with remarkable consistency and determination.

The Russian military puts a special emphasis on the initial period of war. Moscow knows very well it cannot match the West in resources, but focuses on "the imperative to move and strike quickly to not surrender the strategic initiative."[10] In September 2015, Moscow seized a strategic initiative in Syria, and its newly acquired position there offers greater overall military power projection capabilities to undercut the global reach of Western, but chiefly the US military. Thus, the intervention in Syria was always about more than Syria itself. For years the Western military posture had overlooked just how critical the Mediterranean is as a theater of great-power competition, and the Russians knew this.[11]

Even pro-Kremlin Russian analysts over the years, in private, acknowledged that at least one chief Russian goal in Syria has been anti-American. Anti-Americanism was also behind the Kremlin's chief motivation for supporting Assad.[12] Other elements were also at play, such as the situation in Ukraine and Russia's domestic considerations. Terrorism issues did loom in the background, but not in the way the Kremlin had presented them, first because concerns about domestic terrorism emanating from Syria had been severely overblown, and second because Moscow had perceived the West as the chief driver behind terrorism to begin with. To a certain extent, economic considerations also mattered, but more as the icing on the cake. Moscow's Syria campaign had multiple layers: military, diplomatic, and domestic. It also factored in Moscow's foreign policy broadly, including the relationship with the West, and interests specifically in Syria and the region. The next sections and chapters will examine each in closer detail.

A2AD Laydown and Broader Deterrence of the West

The military realm has demonstrated Moscow's priority of deterring the West in Syria like no other. It also showed Putin's Russia had learned a number of lessons from its history. Analysts close to the Kremlin acknowledged privately that when designing the military campaign, it was important to avoid another Afghanistan. From a more tactical standpoint lessons from Chechnya also played a role.[13] Moscow recognized that to compete with great powers in the global arena, its intervention in Syria required innovations. Thus, the weaponry Moscow deployed to Syria revealed its true intent—to create an anti-access/area denial (A2AD, sometimes written as A2/AD) laydown—in short, setting up military hardware to deny others freedom of action.

A caveat is in order. The term A2AD, which entered Western public discourse several decades ago, appears to have originated after the 1991 Operation Desert Storm. At the time, China experts in the West observed that the operation succeeded primarily due to an "ability to deploy forces into theatre with little risk of hostile interference."[14] In response, the Chinese military concluded it had to block or neutralize US military operations in the Western Pacific, and proceeded to develop and field land-attack ballistic and cruise missiles. Western analysts described these efforts as A2AD. The term then spread quickly and entered among others into NATO discourse.[15] Thus, the term originated in a China-, rather than Russia-centered discussion, and as expert on the Russian military Michael Koffman had pointed out, it does not quite fit Russia, which does not tend simply to "sit in defensive bubbles,"[16] though in the maritime domain a conversation about Russian A2AD does make sense.[17] Indeed, the Russian military itself does not use the term A2AD; Moscow's aims go beyond simply establishing a defensive zone. Covington writes that Russian strategic operations "have A2AD actions, along with cyber, informational warfare, offensive action with air, land, maritime, and conventional missiles—while all the time simultaneously posturing and readying other conventional forces and nuclear forces for employment when necessary. In essence, the core purpose of Russian strategic operations involving A2AD capabilities is actually best described as Strategic Area Control—Opponent Options Denial."[18] With these caveats, the term A2AD can be a useful shorthand for a non-technical conversation, and that is how it is used in this book.

Moscow for its part has been working for years on developing A2AD capabilities. Denial of freedom of action is related to deterrence. Historic insecurity and a search for buffer zones, as well as confusion—at least from a Western perspective—over what actions are offensive or defensive, fit within the discussion of A2AD layouts specifically, and deterrence more broadly. Indeed, Russia's military actions show that their primary functions were to save Assad and deter the West. Once Moscow set up these capabilities in Russia, from a broader perspective, it extended the arc of A2AD bubbles, which begin far north, in the Arctic and now stretch further south, ending with Syria.[19] Thus a broader look at Syria as an extension of this one long arc again fits into the bigger pattern of Russian aims in deterring the West and paying special attention to Russia's south.

Other aspects of the campaign showed intent not to get "stuck" in Syria. Moscow attempted to fight the war primarily from the air, which minimizes casualties. Historically, the Kremlin relied primarily on ground forces. It certainly did so in Afghanistan. But in Syria it employed a chiefly areal campaign, using both its air force and the navy. From the beginning of the intervention, Moscow deployed advanced weaponry such as the Pantsyr short-range air defense system and the Almaz-Antey S-400 high-altitude Surface-to-Air Missile (or SAM, as it is referred to in the West) system to the Khmeimim airbase and later to the northwestern city of Masyaf, along with the KRET Krasukha-S4 ground-based electronic warfare system. It has also deployed the K-300P Bastion P coastal defense missile and the 9K720 Iskander ballistic missile system. This weaponry suggested that ISIS was not the Kremlin's primary target—ISIS never had an air force, nor showed any indication of developing one. Moscow's actions indicated intent to protect Assad from both internal and external threats while simultaneously waging an air campaign to destroy Syrians who opposed him. As leading military experts Lester W. Grau and Timothy Thomas observe, ultimately Moscow could not fight the war from the air entirely, a lesson it had to accept,[20] not entirely unlike the West, which faced similar challenges in its desire to win wars solely from the air in Bosnia, Kosovo, and Afghanistan. But a shift towards prioritizing an air campaign showed that the Moscow that came to Syria had absorbed many lessons of Afghanistan and Chechnya. This Moscow was going to be more careful in its employment of military forces to ensure it did not get "stuck" in Syria. At the same time, Grau and Thomas point out that, as far as Russia's ground-based contingent, it is probably Russian military advisors that had the most influence in saving Assad. This shows how careful Moscow was to keep casualties low—military advisors did very little actual fighting, but they did gain a lot of experience in Syria. Indeed, Moscow, unlike Western governments, places entire staffs with their Syrian counterparts and they gain experience working together.

Moscow's intent to coercively deter the West from greater involvement in Syria became readily apparently almost immediately. All the pieces of the S-400 system came in less than a week. In addition to the S-400 and airspace control, Moscow also soon brought tactical ballistic and cruise missiles, and advance anti-ship cruise missiles—all pieces of an A2AD laydown. In the months and years to come, Moscow would maintain a continuous and rapid rotation of weaponry in and out of Syria. Krasukha S-4 deployment immediately signaled use of electronic warfare (EW). Moscow had developed a strong interest in EW since the two Chechen Wars in the 1990s, and began developing new capabilities especially intensely after 2009. As Moscow's Syria military campaign unfolded, Russian forces used electronic warfare, primarily to support its combat operations.[21] "In the context of force protection, EW systems doubtless played a significant role in reducing loss of aircraft in combat, as well as protecting smaller numbers of ground forces deployed in support of the Syrian Arab Army (SAA)," wrote a leading Russian military expert Roger McDermott, "It is likely that some of the EW activity may be directed at collecting EM signature information on NATO aircraft to build their EM database."[22]

As part of this approach, Moscow continued to emphasize the importance of information dominance, that is, to deny the adversary—the United States—the use of information space. Reports note that US troops in Syria have been increasingly forced to defend themselves from Russia's electronic jamming attacks. These attacks can be no less serious than a conventional attack, because electronic jamming can prevent effective self-defense and lead to an inability to understand the picture on the battlefield, thus losing the ability to command and control forces real-time.

Russian behavior in Syria revealed an important aspect of how Moscow tries to erode the US-led global order through subverting the spirit of its institutions. Those who interact with Russian officials and military personnel often note that the Russians pedantically adhere to the letter of agreements, but violate their spirit. From a Western perspective, international obligations are not only about codified texts, but also unspoken norms, but the Kremlin conceptualizes international law narrowly, and instead focuses on the UN charter and resolutions. Russian foreign minister Sergei Lavrov for example once scoffed, "Today a tendency is traced to change international law in how we understand it, with some 'rules-based order.' This is what a number of our creative Western friends call it."[23]

Narrow adherence to technicalities allows Moscow to manipulate the international system to its own advantage. In the military realm in Syria this effort became apparent with the so-called deconfliction mechanism. Originally created in October 2015 and made more robust two years later, the deconfliction process was meant to be an open and narrow channel of communication between Washington and Moscow to avoid clashes and generally dangerous situations. Indeed, it started out informally, almost as a gentleman's agreement. But Moscow used the agreement to complicate and limit efforts of the United States and their partners, chiefly the Syrian Democratic Forces (SDF), while claiming that they warned the proper channels about their air, artillery, and missile strikes. This behavior showed Moscow's true priorities. Robert E. Hamilton, former US Army officer who ran the US deconfliction channel for several months in summer and fall of 2017, says the Russians would often contact the Americans, claim to see ISIS in a certain spot, provide the coordinates, and strike—but dangerously close to the SDF. "They would say, 'we de-conflicted', it was that sort of game. But we would not de-conflict because what they were seeing was not ISIS, it was us . . . and they knew it," he explained.[24]

The SDF force was approximately 65,000 strong, and Russian forces had drones in the air and flew reconnaissance. It is difficult to imagine they could mistake it for much smaller ISIS forces. To be sure not every instance was clear-cut. "Sometimes we would sort of scratch our heads . . . is their intelligence bad or did they mean to do it?" recalls Hamilton. Still, it was clear to the Americans on the ground that even with much uncertainty, Moscow was committed to deterring the United States and its partners, and was using the existing rules to do so as they technically called to deconflict. Indeed, such Russian behavior goes far beyond Syria when it comes to interaction in the air or the sea—it goes straight to the heart of erosion of the US-led global order on all fronts, using all resources the Russian state has available.

The Campaign

Moscow predicated its overall Syria strategy on Tehran and its proxies doing the heavy lifting on the ground to keep Moscow's costs low, both in terms of blood and treasure. This is a major shift as compared to the Soviet Union's direct involvement. More broadly, Putin's Russia has focused on utilizing proxies to gain control in the region overall. In Syria, this approach was also predicated on building leverage against the West and its allies to support Moscow's objectives. Lastly, it was designed to be flexible and adaptive. Thus, it would be easy to pivot in a different direction when mistakes or setbacks inevitably occurred. Indeed, Dima Adamsky notes that the learning process Moscow has demonstrated in recent conflicts "seems to be tolerant of failure and has demonstrated conceptual flexibility and dynamism."[25] This is an assessment that other military analysts share. "The modern Russian approach is far more flexible, more multi-variant than its Soviet predecessor,"[26] wrote Covington. Indeed, the command and control system Moscow set up in Syria made it possible to respond to rapidly emerging threats and by many accounts was a success story.

The objective of the Russian military campaign was to keep Assad in power. Moscow's first strikes hit areas with large numbers of anti-Assad opposition, such as the suburbs of Homs in Western Syria, the country's third largest city, which analysts described as the birthplace of the Syrian revolution. ISIS strongholds that included Palmyra and Raqqa were miles away. Russia's political track went hand in hand with the military one. Militarily, the campaign aimed to destroy, with relatively few resources, any opposition to Assad so as to confront the West with a choice—either ISIS or Assad. This was a situation where the West would really have no choice but to accept Assad. Through coercive tactics, Moscow built leverage both militarily and politically. These included information operations, testing the West and creating dangerous situations to pressure the United States and its allies and force them to cooperate. A perception of a dangerous and unpredictable Russia helped create fears in the West that Russia would fight a war over Syria, which contributed to the desire to back down to avoid a war with Russia. Perception often matters far more than reality. It is highly doubtful at best that the Kremlin would have fought a direct war with the United States over Syria.

Simultaneously, on the diplomatic track Moscow marginalized opposition that demanded Assad's departure as a precondition for peace talks (taking the playbook from its Chechnya policy in the 1990s and 2000s),[27] and when it engaged regional opponents to Assad it created conditions for negotiations on Russian terms, to lay the groundwork for a slow acceptance of Assad staying in power.

Prior to Syria, Moscow reportedly struggled with precise targeting and delivery of munitions.[28] One might argue that Moscow simply had no ability to deliver precise strikes, and its historic indiscriminate campaigns that killed civilians were only a reflection of an inability to do things differently. But in Syria, evidence suggests that Moscow's delivery was more precise, even though the majority of munitions Moscow delivered were unguided. It is with greater precision than in the past that Moscow hit civilian targets, such as hospitals, bakeries, and gas stations where people lined up for gas and this speaks volumes to Moscow's fundamentally different approach to counterinsurgency to that taken by the West, regardless of technological improvements.[29] After Russia entered the Syrian theater, attacks on health-care facilities only increased, as Moscow helped Assad double-down on eliminating opposition. While no party was innocent in Syria, the Assad regime bore by far the greatest responsibility.

A study published in the peer-reviewed *BMG Global Health* journal found that the Syrian and Russian regimes "weaponized healthcare" by deliberately targeting ambulances.[30] Officials and activists also observed that after hospitals had voluntarily provided their GPS coordinates to the UN "no-strike" list, they became targets of strikes, raising questions about whether Moscow used the UN system to its own ends,[31] while a UN-led investigation into bombings of civilian targets in Syria released in April 2020 had concluded that "Assad and his allies" committed most of the attacks but did not name Russia directly. Richard Gowan, UN director at the International Crisis Group, said about the report, "on a less charitable reading, this is an effort to minimize offending Moscow that reflects the fact that UN officials believe that continued cooperation with Russia is key to the future of humanitarian operations in Syria."[32]

Thus, Moscow's air campaign ran in tandem with that of the Syrian regime in terms of terrorizing and demoralizing the general population and anti-Assad opposition. It had little to do with specifically targeting ISIS with any consistency. Thus, while Moscow talks about its SAM systems as an inherently defensive weapon—in Syria, necessary for the protection of the Russian air force—their employment extended far beyond protection as it related to the actual civil war.

In terms of personnel, based on open sources, at any given time Moscow typically had between 4,000 and 6,000 military personnel on the ground, primarily their elite forces, though over time it rotated tens of thousands. According to official Kremlin reports, the number is at 63,000.[33] Although the real number remains unknown, the available information gives a convincing sense of Moscow's relatively light footprint in Syria. It shows again that, even if we do not know the exact numbers, the Syria campaign was very different from the Soviet operation in Afghanistan.[34] Russian General Staff often touted the numbers that have gone through Syria but its meaning was likely lost on the Western audience. Their real impact is the experience Russian air, naval, and army forces gained in being able to integrate high-end combined arms in an effort to coercively deter a peer adversary—that is, the West—not those who deployed to train and win a counter insurgency though limited intervention.

To that end, another critical aspect of Russian military operations has been to test Western resolve. While Moscow's entry into the Syrian theater automatically made the airspace more crowded and naturally created greater potential for accidents, this is not the full story. Reports suggest that Moscow also purposely tested the West. And Andrew Weiss, former member of US National Security Council staff, writes that there is a connection between Moscow's testing in other theaters and Syria:

> That the risk of escalation has not been completely eradicated is a reminder that events in Syria are not occurring in a vacuum and are merely one element of a very difficult bilateral relationship. Too-close-for-comfort intercepts and barrel rolls performed by Russian jets over Western military planes and ships along Russia's increasingly contested frontline with NATO in the Baltic and the Black Sea regions. These in-your-face tactics have helped cement deep reluctance in US policy and military circles about the potential benefits of expanded cooperation with a government that intentionally exploits the threat of military accidents as a political tool and source of leverage.[35]

These tools of political leverage were very relevant to Syria and relate, among others, to Moscow's A2AD layout. A2AD layouts are not one size fits all. Moscow's layout in Syria is quite capable, but relatively limited. Indeed, Moscow did not succeed in creating a complete A2AD bubble—a complete bubble means no external power can operate in the space. This did not happen and US coalition forces continued their operations, but with greater complications and limitations. (More details on this follow in the upcoming section.) But this is no cause to dismiss Russia's position in Syria—the aim was never to create the same A2AD bubble as in Kaliningrad, for example. It was enough to intimidate, which helped push the West to self-deter—something the West was already pre-disposed to do, given its hesitancy to become involved in Syria.

Lastly, an element of Moscow's military campaign was coordination not only with Assad but also Iran and Hezbollah.[36] Moscow never considered the latter a terrorist organization, unlike Sunni terrorist groups. Several reports indicated Hezbollah learned from Russia by operating side by side with the Russian military.[37] Other, more recent reports suggested that Hezbollah used the Russian flag as cover to evade Israeli strikes.[38] Moscow also supplied Hezbollah with light arms, through Qasem Suleimani. Not only had the Kremlin invited Hezbollah to

Moscow over the years for official visits, but more recently, in Syria, then-Russian ambassador to Lebanon Aleksandr Zasypkin publicly praised Hezbollah.[39] Moscow also worked especially closely with the Shia militias.[40] Some reports also noted that Iranian fighters switched to Assad uniforms to avoid getting hit by Israel.[41] Moscow's coordination with Iran and its proxies is important for several reasons. One of them, as it relates to Russia's military campaign is that Iran and its proxies, rather than Russia, did the heavy lifting in Syria. This is a crucial aspect that allowed Moscow to keep its footprint light. During the Soviet war in Afghanistan, thousands of body bags came home, in addition to even more wounded soldiers. This did not happen with Russian Syrian operations in Syria. Instead, body bags and wounded soldiers went home en masse to Iran.

The broader picture here is that in Syria, Moscow was actively competing with the United States and the West, even if the West did not see it that way. To be successful in this competition, Moscow understood that it had to deter its adversaries by deploying high-end systems across a broad range of spectrum of capability. The Syrian rebels had captured significant quantities of armor and artillery. To help Assad re-establish regime control, Moscow deployed an air armada meant to support achieving decisive victory on the ground. These actions coercively deterred any further involvement of other major powers that could have influenced the Syrian conflict through limited military intervention. This is why Moscow deployed high-end military capabilities to Syria that had nothing to do with the actual conflict on the ground.

The wars the United States has fought since 1991 have focused on a militarily weaker adversary, rather than keeping a stronger peer competitor on the sidelines. When the United States went into Fallujah in 2004, for example, it had no periphery concerns of external military intervention at a conventional level. Over these years, Moscow by contrast has never lost sight of the importance of keeping a stronger competitor at bay and Syria has put this out on full display. When the Russians executed their campaign in Syria, they brought to bear a gamut of air and naval forces to coercively deter great-power intervention (including Turkey), as well as those that would support winning the fight on the ground.

By March 2019, Valeriy Gerasimov announced that Moscow had been pursuing a strategy of "limited action" in Syria, and one that it hopes will guide future military action.[42] By that point it was a description of actions that had already taken place in the previous years, and more to the point, this strategy reflected a return to Soviet and tsarist methods of "limited war."[43] These developments show the extent to which Moscow under Putin prioritized great-power competition with the West, and how this competition played out in Syria.

What did Moscow Gain?

Moscow's intervention unambiguously saved Assad from an imminent fall and projected great-power status. That alone is a major gain for the Kremlin and its allies. Moscow also established control over Syrian airspace, which holds major implications for Israel. Russia now has a permanent military presence on the Mediterranean, at least until the year 2066, with the option to extend afterwards for an additional twenty-five years.[44] This matters not only for Russia's ability to project power towards NATO's southern flank and into the region, but also for expanding operations further, for example in Africa, and towards the Red Sea, as Moscow has started doing. Russia's position in Syria enabled it to have a deeper involvement in Libya, another strategically vital country on the Mediterranean—and one where Moscow has the most chances of gaining naval basing rights. Indeed, as mentioned earlier, on the Eastern Mediterranean, Moscow could not get this access from Cyprus and Montenegro, but Libya has not closed that door. Indeed, Russian operations show that increasingly, Moscow projects what it calls its "southern line of defense" further than in earlier years—not only across the Black Sea, but also into the Levant. This gain eluded even the Russian tsars.

Overall, from a military perspective, Moscow has demonstrated greater competence than it has for a number of years previously, coupled with high ambitions. Despite clear problems, the Russian military demonstrates growth, improvement, greater flexibility and learning. Perhaps even more importantly, it is clear that the Syrian experience, more than any Russian post-Cold War Russian military engagement has impacted Russian military thinking with regard to future warfare and military operations. Indeed, the Syria experience is the one Russian military officers cite most often when they talk about the future of warfare, while service in Syria has become much sought after.

Along those lines, Moscow improved the Syrian air defense system and demonstrated that, in spite of some difficulties, they can put Russia's only aircraft carrier *Admiral Kuznetsov* on the Mediterranean and fly aircraft off of it. While many rightly criticized if not laughed at many of *Kuznetsov's* shortcomings, the carrier occupied space in a vacuum, and it was enough to demonstrate relevance by simply being there when the United States was absent. Moreover Kuznetsov helped facilitate a quiet meeting with Libya's Khalifa Haftar which helped Moscow gain more influence in Libya.

In addition to expanding the Russian naval facility in Tartus and putting it on the path to becoming a full-fledged base, Moscow also opened an air base in

Khmeimim, or the Basel Al-Assad airport, as it is typically referred to by the Department of Defense.[45] Khmeimim is the main operating base for Russia in Syria, and it is right next to Tartus. Both are on the Eastern Mediterranean coast, and are major components of Moscow's A2AD layout in Syria.

That said, Moscow had military assets stationed in several other locations throughout the country. One is the Shayrat airbase at Homs. Since 2015, Moscow has operated and gradually expanded the airbase in support of Russian Aerospace forces operations Moscow used and expanded since 2015 to support Russian air force operations.[46] Another is the Tiyas air base, often referred to as T-4, located in West Palmyra. Most recently, after Trump announced US withdrawal from Syria in October 2019, Russian deployments are increasingly appearing in northern Syria, including in Manbij.[47] Russian official news sources also show that Moscow established a helicopter base in Qamishli.[48] Whether Moscow is entirely in control in these areas is a matter of debate, but Russian deployments are there and working on entrenching themselves, exploiting a vacuum left by the US withdrawal.

Some reports suggest Moscow is converting it to its main center of aerial operations in Central Syria to provide backup for Khmeimim. Since these are not considered permanent military bases, Russian forces rotate in and out. An added element to this is Iranian operations that overlap with Russia's in these locations, for example in Palmyra (Tadmur) and others. Indeed, some reports suggest for example that Iran is also building a base in Shayrat along with other bases in Syria.[49] These additional operations are an important element of Russia's military activities. While the center of Russian operations is on the West coast of Syria, on the Mediterranean, these additional operations show the evolving and expanding nature of Moscow's military operations.

The United States and its allies are still able to operate, throughout the Syrian battlespace, even with the increased complexities. The laydown Moscow set up is powerful, but limited primarily to Syria's West coast. This also accounts for why US missile strikes in 2018 on the Syrian regime's chemical warfare facilities came primarily from Iraq and its air forces based in Qatar instead of the Mediterranean. The mountain range in Khmeimim and Latakia makes air surveillance difficult, and this is one of several critical components of making a complete, impenetrable bubble so the Russians had to rely on the Syrians for information—and their system is old and unreliable. The same limitation applies to electronic warfare. Before you can jam an object you have to know where it is. If you are at sea level surrounded by mountains, where most of the Russian systems are, identification can become an issue. In addition, the flip side of Moscow's jamming is that it also provides the United States with opportunities to learn more about Russian technology. And, as mentioned earlier, Moscow had to accept it could not win a war utilizing an air campaign alone.

Ultimately, for the West, lack of political will was a more difficult hurdle than Russian weaponry in Syria. Putin understood this and took full advantage. While it has been customary to describe Putin in the West in narrow, dichotomous terms, as a mere opportunist, an ability to read your adversary correctly is a strategic skill—and the West had yet to even admit that Moscow was looking at the West as an adversary to begin with. More to the point, Moscow's activities demonstrate consistent intent and commitment to deter the West, test to see where it can be intimidated, and project power in the Middle East to ultimately undermine the US position. And it was Syria that provided the Russian military with unparalleled opportunities for experience and improvement, not seen since the war in Afghanistan.

Arms Sales and Military Training

Moscow has for some time vied for the position of an arms supplier of choice for the Middle East and North Africa region. For years, it has been second only to the United States—both in the Middle East and in North Africa, but also worldwide, and this remains the case at the time of writing. Moreover, it is safe to predict that this situation is unlikely to change in the near future.

Syria has provided a valuable opportunity for Moscow to test and advertise new arms, dispose cheaply of old munitions, and train the Russian military. These were not the reasons why Moscow went into Syria—they are by-products of the intervention that Moscow has fully exploited, and which has helped to create a perception of a Russian reemergence as a global power broker. Russia's economy remains over-reliant on raw materials and natural resources, but the defense industry as a technology-intensive sector has proved to be more than just an important source of revenue. Domestically, Russia's defense industry is a major source of employment. Putin renewed his emphasis on modernizing the armed forces, especially the navy, on May 7, 2012, on the same day as he took office as president for a third term.[50]

Thus, in July 2012, Putin complained about Iraq and countries undergoing the Arab Spring, "Russian companies are losing their decades-long positions in local commercial markets and are being deprived of large commercial contracts."[51] As Sergei Chemezov, chief of the powerful state industrial holding Rostec, said in February 2015, "As for the conflict situation in the

Middle East, I do not conceal it, and everyone understands this, the more conflicts there are, the more they [clients] buy weapons from us. Volumes are continuing to grow despite sanctions. Mainly, it is in Latin America and the Middle East."[52]

While arms sales are one objective, for Moscow they are also an instrument of foreign policy. Three years before Chemezov's comment, in July 2012, Putin said that arms exports are "an effective instrument for advancing [Moscow's] national interests, both political and economic."[53] Next year deputy prime minister Dmitry Rogozin said that the Federal Service for Military Technical Cooperation, which leads arms sales to other countries is Russia's "second foreign policy agency." He also said that the main goal behind arms sales is influence in other countries.[54]

In Syria, testing and the advertisement of arms was a key component of its campaign. In early October 2015, only days after Russia's Syria intervention—and on Putin's birthday—Moscow fired twenty-six cruise missiles from primarily small corvettes in the Caspian Sea to hit targets in Syria.[55] Moscow made a public display of the event, not only to demonstrate Russia's own might, but also to show other countries they need not purchase large expensive ocean-going warships to achieve and project decisive influence and power. And of course, Moscow has expressed that it is more than happy to aid countries in achieving these goals.

As the campaign unfolded, Moscow continued to test weaponry, rotate many different weapons systems in and out, and watched its arms sales grow.[56] In the same vein, Syria became a useful and cynical ground for disposing of older munitions more conveniently than on Russian territory.

Electronic warfare is another example. Experts note that Russian electronic warfare equipment is sophisticated, and close proximity to US troops and technology allows them the opportunity to constantly test their technology, and learn.[57] Roger McDermott notes that a secondary reason for Moscow's use of this weaponry was to test them in live combat—as he writes, the Krasukha-S4 deployment also mattered with regard to field testing the system in operational conditions. Indeed, McDermott writes that since 2009 Moscow has consistently invested in modernizing its electronic warfare capabilities, with the overall aim of asymmetrically challenging NATO on Russia's periphery "and maximi[zing] its chances of success in any operation against NATO's eastern members."[58]

While Syria largely disappeared from Russia's domestic news by approximately 2017 (this campaign is discussed in greater detail in the next chapter), testing and development of military hardware, along with training for the Russian military, is one point that Putin had continued to bring up in his subsequent speeches as of the time of this writing. In March 2016, in his first address to the Federal Assembly after the Syria intervention, Putin said, "The Russian Army and Navy have shown convincingly that they are capable of operating effectively away from their permanent deployment sites."[59] In 2017, on the one-hundredth anniversary of the Bolshevik revolution, Putin did not give an address, perhaps because he did not consider the revolution anything to celebrate. But in March 2018, in his address to the Federal Assembly, Putin, went into great detail and emphasized the arms sales and training boon provided by the Syrian campaign:

> The operation in Syria has proved the increased capabilities of the Russian Armed Forces. In recent years, a great deal has been done to improve the Army and the Navy. The Armed Forces now have 3.7 times more modern weapons. Over 300 new units of equipment were put into service. The strategic missile troops received 80 new intercontinental ballistic missiles, 102 submarine-launched ballistic missiles and three Borei nuclear-powered ballistic missile submarines. Twelve missile regiments have received the new Yars intercontinental ballistic missile. The number of long-range high-precision weapons carriers has increased by 12 times, while the number of guided cruise missiles increased by over 30 times. The Army, the Aerospace Forces and the Navy have grown significant stronger as well. Both Russia and the entire world know the names of our newest planes, submarines, anti-aircraft weapons, as well as land-based, airborne and sea-based guided missile systems. All of them are cutting-edge, high-tech weapons. A solid radar field to warn of a missile attack was created along Russia's perimeter (it is very important). Huge holes appeared after the USSR disintegrated. All of them were repaired.[60]

Lastly, in his February 2019 address to the Federal Assembly that focused primarily on domestic issues, Putin's only mention of the Middle East was the following, "We continue developing our Armed Forces and improving the intensity and quality of combat training, in part, using the experience we gained in the anti-terrorist operation in Syria."[61]

Few would dispute the significance of live training. Putin has highlighted this point publicly during the annual direct line question-and-answer session with Putin on June 7, 2018, when a pensioner asked him about when the Russian military contingent would withdraw from Syria. Putin began by saying, "First, the use of our Armed Forces in combat conditions is a unique experience and a unique tool to improve our Armed Forces. No exercises can compare with actually using the Armed Forces in combat conditions."[62] In his elaborate answer that touched on several other issues, he particularly stressed the training opportunity for the military.

Use of PMCs

The introduction of so-called private military contractors, or companies (PMCs, abbreviated as ChVK in Russian), such as the Wagner group (owned by Yevgeny Prigozhin, an oligarch close to the Kremlin known as "Putin's chef"), in Syria has made many headlines over recent years. These semi-state security forces, while few in number, played another important role in helping to prevent Russia from getting "stuck" in Syria, and while accurate information about them remains scarce, they will increasingly matter as a Russian foreign policy instrument.

Journalists routinely describe Russian PMCs as mercenaries or use the two terms interchangeably, but this is inaccurate. Mercenaries provide a very narrow service—they kill for money, whoever pays, and do not think long term. But as scholar Kimberly Marten points out, the activities of Russian PMCs overlap across of a whole host of categories. Sometimes, they do indeed include mercenary behavior, but they also provide a wide range of other services including leadership security, training, campaign advice and natural resource extraction. They also tend to think more long term about their client base.[63] The very term "private military company" is understood differently in Russia than it is in the West—it assumes a connection with the state, an association that does not exist in the West. Historically, when Russians use the term "volunteer" they often mean it in quotes, an experience that goes back at least to the Soviet Union when the state "volunteered" people.

A Russian military journal of the Russian Ministry of Defense, Voeynnaya Mysl, defined PMCs in the following way:

> Private military company (PMC) is a registered private for profit commercial structure, staffed by highly qualified technical specialists, controlled by the state and working in the interests of the state, and this is its fundamental difference from the classic detachments of mercenaries and terrorists. PMCs are private only relatively, because they work practically in the interest of the state, follow the same plans and pursue the same goals as regular armies, although they are given some freedom in choosing the means to achieve them.[64]

Russia has a long and unique history of utilizing semi-state security forces which predates the Soviet Union. Russian tsars had utilized them for centuries, often including non-ethnic Russians. As mentioned earlier, a small number of Russian "mercenaries" appeared in Yugoslavia in April 1999 in the context of Moscow's disagreement with the NATO intervention in Yugoslavia. In the Putin era however the emphasis on PMCs has intensified. In this context, PMCs first emerged in Ukraine according to press reports. In 2013, Slavonic Corps Limited, a private military company, began operating in Syria approximately two years before the official intervention in September 2015. Some recent Russian sources suggest that Slavonic Corps was created specifically to operate in Syria.[65] The Wagner Group, the best-known PMC, came out of the Slavonic Corp. Indeed, according to one report by a Norwegian Defense Ministry think tank, "The story of Wagner starts with a request from the Syrian government to Moran Security Group in 2013 to assist in retaking from the Islamic State Syrian oil and gas infrastructure that the latter controlled."[66] The personnel, especially at the leadership level of PMCs, are all associated with the GRU, Spetsnaz, naval infantry, and so on; they associated with the Ministry of Defense, and are "the core of Russian expeditionary forces and capabilities."[67]

Indeed they have proved to be an effective foreign policy tool for the Kremlin. Their involvement in Syria has been fairly limited, but their use fits within a strategy of limited means—how do you deploy your military around the globe when it is not only against the law, but you also do not have the means do it? This is why their use is growing and, ultimately, we tend to see PMCs increasingly wherever the Russian government is involved. The entire system of utilizing PMCs is very different in Russia than it is in the West, where military contractors are legal and their activities are transparent and clearly defined. Moreover, they are officially illegal under Russian law.

The aspect of plausible deniability appears to be useful to the Kremlin.[68] It fits with Putin's strategy of creating confusion through information operations and aligns with creative and adaptive thinking that Russian military reforms have emphasized in recent years, especially given Moscow's weaker position vis-à-vis the United States in terms of conventional weapons. Still, as time went on, denial became less and less convincing. As Marten has argued, keeping PMCs illegal likely fulfills an additional purpose—to maintain a grip on power over oligarchic groups circling the Kremlin.[69] Illegality hangs a sword of Damocles over these groups when the possibility of criminal prosecution is always an option. Moreover PMCs can be used to settle personal scores and send a message.[70] This also highlights that domestic elements continue to underpin Russia's foreign activities in a way that is very different from the behavior of Western countries, and paradoxically highlights the weakness of the Russian state which has to resort to such measures to maintain control.

The use of PMCs is likely to grow as a national security tool for the Kremlin in the Middle East and Africa, as they have been shown to be a useful innovation. Specifically with regard to the Syria campaign, PMCs were only one, and not necessarily the most important tool in the broader toolkit—as mentioned earlier Russian advisors played a more important role in keeping Assad in power, and Russian military police played perhaps another important role. But the use of PMCs says something broader about Russia. Domestically, their use created less apprehension than sending conscripts to Syria—after all, these individuals had chosen to go to Syria and got paid for it. They knew the risk. This is why the infamous Der Ezzor incident that resulted in the deaths of roughly 200 Russian PMCs did not cause widespread domestic outrage in Russia. This incident occurred in February 2018, when several hundred Assad-backed forces, that included members of the Wagner Group, violated the 2015 deconfliction agreement between the United States and Russia in Syria by crossing the Euphrates and attempting to capture an oil refinery near Deir Ezzor, a city in eastern Syria. These fighters used Russian heavy weaponry to attack a US-supported Kurdish opposition outpost. US forces first shot back in response, but the fighters did not cease. US forces had little choice but to call in larger air strikes in self-defense. They continuously communicated with Moscow before, during, and after the strikes. According to the Pentagon and press reports at the time, between 200 and 300 fighters died as the result of the strike, most of them from the Wagner Group. Moscow for its part at first denied any Russian involvement at all, and then downplayed the number of deaths—again, conscious of public opinion. But, in the end, this event simply did not cause a significant reaction domestically. Many questions about the incident remain unanswered, chiefly why Moscow allowed it to happen. Marten's explanation seems most plausible—the incident likely centered on domestic Russian politics and "ruthless infighting between Russian security forces that goes on regularly, while Russian President Vladimir Putin looks the other way." She suggests that the events at Der Ezzor "may actually have centered on domestic politics inside Russia."[71]

More broadly, another interesting aspect of use of PMCs is that they created job opportunities, even as the people knew the risk involved. There was an element that one Russian analyst described as "we don't care about our lives because our lives already don't have meaning."[72] This element of the Syria campaign highlighted the lack of prospects for the Russian youth even as, paradoxically, the PMC element helped to sustain the Syria campaign without the costs that many considered prohibitive.

On the foreign policy front, the use of PMCs allows Moscow to exploit a loophole in international law. Once again, Moscow is exploiting the international system to erode behavioral norms. Once Moscow reaches agreements on economic or military cooperation in a given country, technically it has a legitimate reason to send personnel there, for example to provide security for companies undertaking resource extraction. Again, this was not Afghanistan where Moscow struggled to find written justification for being there. Technically nothing prohibits PMCs from being in a country after the two governments have reached certain agreements. This situation then gives Moscow a foothold, which it can then use to engage in other shadowy activities that are hard to monitor, to expand Russian influence in a country (be it Syria or elsewhere) and thus alter the regional balance of power.[73] This is why the use of PMCs is another instrumental tool that the Kremlin has used as a safeguard against getting "stuck" in Syria, and what made this intervention so different from the Afghanistan experience.

And there is a broader connection to why PMCs are so important in Moscow's competition for dominance in the international arena. Moscow knows it cannot counter the West symmetrically. The United States bases its power on global freedom of navigation. Moscow cannot match this ability, but it can impose costs on the United States across the spectrum of a conflict, to require it to increase its investment of resources. PMCs can operate under the table, without provoking a serious reaction from the West, without a realization that Moscow is using them to alter the balance of power, as it is currently attempting to do in Libya, where Russia's existing position has helped bolster Russian PMC activity. As one anonymous US military source said, the US intelligence community is not connecting PMCs with a broader military strategy to its own detriment. "What makes this more detrimental is an uninformed notion that Vladimir Putin and those at the top are not strategic thinkers. We're not even going to have strategic discussion about the potential of the Russian military strategy."[74] PMCs thus are important perhaps less for what they have done, but because of what they can potentially accomplish in the future for the Russian state.

7

The Domestic Campaign

"Russia will not participate in any military operations on the territory of Syria or other states, at least currently we are not planning it," Putin told CBS journalist Charlie Rose on September 28, 2015. Still, Putin did not rule out sending troops if Assad asked for help.[1] The following day, after a ninety-minute meeting with Barak Obama, Putin said that the Kremlin was thinking about additional help to Assad's army, but "(i)n terms of ground troops ... Russian involvement is out of the question."[2] While Putin spoke to American audiences, his message also mattered domestically. Within Russia, discussion about a possibility of a Syria intervention took place before September 2015. Moreover, Putin's domestic campaign is relevant to the Syria intervention. This is the subject of this chapter.

Only two days after speaking with Charlie Rose, on September 30, Putin met with the Russian Federation Council.[3] The meeting focused on measures to address the economic recession in the next year, and "separately devoted attention" to "Syria and international terrorism issues."[4] Russia's main international propaganda channel RT reported on the meeting along similar lines.[5] The Council ostensibly held a vote precisely on this issue. The result was a unanimous "yes," with 162 votes.[6]

The Announcement

After the Council vote, Putin announced the intervention to the public.[7] The announcement deserves a detailed look. Putin's statement encapsulated the single thrust of the overall state message to the Russian people—if Russia did not kill terrorists in Syria, they would inevitably return to their home countries, including Russia, and stage terrorist attacks there. The intervention in Syria was about Russia's self-preservation—with a shade of anti-Americanism:

The only sure way to fight international terrorism—and, it is precisely gangs of international terrorists who are raging in Syria as in the territories of its neighboring countries—is to act to prevent, fight and destroy militants and terrorists in the territories they have already seized, not to wait for them to come to our home. It is well known that in the ranks of a terrorist organization, which is the so-called "Islamic State"—and I want to emphasize once again that this has nothing to do with real Islam—today there are thousands of immigrants from European states, Russia and the post-Soviet countries. You do not need to be an expert on these issues to understand: if they succeed in Syria, they will inevitably return to their countries, and come to Russia.[8]

Putin stressed Russia's support for international efforts to fight terrorism and in line with his earlier UN speech, and stressed Russia's (at least ostensible) willingness to work with partners. He emphasized that Russia was acting within the framework of international law, a consistent Kremlin theme in and of itself—but Putin added that the intervention is upon "the official request of president of the Syrian Arab republic." The anti-American shade to his message was that the Syrian conflict had deep roots and was worsened by "external interventions."[9] The "external interventions," of course, were led by the United States in this interpretation. Importantly, the intervention, Putin said, would be limited—Russia will support the Syrian army from the air and *intends* to do it for a limited time—though Putin did not give a precise end date:

> Considering all these circumstances, we, of course, do not intend to dive into the conflict, as they say, immerse ourselves completely. Our actions will be carried out strictly within the specified framework. Firstly, we will support the Syrian army exclusively in its legitimate struggle with terrorist groups. Secondly, support will be provided from the air without participation in ground operations. And third: such support will be limited in time—for the duration of the offensive operations by the Syrian army.[10]

Overall, several features stand out about Putin's announcement of the Syria intervention. First, the terrorism issue already loomed large in the Russian public consciousness along with a Kremlin-spun message that the United States trains and supports terrorists. Second, while the announcement superficially resembled the Soviet announcement of the invasion of Afghanistan, here Putin could credibly point to an official invitation from Assad in a way that the Soviets could not, since Putin did not install Assad himself. Indeed, it was clear that Putin very much wanted to signal to the Russian public that this intervention would be brief and limited; it would cost little and win a lot. This was not going to be another Afghanistan.

Anti-Americanism stood in the backdrop of paying lip service to international law—a Kremlin claim that Russia, unlike the United States, adheres to international law, a persistent Kremlin theme—with a caveat that Moscow understands international law differently from the West. Fourth, the announcement seemingly suggested a limited intervention, but also left plenty of flexibility in terms of how long Russian troops could remain. In addition to the vague overall language in terms of a pullout deadline, Putin even said that Moscow did not "intend" to immerse itself in the conflict, which is different than simply saying that it would not become involved at all. The carefully phrased announcement opened a window into the Kremlin's thinking, and demonstrated a degree of awareness of public opinion.

Another important element is worth highlighting. Immediately after Putin's announcement, Kremlin spokesman Dmitry Peskov said that Russia was the only power to use force in Syria legitimately: "[T]he use of armed forces on the territory of third countries is possible either by a UN Security Council resolution or at the request of the legitimate leadership of that country. In this case, Russia will in fact be the only country that will operate on a legitimate basis, namely at the request of the legitimate president of Syria."[11] This point, which seemed primarily aimed at the United States, and the West more broadly, foreshadowed Moscow's comments several years later in discussions about Iran, where Moscow again stressed that Russia was the only external actor who was in Syria legitimately. This early statement however suggests that the groundwork for these later comments was laid out from the beginning, or at least demonstrates consistency in the Kremlin's thinking. It also supports the argument that Moscow was looking to limit the presence of the United States in the Middle East with its intervention.

When it comes to Assad's invitation to Russia, the Kremlin clearly learned the lesson from Afghanistan. However he arrived at this decision, there is little doubt that Assad sent a letter to Putin asking for help—a letter which also cited Russia's efforts to fight "terrorism" as the reason for the request for help.[12] Over the years, Assad repeatedly talked in public about the need for Russia to be in Syria and, over time, began emphasizing the need for its long-term presence. For instance, he said in July 2018, "Russian armed forces are needed for balance in our region, at least in the Middle East, until the political balance is restored in the world."[13]

The issue of Assad's own legitimacy is another matter. A man who was ultimately deemed illegitimate by the majority of his own people, a man who unleashed one of the worst humanitarian tragedies since World War II and himself served as the largest recruitment tool for terrorists, had no legitimacy left—at least from a Western perspective. Yet the West ultimately never took a firm position on the issue of Assad's legitimacy. To be sure, Assad lost all credibility in the eyes of Western and Middle Eastern leaders, but they never made a firm commitment to his removal beyond declarations. Indeed, the UN Geneva communiqué of 2012 and the subsequent Security Council Resolution 2254, that outlined the map for transition in Syria and called for a transitional government and elections, ultimately remained vague on the status of Assad—2254 does not mention Assad at all. From the Western perspective, the spirit of these documents envisioned Assad's eventual departure, but the ambiguity of the actual language left room for Moscow's interpretation. This will be discussed in more detail in other chapters.

As far as the Russian public is concerned, when it comes to terrorism claims, another aspect is important. The Kremlin had spread the message domestically for years before the Syria intervention that the West had created ISIS and used it as an instrument of geopolitics, including the killing of Christians in Syria, along with the message that the West is only interested in removing the "legitimate" government of Syria to assert its hegemony in the Middle East.[14] Putin himself advanced the idea that the West supported terrorists inside Russia. While it is hard to gauge exactly how much the Russian public truly believed the announcement about Syria, it is reasonable to conclude that the earlier propaganda message on terrorism helped to create a degree of receptivity.

The Public Message

If Putin's announcement was resolute, and the Kremlin had a clear sense of purpose on the strategic level, in the immediate aftermath of the announcement of the intervention, the Kremlin's propaganda machine briefly struggled when it came to the details. But a unified message quickly emerged on Syria that went into greater detail beyond Putin's announcement. According to this narrative, Syria was a beautiful, peaceful, and tolerant country that was thriving until "terrorists" came, with their "Western" ideas of "freedom," and tore the country apart in a matter of months.[15] Meanwhile, in this narrative, the West was responsible for the rise of terrorism in Syria and continues to support terrorist groups in a geopolitical struggle to undermine Russia. Putin, in this view, is leading the true effort on eradicating terror—although the Russian government never provided a clear definition of terrorism. An image of a great Russia thumbing its nose at America, an image of a Putin who "outsmarted everyone," a Russia that everyone respects and talks to, was a critical component of the state's domestic messaging, and one that genuinely appealed to many Russians. For the first time in many years, Russia's resistance to the United States was on full display.[16] This big-picture aspect of great-power competition seemed lost on Western officials that saw only narrower short-term goals with Putin's move in Syria. They underestimated its true significance and scope.

Overall, media reports about the Syria campaign, unlike those on Ukraine, by and large presented sterile images to the Russian public—a very clean, easy campaign, and cheap in terms of blood and treasure.[17] State-controlled media reports were often reminiscent of action movies or video games: planes took off and bombs fell onto buildings, while commentators discussed, for example, whether the weather in Syria was favorable for air strikes. The Defense Ministry provided regular news briefings with colorful maps and reports of successful missions. There were interviews with Assad's forces who were grateful for Russia's help. Reports indicated that the Russian side was treated well—another subtle way in which the Kremlin aimed to reassure the public that Russia was not bearing serious costs. For instance, according to some reports, Russian pilots in Latakia received plenty of rest, read books, and ate hearty meals in clean facilities in their free time.[18] This is another indicator of how conscious the state was of the public mood, wary of another Afghanistan. In May 2015, Putin amended an existing decree on state secrets. Among other changes, he put Russia's military losses on the list of state secrets even in peace time, "during special operations,"[19] which shows how much the Kremlin wanted to avoid the public knowing true losses in Syria.

To some extent, emotion had a place in the discussion. A lyrical song, "Syria, my sister, your Russian brother will save you!," originally performed at a Putin rally as early as September 2013, gained traction after the intervention.[20] Media provided detailed interviews with Syrians about the brutality of the Western-backed "extremists" and promoted the message that all those in Syria fighting against Assad were monsters who tortured and killed in the most horrific ways. Images of innocent people, especially children, being blown up showed blood and gore, and reinforced the message that there were no other alternatives to Assad—who himself was the only source of order and peace.

One talk show, from as early as March 2014, for example, focused on Bashar al-Assad's cousin, Siwar Assad, and his Russian wives in Paris: images of Siwar as a caring father holding his children, a family that jokingly calls itself "Assadov" to emphasize closeness with Russia, and Russian women who entered fairy-tale lives with an Arabian prince who swept them off their feet.[21] It is noteworthy that the show begins by saying that Syria is thankful to Russia for preventing a Western intervention. But in terms of what Russia was actually doing in Syria with its 2015 intervention, the Kremlin clearly wanted the Russian public to see a painless, faraway campaign.

News about Syria quickly—and briefly—replaced news about Ukraine, which pointed to a short-term goal—a distraction from the earlier failure to subjugate Ukraine. Political analyst and later refugee from Putin's regime Andrei Piontkovsky called it an "imperial narcotic" that allowed the public to "forget about the failed Ukrainian embarrassment, return the intoxicating air of triumph of Russian Spring 2014, and at the same time remove the awkwardness and discomfort that Russians still experienced when killing the so-similar-to-them Ukrainians."[22] The failure in Ukraine reflected a broader failure of the *Russkiy mir* (Russian world) project, a concept many analysts close to the Kremlin developed in the late 1990s, and one that goes back to Putin's public discussion in the early 2000s of Russia in being danger of losing its unity.

This idea linked to the concept of Russia as a unique civilization, with its compatriots scattered and in need of protection from external enemies, chiefly Western ones. Indeed, this is the concept Putin invoked when he annexed Crimea from Ukraine; a concept of a short victorious war that distracted the public from failures in Ukraine and forced the West into a dialogue clearly played a role. This distraction had a short shelf life, and after several months, it was clear Moscow was in Syria for the long-haul. Furthermore, drawing Europe into a dialogue had more potential than doing the same with the United States, which viewed Russia at this point in relatively more nefarious terms than did Europe. The Kremlin, at least in part, genuinely believed that the United States has been a destabilizing force in global affairs and in the Middle East, and in particular that the US was out to get Russia and sponsor protests against authoritarian leaders, including within Russia itself. At the same time it needed to use the narrative of the United States as the enemy as a tool for domestic mobilization and a source of domestic legitimacy, and this need was not going to disappear. More broadly, the United States fits the role of an external enemy too well—it will always be there, and it is not going to attack.

The Russian Orthodox Church—which was aligned with the state and had operated as its unofficial arm—expressed support for the Syria operation. Head of the church's public affairs department Vsevolod Chaplin said, "the fight against terrorism—is a moral struggle, if you like—a holy struggle, and our country today is probably the most active in the world that resists terror."[23] Russia's

Central Spiritual Board of Muslims expressed public support for the campaign as well.[24] The World Congress of Russian Compatriots Living Abroad—a soft-power Kremlin propaganda tool—noted in November 2015 in Moscow an "extraordinary sense of elation" after Syria.[25]

Over the years, the Kremlin narrative by and large remained the same when it came to these main points about involvement in Syria, though the narrative slowly and very subtly changed to a long-term presence, without a heavy involvement and investment. For example, at a December 2017 press conference, pro-Kremlin journalists asked Putin several questions about Syria, including about how long Russian troops would remain there. Putin did not give a direct response. Rather, he went into a discourse about the roots of terrorism: in his view it comes from a lack of education, poverty, and "injustice." Without directly naming the United States, he said the most important thing is not to think short-term, because such thinking "created al-Qaeda, to fight the Soviet Union in Afghanistan," which then attacked the United States on September 11, 2001. Then he said, "We tell our American partners [about terrorists] where they travel and they ignore this. Why? Perhaps to use them [terrorists] to fight Assad?"[26] And there it was again—the message that the United States was ultimately the enemy out to get Russia—and that the United States recklessly undermines world stability and supports terrorists. And there was something else—the conflation of the Afghan mujahedeen with al-Qaeda—groups with their own separate identities. This was an anachronistic and at best misinformed argument that, to be sure many commentators have also made in the West. Al-Qaeda formed as an organization in August 1988, the final year of the Soviet occupation of Afghanistan. It aimed to look into the future after the Soviets left Afghanistan and its work began the following month.[27] The Taliban for its part was not a direct CIA creation, and while it is true that so-called Arab volunteers appeared in Afghanistan to resist the Soviet occupation, the CIA never supported them, while their role in fighting during the 1980s was minor. They only emerged as a coherent force in Afghanistan in the 1990s, after US involvement and Soviet occupation ended, while Osama bin Laden, the founder of al-Qaeda came to Afghanistan only as late as 1996.[28] But perhaps most importantly, the Soviet Union had to be fought, and the Cold War context is crucial for understanding US actions. And herein lies one key to Putin's hostility towards America—his misunderstanding of it, and desire to continue to fight the Cold War and create an alternate ending. If one follows this logic, it will come as no surprise that Putin also believed that the United States supported terrorists in the North Caucasus—if anything it was the only logical conclusion for a man for whom the

Cold War had not ended. Putin said in an infamous interview with Oliver Stone in June 2017 that during George Bush's presidency, the Kremlin "hoped" that the United States would support its struggle against "terrorists" in Chechnya, but "instead we saw that American special services precisely supported terrorists."[29] Again, the chief adversary was the United States, as far as the Kremlin was concerned. The United States had moved on after the fall of the Soviet Union; the Kremlin had not.

Meanwhile, over the course of the campaign, Putin announced, with much fanfare, triumphant yet unspecified withdrawals from Syria, in March 2016 and December 2017, only to boost Russia's actual presence immediately afterwards. From a domestic standpoint, it is difficult to imagine what purpose these announcements of faux withdrawals may have had other than to demonstrate brief and victorious campaigns to the public. This is not to exclude an international dimension—to confuse the West about Moscow's genuine intentions, but the announcements clearly served a domestic purpose.

Another interesting element of domestic messaging in Syria deserves a discussion. Narratives emerged that Syria is intrinsically connected to the very creation of Russia. These do not appear been state-led and did not dominate. A controversial thesis was advanced by historian Vadim Makarenko who, in December 2010, published an issue of *New Geography of the Ancient World*, where he claimed that Russia's ancestors were kicked out of the Middle East and into Europe. "Europe in the distant past existed in completely different coordinates and included a huge part of the Middle East and East Africa, inhabited at that time by white people. Among them were our ancestors—the Slavs," he wrote.[30] In line with this narrative, one Russian parliamentarian Semyon Bagdasarov boomed on main state Russian television's leading talk show that Syria is "our land . . . sacred land!" and that "if there was no Syria, there would be no Russia . . ." The first monks in Rus were Syrian by birth, he said, and without Syrians there would be no Orthodoxy in the Rus, and when Russia celebrated 300 years of the Romanov dynasty, the entire liturgy was read not by the Russian Orthodox Church, but by the Antioch Orthodox Church.[31] While some of the facts Bagdasarov cited in and of themselves may be accurate—and that is more for historians to judge—the narrative appeared to cherry pick at best, and sprang out precisely at the time of the Syria campaign.

Prior to the intervention, the idea of Syria as the birthplace of Russia had not been part of the discourse at all. As one anonymous internet blogger observed sarcastically about the narrative of Syria as Russia's birthplace:

From the depths of the internet the name of Vadim Makarenko had floated up ... Suddenly there's a song and dance around Syria, Egypt, Turkey and the entire Middle East acquires a deep-holographic dimension. We were there. We lived there. Our roots are there ... It was from there that we had to go north under the pressure of the Turkic and Arab conquerors, who later appeared in the history of Russia as the supposedly Tatar-Mongol yoke. And we built new cities, which we gave the old names ... And on the former land of our ancestors the names of cities and rivers, the names of our heroes and commanders were altered in Arabic manner, although they remained largely consonant: Novgorod—Nablus, Moscow [pronounced Moskva in Russian]—daMASK, Ryazan—Deir-ez-Zor, Staraya Russa—Jerusalem [pronounced Iyerusalim in Russian] ... For those who are familiar with the New Chronology of Fomenko, research by Makarenko will not seem too fantastic. The past is rewritten, redone, retouched, edited.[32]

The point about Syria's connection with Russia did not get lost on more mainstream observers. Another Russian blogger writing for major, and relatively liberal *Echo Moskvy*, wrote sarcastically in March 2016, "It turned out that Syria is our sacred land. That exactly in Syria is the fate of our country, or perhaps the whole world, is being decided." Because by this point Syria was disappearing from the news, he concluded no less sarcastically, "Who did you leave us for, Syria, mother of Russian cities?"[33] These additional narratives about Syria's fate being tied to Russia's highlight the role of the mystical over the rational that often prevailed in Russia—of history—and Russia's tradition revision of it—as it played out domestically in Russia's Syria campaign.

Public Reactions

Narratives are one thing. Public reactions to them are another matter. Grani.ru, which over the years has featured anti-Kremlin analysis, published a brief video interview in October 2015, in which a journalist stopped people on the street and asked what they thought about the Syria intervention.[34] Tellingly, and perhaps somewhat sarcastically, it was titled "Syria, my sister," possibly a reference to the song, "Syria, my sister, your Russian brother will save you" mentioned in the previous section. The majority of those in the video said they supported Putin's intervention in Syria. Usually they repeated Putin's line—killing terrorists was better there, before they come to Russia. Several respondents were asked to find Syria on a map, and they seemed to struggle with this task. (One person seemed to finally point to Syria, but it is hard to tell based on the video if was correct.) Asked if they would send their children to fight in Syria, some of the respondents said they would, though there was more hesitation, and some emphasized a preference for safety and use of air rather than ground forces. A number expressed negative views about US actions in Syria.

To Putin's Russian critics, the Syria campaign was reminiscent of another Afghanistan and a desire to distract the public from the state's internal failings. Their comments highlight the public fear of getting bogged down in Syria as the Soviet Union had done in Afghanistan, and a desire for the state to focus on domestic issues rather than foreign adventures. On September 7, 2015, the then one remaining anti-Putin opposition member in the Russian parliament (Duma) Dmitry Gudkov, sent an official request to Russian Defense Minister Sergei Shoigu. "Two things interest me," Gudkov wrote on his Facebook page, "First, are our soldiers really fighting for Assad, and second, if yes, why is this done in secret, without the parliament's approval? On the one hand, we strongly criticize America over Iraq, NATO over Yugoslavia—and on the other, it seems we send troops to support a far-from-pleasant regime."[35]

In trying to explain Putin's motivations for increased involvement in Syria, journalist Evgeniy Kiselev wrote for *Echo Moskvy*, "[Putin's] authoritarian regime, faced with internal problems, seeks to compensate for them in the direction of foreign policy," adding that this scenario was very similar that of Afghanistan thirty-six years ago.[36] Along the same lines, analyst Oleg Ponomar asked "Does this situation not remind us of Afghan history? As back then, the top [leadership] of the USSR, without any public discussion made a decision to introduce a 'limited contingent' of Soviet troops in Afghanistan. During this time, the already decrepit Soviet economy collapsed under the weight of military spending and social discontent, dragging to hell the whole Soviet regime."[37] Even so, the view that this would turn into another Afghanistan was not unanimous. Economist and Putin critic Sergey Aleksashenko wrote in October 2015 for the Brookings Institution that Russia's partnership with Iran is stable and long lasting despite problems, and that Russia's strategic goals in Syria are limited. His comments suggested that rather than spiral out of control, the Syria situation could drag on slowly, which would not necessarily be another Afghanistan. An interesting comment came from Russian military expert Alexander Golts in September 2015, which highlighted a degree of difference between Syrian and Afghanistan operations, "I have seen many speeches by Soviet and Russian leaders which were prepared as a military operation," he told Svoboda (Russian RFE/RL), "This, in my memory, is the first time when a military operation is timed to the leader's speech and is happening because of the leader's speech."[38]

The Kremlin had also revived the Soviet-era practice of utilizing *agitpoezd* (agit-trains)—trains going across the country to show off military trophies, with guides explaining that much of the ISIS-confiscated weaponry could have been delivered by Americans.[39]

Yet for all the comments that Russian observers and the public had made, what they did not say is perhaps even more important. Over the years, in my conversations with Russians, the main thrust of criticism of the Syria campaign among Russians has been about its costs for Russia—an unnecessary diversion of resources to Syria when Russia needs it the most, a pathetic display to try to divert attention from previous government failures, fear that the Syria adventure will turn into a quagmire—in other words, the criticism had primarily been that being in Syria only compounded Russia's own problems. Rarely have I heard the criticism of civilians, especially children, dying as a result of Russian carpet bombings and other support for the brutal Syrian dictator. Individual human life has historically held little value in Russia, something Russians themselves talk about. When discussing Syria and lack of overall empathy to the plight of the Syrian people, one Russian analyst, Natalia Kanotovich told me, "maybe there is empathy ... but it doesn't hurt [the Russian] people, it doesn't wound."[40] This echoes comments I've heard over the years from other Russians, such as "we have our own problems."

There are multiple reasons for this outcome. Russian media is mostly state controlled and devoted little attention to the real suffering that the Russian intervention inflicted, and what Assad has done to his own people. Instead, the primary message that the Russian public hears is that the United States is the source of Russian and global problems. If the Russian people knew the truth about Syria, Assad, and the Russian campaign, it would undoubtedly cause greater public outrage. And to be sure, I have met Russians who did feel outrage for the suffering their government has inflicted on the Syrian people. Indeed, when protests first broke out throughout Syria, several years before the Russian intervention, Russian liberal opposition expressed support for the protestors in the face of a brutal dictator. This went largely unnoticed, both domestically and in the West, domestically this was most likely due to state control of the press. Moreover, several brief episodes generated greater public reactions. For example, on December 26, 2016, Putin officially declared a day of mourning after a Russian military Tu-154 plane headed to Syria crashed in the Black Sea and claimed the lives of all ninety-two passengers on board, including sixty-four members of the famous Red Army choir. That Putin declared a day of mourning again shows his sensitivity to losses in Syria, but these events did not cause enough public outrage to demand a withdrawal from the country.

But deeper societal issues are also at play. Soviet Russia believed in communism. Yeltsin's Russia struggled to find what to believe in, and Putin's Russia found an answer in universal cynicism and militarization—not only of the country but also of the consciousness. Russia never experienced true democracy and what was supposed to be a transition to democracy in the 1990s led to widespread societal disillusionment, resentment of the West mixed with a fundamental misunderstanding of how Western democracies function, and a selfish cynicism that reveals itself in such expressions as "don't do good, you won't get bad." In the twilight days of the Soviet Union, people openly mocked the Soviet authorities, something I remember vividly as a child growing up in Moscow in the late 1980s. Putin's Russia is a different beast, even as it builds on previous experience. The vast majority of Russians are unaware of how many neighboring countries took in Syrian refugees, but they are aware of how many flooded into Europe, and in the context of ramped-up resentment towards the West, the possibility that Syrian refugees could destroy the European Union genuinely delighted a segment of the Russian population.[41]

The traumas of World War II and Afghanistan are far enough in the rearview mirror that the state has managed to ramp up narratives of militant patriotism that many sincerely find appealing.[42] The Soviet Union's tradition of double speak, when people said one thing in public and in private, in their kitchens, criticized the authorities, is gone. While the true number of Putin's supporters is a matter of considerable debate, there is no doubt that he has managed to gain support from a significant proportion of the population, and some are genuinely ready to tear apart any interlocutor who dares to criticize him. As Russian military expert Alexander Golts wrote, "The Afghan and Chechen syndromes have healed. Indeed, now several decades in the past these bloody escapades are perceived as a heroic epoch."[43]

Public Opinion Polls

As mentioned at the beginning of this chapter, discussion about the possibility of an intervention in Syria took place in Russia before September 2015. While public opinion polls in Russia, where people are not simply afraid to speak the truth, but whose state from its inception excelled at manipulation of the truth—should be taken with a large pinch of salt—and state-funded ones are almost entirely engineered. But within this framework, discussion of the polls is still useful. First, because some independent polls are still available, and overall, even if we cannot completely trust the actual percentage findings, they can still show helpful trends over time. Second, polling results of state-funded pollsters can help drive public opinion—similarly to how Kremlin-invented stories generate a certain psychological response, and their very language reveals the direction of the Kremlin's thinking.

The most trustworthy pollster in Russia has been the Levada Center. It remains independent and in fact the Kremlin put it on its list of "foreign agents." Other pollsters in Russia include FOM, VTsIOM, ROMIR, and Bashkirova and Partners. VTsIOM is openly Kremlin-funded, the rest appear more opaque. A search in the databases of these organizations shows that Levada did the most polling on Syria over the years, including before the Syrian intervention. FOM and Bashkirova and Partners do not show any polling results on Syria. ROMIR tends to reflect international trends, rather than domestic Russian public opinion. A search on the VTsIOM database with a keyword "Syria" in Russian results in four polls (all after the intervention), and four brief articles.

Prior to the Russian military intervention, Levada polls showed little public interest in military interventions in Syria in general and, overall, the polls showed distrust of all major actors in Syria. For instance, as early as October 2013, a poll found that 69 percent of Russians did not want an international military operation in Syria,[44] while an August 2013 poll found that a slim majority (just over 50 percent) did not support any side in the civil war even as both polls indicated that few paid close attention to the events in Syria, though a higher number always supported Assad than the rebels.[45]

On September 28, 2015, just a couple of days prior to Putin's announcement about the intervention, Levada posted a poll that indicated the majority of Russians opposed their country's military involvement in Syria: 69 percent said they either firmly opposed or probably opposed deploying Russian troops to help Assad, and only 14 percent believed Russia should provide "direct military support" by sending troops; 67 percent backed Russian "political and diplomatic support" for Assad's government. The picture was more divided on support that did not involve Russian troops: 43 percent supported providing Assad with weapons and military consultation—as Moscow had already been doing regardless—while 41 percent opposed it.[46]

Compare these findings with VTsIOM's. The language of the organization's press releases and the questions it asks, in and of itself, is reflective of the Kremlin narrative. It is not as objective as Levada's. On October 9, 2015 VTsIOM reported that 56 percent of Russian citizens were leaning towards blaming the United States and its allies for the bloodshed in Syria. In terms of overall support, the poll reported that 64 percent agree that "Russia needs to participate in the Syrian crisis to stop Islamic terrorists from far away, rather than on our own territory."[47]

In March 2016, VTsIOM found that, after six months of "sending Russian armed forces to Syria to fight terrorism," the support was up at 70 percent. Mikhail Mamonov, head of research projects at the VTsIOM commented: "not only in media support, but also in the fact that the actions of the Russian military were largely successful: almost half of the respondents stated that the situation was normalizing." It is noteworthy that he does not say Moscow's actions are perceived as successful, which would be the typical language a pollster would use; rather he accepts success as given. In addition to the way he openly attributed media influence to approval ratings, the issue of a "normalization" of the situation is also matter of perception, yet he didn't mention the perception part and simply stated normalization as fact. Mamonov's next comment is also illustrative, "Under these conditions, a request is being formed to reduce the participation of Russian troops in the Syrian conflict. And this means that the decision of the President regarding the reduction of the Russian military contingent in Syria meets the expectations of the majority of the population."[48]

In June 2017, VTsIOM found that over a third of respondents "perceive a military threat," and 63 percent within this group believe that the primary threat comes from the United States, followed by Ukraine (31 percent). Syria is at the bottom of the list, with only 3 percent.[49] And in February 2019, it found that 84 percent of Russian citizens are interested in Syria but "only" 22 percent follow it regularly. Interestingly, only 9 percent feel that the situation in the region stabilized and only 8 percent perceive the war as "an American intervention," while the perception of the situation in the previous six months "worsened," with 17 percent perceiving the situation as deteriorating, while the approval rate of the Russian armed forces remained high, at 73 percent—this percentage feels that the army "reached the stated objectives," and 34 percent supported the Russian government's policy.[50]

Another point is relevant when it comes to the discussion of public opinion polls. Did Putin go into Syria to boost his falling ratings? And did Syria provide a distraction for the domestic audience? Below is a snapshot of Putin's approval ratings, from coming to power until 2019. Overall, the lowest approval ratings Putin ever had were in August 1999, with 31 percent. Other low points were in 2003–4, 2007–8 during the financial crisis, and prior to annexation of Crimea in 2013–14, hovering at 61 percent. There is a clear correlation with Crimea, because after the annexation approval rose almost 30 percentage points, raising approval to 88 percent. Looking at Putin's approval ratings immediately prior to

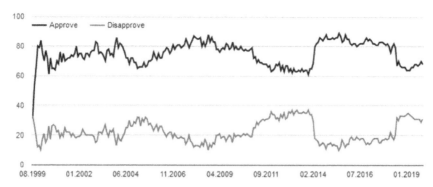

Figure 1 Putin's approval rating.[52] Source: Levada Center, accessed June 20, 2019.

the Syria intervention, the rate was already high, in the 80s. The Syria operation merely gave them a small boost.[51]

Does this mean we should write off the domestic aspect entirely? No. Domestic factors still mattered. This is why analysts such as Piontkovsky (cited earlier) talked about an "imperial narcotic" that distracted the public from the killing of Ukrainians and provided a vision of victory. This aspect is hard to capture in a poll. But these findings do suggest that the domestic factor was just that—a factor, not the primary motivation.

Here is another insight into Putin's approval ratings. When Putin came to Sevastopol in Crimea on May 9, 2015 (Russia's Victory Day) to observe the parade held annually to commemorate victory over the Nazis, he was greeted by tens of thousands chanting thanks for "returning" Crimea to Russia. But in face-to-face conversations with at least one Russian journalist, Sevastopol residents pointed to economic and other problems that Russia's annexation created. "But if the people have major problems, why did they welcome Putin so much today?" asked the journalist. "Because so far there has been no disillusionment," responded one resident, "We are hoping for the best. For now, we are waiting."[53] This incident shows the elusiveness of the true public mood in Russia, and opinion polls, at least the more credible ones, can help but do not give the full picture. The Kremlin knows its audience. This is why Putin himself, it is said, does not trust high approval ratings, and obsessively asks for more polls to be run—why does he need constant reassurance, if he believes support for him is so high in reality?

Another relevant example is the growing trend of Stalin approval ratings in Russia in recent years, which has accompanied a government-led rehabilitation of Stalin. Clearly, many factors matter with regard to this subject, and these go beyond the scope of the Syria discussion. The relevant aspect for the Syria discussion is the debate among Putin critics about the validity of the polls. While some tried to look for excuses for the results, feelings of hopelessness in the present and questioning the validity of results in the first place, analysts such as Konstantin von Eggert, a prominent Russian journalist, and Putin critic, said that the majority who approved of Stalin had no excuse given all the information available about Stalin today even to the Russian public. No matter how much you may discount the actual number as an exaggeration of true support, the trend still matters. We cannot discount the trend and it is one of clear growth.[54] This snapshot of a discussion can be applied to Syria and Putin's approval ratings.

An incident with VTsIOM is also illustrative. In a May 2019 poll, the organization found that trust and approval ratings differed—trust fell to historic lows of approximately 30 percent, while approval was at 65 percent. When the Kremlin asked for an explanation of the difference, VTsIOM instead published a new poll, just hours after the Kremlin made the request. This showed trust at about 72 percent. Analysis of the difference between the two polls came down to whether questions were open-ended, or yes or no questions. Many respondents simply chose not to answer open-ended questions, and in this survey trust came down to 30 percent. But when they could answer with a choice of yes or no, trust rose to 75 percent.[55] This incident shows the complexities of public opinion polling in Russia and that even a state-run poll can yield useful insight. Indeed, another state-run poll from June 2019 showed that Russians are increasingly disinterested in foreign affairs.[56] As for Levada's polls, in August 2017, 49 percent of Russian citizens supported ending the Russian Syria campaign, and a May 2019 Levada poll found that 55 percent wanted to end the Syrian operation.[57] These are important findings and suggest that the Russian public is becoming more casualty averse than it was historically.

8

Diplomatic Efforts

With so much focus on Russian military activities in Syria, one might wonder if Russian diplomacy mattered at all. With scores of images over the years of the Kremlin shaking its angry fist at its immediate neighbors and Western countries, the Russian military rolling into Georgia and Ukraine, as well as of poisonings and murders of Kremlin critics, Russian officials do not exactly come across as charmers to an average Western audience. Yet dismissing Russian diplomacy as irrelevant or ineffective in Syria would be a big mistake. Indeed, Moscow worked consistently to enlist support to cast itself as part of a solution in Syria, and Western officials were often inclined to believe it. Putin would not repeat the mistake of international isolation that the Kremlin experienced during the Soviet invasion of Afghanistan.

Moscow's diplomatic involvement in Syria began early. The Kremlin watched the beginning of protests in Syria carefully and in September 2011 sent a Russian Federation Council (parliamentary upper house) delegation to Damascus to talk to the Syrian regime and the opposition "to avoid a Libya scenario."[1] The Assad regime thanked Moscow for its "balanced" position.[2] These diplomatic efforts boosted Moscow's broader political, military, and geostrategic goals discussed in earlier chapters. The short term goal was to keep Assad in power. Thus the Kremlin blocked UN Security Council resolutions that called for action against Assad that went beyond mere rhetoric, over a dozen at the time of this writing. The Kremlin also used diplomacy to stall for time to help Assad, and create processes to sideline the United States and bolster its own position.

The First Veto

In October 2011, Moscow (along with Beijing) blocked the first draft UN solution, which called for an end to the Assad regime's human rights abuses as well as an independent investigation into human rights violations in Syria overall. Moscow rejected the "threat of an ultimatum and sanctions" against the Assad regime and stressed several times a "Syrian-led" and "all-inclusive dialogue."[3] Nor would Moscow accept being ignored. "Our proposals for wording on the non-acceptability of foreign military intervention were not taken into account," said Vitaly Churkin, Russia's permanent representative to the UN from 2006 to 2007, "and, based on the well-known events in North Africa [meaning Libya but likely also the Arab Spring] that can only put us on our guard."[4] Churkin mentioned sanctions but the resolution put to the vote had made no mention of sanctions; earlier versions did. As the draft progressed the version continued to be diluted on Russian insistence, to the point where Western representatives removed the word "sanctions" entirely.[5] Even so, Moscow vetoed the resolution in October 2011.

Several key themes stood out in Churkin's statement and continued to play out over the coming years from Moscow. First, Moscow stood firmly against even a hint of a possibility of regime change in Syria, and labeled the idea as aggressive and confrontational. The draft resolution Moscow vetoed from the beginning mentioned absolutely nothing even close to regime change. Even so, a mere condemnation of Assad alone was too much for the Kremlin.

Second, Moscow clearly stood by Assad. Yet it simultaneously claimed it was not wedded to Assad—merely to a "legitimate government" in Damascus—which, according to Moscow, fit Assad's profile. This dual claim opened the door for an interpretation that it was possible to work with Moscow to remove Assad in the future—as long as the Kremlin was satisfied with the conditions for such a deal. Such engagement with Moscow implicitly redirected the discussion away from the West acting outside the Security Council. To be sure, such a discussion did take place over the coming years when some analysts (myself included) called for a protected no-fly zone in Syria for which there was a precedent (the 1991 Operation Provide comfort, for example). But Western leaders doubted the extent of Moscow's commitment to Assad. An argument for action outside the Security Council may have had more resonance, if it was clear that all effort to work with Moscow was futile. The ambiguity in Moscow's position may have reduced the perception of the futility of working with Russia.

Third, the Moscow interpretation of the Libya experience and the Arab Spring—that is, a direct connection with regime change and perceived threat of the "chaos" it entailed—loomed large in the Kremlin's thinking. The idea of "foreign interference" in "internal affairs" appeared to matter most to the

Kremlin based on numerous official comments over the years. Fourth, Moscow's position on terrorism as coming only from the Syrian opposition fit within Moscow's overall position on "working together" globally to fight terrorism.

Assad, however, was ill-suited to being a partner in the fight against terror. He was both responsible for the vast majority of civilian deaths throughout the entire Syrian tragedy, and his brutality began and remained the largest source of recruitment for jihadists. Nor did the Assad regime consistently go after ISIS once it had taken root in Syria—rather he went after civilians. Moscow never accepted this reality. Instead, in the Russian narrative, Assad, like Moscow, was a victim of foreign (Western) aggression.

Lastly, Churkin's brief mention about working with the part of the Syrian opposition that wanted "no foreign interference" went unnoticed in terms of its deeper meaning. It foreshadowed exactly what Moscow would soon do— selectively work only with those members of the Syrian opposition that accepted Assad staying in power, while marginalizing opposition that called for Assad to step down as a precondition for peace talks. To be sure, when protests began in Syria in March 2011—peacefully—at first the protestors did not demand that Assad step down. They were merely calling for government accountability and reforms. But in response to Assad's swift and brutal suppression in the first month of protests—most notably the torture and murder of children, some as young as ten—demands for Assad's departure escalated.[6] These demands were being made by the time Moscow vetoed the first UN Security Council resolution. More broadly, Moscow's insistence on loyalty to the "legitimate government" in Damascus based on "international law" said something broader about Moscow— by sticking to technicalities, Moscow pushed for its own vision of international law that ran contrary to the rules-based order built by the West. The clash of these ideas—Moscow's rejection of human rights as a universal value, its own definition of what makes a great power, what gives a country true sovereignty (indeed Putin famously said once that few countries are truly sovereign)[7] stood in the backdrop of divergent Russian and Western interpretations of UN legal documents and principles as they applied to Syria. The broader effect of Moscow's action at the UN was erosion of these ideas as they were envisioned by the founders of the post-World War II global order based on institutions as an alternative to balance of power. Thus, Moscow was eroding the US-led global order politically and diplomatically, not only militarily, because at the end the institutions allowed themselves to bend to accommodate Moscow.

2012: Geneva Communiqué, Peace Talks, and the Red Line

The year 2012 saw a number of key diplomatic developments on Syria, and Moscow played a crucial role in these events. Yet Moscow's role also mattered in relation to Western and especially US politics and cannot be separated from it. European leaders, especially France, called for Assad to step down, and urged military intervention. However, many in Europe concluded that an intervention would be impossible without a major commitment from the United States.[8] And the Obama administration had little appetite for intervention. Obama, after all, had campaigned in 2008 on pulling US troops out of Iraq and more broadly curtailing American involvement in the Middle East.

Moscow meanwhile continued to stick to its position of non-intervention in Syria. In January 2012, Churkin reiterated Russia's position in response to another draft UN Security Council resolution, proposed by Morocco, which called for Assad to step down. "Once you start, it is difficult to stop," Churkin said, referring to asking Assad to step down—if this resolution was to pass, the Security Council would soon announce "what king needs to resign, or what prime minister needs to step down."[9] In the same vein, Churkin forwarded the next month a Duma declaration to the United Nations addressed to the Secretary-General, which said that in the view of Russian deputies, "the scenarios proposed by a number of Western and Arab States seek something quite different from the United Nations and the international community as a whole. In fact, these scenarios prejudge the outcome and see political regime change as an absolute prerequisite for resolving the issues in Syria."[10] The Duma in Russia has long ceased to be independent, yet the Kremlin felt it important to add a veneer of legitimacy to its actions through approval of a rubberstamp parliament.

Another episode that occurred highlights the perception of the Russian position among Western leaders. In February 2012, Moscow (along with Beijing) vetoed another resolution on Syria.[11] The same month, former Finnish president Martti Ahtisaari claimed in an interview that during a course of discussions, Churkin laid out a plan that had included a proposal for Assad to leave power some time after peace talks had started between the regime and the opposition. Ahtisaari also claimed that Western powers ignored the Russian proposal because they were convinced Assad would soon fall. Ahtisaari said he recalled that Churkin "said three things: One—we should not give arms to the opposition. Two—we should get a dialogue going between the opposition and Assad straightaway. Three—we should find an elegant way for Assad to step aside."[12] Churkin himself refused to comment on what he described as a "private" conversation, but Ahtisaari

persisted in his version. Other Western diplomats involved at the time saw a
different story. Sir John Jenkins, former director of the Middle East department of
the UK's Foreign Office said that in his experience, Moscow resisted attempts to
bring Assad to the negotiating table "and I never saw a reference to any possible
flexing of this position ... the weakest point is Ahtisaari's claim that Churkin was
speaking with Moscow's authority."[13] In other words, this message would have
meant a lot more if it came directly from Putin; but such a message never came.

This widely reported episode captures divisions among Western leaders and
officials from the very beginning, with some believing Moscow both could and
should be a part of the solution in Syria, and others wary of Moscow's clear
preference to keep Assad in power. Some Western officials also privately believed
that if the United States and Russia managed to work together on a peaceful
solution, despite their differences, other countries would follow, and it would be
possible to advance a real peace settlement.[14] Given Moscow's historic role in the
Middle East it is not unreasonable that some would come to this conclusion—
recall how important Moscow's presence was in the Madrid conference, if only
as window dressing. Another problem is that Moscow's views often sounded
reasonable—especially when taken at face value, or out of context. And many
Western officials wanted to believe that the Kremlin could be constructive in
Syria. Over the years, Secretary of State Kerry had periodically described Russia's
role as "constructive" in Syria.[15] Western Europeans for their part believed in
engaging Russia overall—what one official described as a "more for more
approach."[16] Eastern Europeans continuously warned about the dangers of this
approach but countries such as Germany, France, and Italy, "tried different forms
of engagement, assuming trade (with German companies) or strategic
engagement (through projects like the Mistral military ship with France) could
gradually induce a more constructive dynamic with Russia."[17] This dynamic was
not in sight, but these governments persisted.

The idea of Moscow as a peacemaker in Syria had taken root, and Western
leaders themselves helped push it. These efforts helped lay the groundwork for a
degree of recognition of Russia's legitimacy as a powerbroker. Legitimacy is
about perception in the eyes of others, and Moscow learned its lesson from
Afghanistan—it was not going to go it alone in Syria. Moscow did not veto
Security Council resolutions alone. China typically followed suit, and a minority
of non-permanent members of the Security Council also periodically expressed
support for Moscow's position. Still, Moscow took the lead on the Syria issue.

In response to the Russian and Chinese vetoes in February 2012, France
spearheaded efforts to set up an international "Friends of Syria group"[18] tasked

with finding a solution to the Syrian conflict, which included (in addition to the United States and France) the United Kingdom, Saudi Arabia, Turkey, and Qatar, along with other members.[19] The group first drew big gatherings from all relevant international actors, and in April 2012 it recognized the opposition Syrian National Council (SNC) as the legitimate representative of the Syrian people. The West, however, hesitated to overtly provide arms to the opposition due to concerns over radical elements within this opposition. (Covertly, the administration began arming Syrian rebels in 2013 against ISIS—rather than Assad. It was too little too late, and the program ultimately failed.)[20] Over the coming years, the group stuck more to rhetoric than material support for the opposition overall, and the group's attendance—along with its relevance—slowly dwindled.

In March 2012, the UN Security Council gave its "full support" for the Joint Special Envoy for the United Nations and the Arab League to bring about a ceasefire in Syria in what became known as the six-point Kofi Annan peace plan, or Geneva I, released the next month, in April.[21] Russian officials for their part continued to worry the most about a US-led intervention that in their view would create a vacuum that terrorists would fill.[22] The ceasefire the plan called for quickly failed, and the UN suspended its monitoring mission there by mid-June—a mission which some criticized as too small to adequately complete the work it was tasked with. Reportedly, both sides violated the agreement, yet at the time, Assad had more resources and could do more damage than the other side.[23] Speaking about the ceasefire, for example, German envoy Peter Wittig said, as summarized by a UN press release in July, "Instead of implementing the plan, instead of silencing the weapons, Mr. Assad had unleashed tanks and helicopters. The Council could not continue business as usual."[24] His comment came after Moscow and Beijing had vetoed a third UN Security Council resolution on Syria, which demanded that all sides cease violence to provide support for the UN mission. The only party in the conflict with heavy weapons was the Assad regime, and merely threatened it with a possibility of sanctions if it continued to use force against its own citizens.[25] Moscow held its position firm in the coming months. By August that year, Annan resigned from his position, saying, "As an envoy, I can't want peace more than the protagonists, more than the Security Council or the international community, for that matter."[26]

Nonetheless, prior to Annan's resignation, the international community had agreed on another important document, initiated upon Annan's initiative—the Geneva communiqué of June 2012. Specifically, it was agreed upon by the so-called "action group" for Syria, comprised of the Secretaries-General of the United Nations and the League of Arab States, and representatives from China,

France, Russia, the United Kingdom, United States, Turkey, Iraq, Kuwait, Qatar, and the European Union. The document called for, "The establishment of a transitional governing body which can establish a neutral environment in which the transition can take place [in Syria] . . . All groups and segments of society in Syria must be enabled to participate in a National Dialogue process."[27] The spirit of the document, from the Western perspective, envisioned Assad's departure, but its actual language remained vague on this point upon Russian insistence. In fact, the document never mentions Assad. Thus, Assad could very well be included in the process.[28]

At the end of August, even Tehran presented its own peace plan, claiming that US efforts to isolate the Islamic Republic had failed,[29] while later in the year, in October, Lakhdar Brahimi, who replaced Kofi Annan, went as far as to seek Iran's mediation assistance.[30] This attempt did not produce tangible results but is illustrative of the overall complexity of the Syria situation. Indeed, the complexity surpassed even that of Bosnia in the 1990s. Moreover, Iran for its part would soon play a far more prominent role in Syria.

More to the point, a far more critical event took place the same month. During remarks to journalists on August 20, 2012, then-US president Barak Obama made the following comment in response to a journalist's question:

Question Mr. President, could you update us on your latest thinking of where you think things are in Syria, and in particular, whether you envision using US military, if simply for nothing else, the safe keeping of the chemical weapons, and if you're confident that the chemical weapons are safe?"

Obama I have, at this point, not ordered military engagement in the situation. But the point that you made about chemical and biological weapons is critical. That's an issue that doesn't just concern Syria; it concerns our close allies in the region, including Israel. It concerns us. We cannot have a situation where chemical or biological weapons are falling into the hands of the wrong people. We have been very clear to the Assad regime, but also to other players on the ground, that a red line for us is we start seeing a whole bunch of chemical weapons moving around or being utilized. That would change my calculus. That would change my equation.[31]

This is how the US president drew the famous "red line" in Syria. Reportedly, the comment drew some surprise from his aides, but they stood by it and reiterated it the next day, and in the weeks and months after.[32] Some argued that a comment made at a press conference is less significant than a prepared statement, but the fact of the matter is, the administration continued to reiterate it. Obama indeed continued to reiterate it several months into 2013.[33] The red line was drawn, loud and clear. The consequence of its subsequent non-enforcement reverberated far beyond Syria, though in all fairness, the non-enforcement itself was only a logical conclusion of previous efforts to avoid getting involved in Syria.

Chemical Weapons: An Opening for Moscow

The first public report of Assad's alleged use of chemical weapons came in December 2012.[34] In early 2013, more allegations came to light, and investigations into chemical weapons continued. Damascus blamed the Syrian opposition for the use of chemical weapons, and Moscow supported this view. In a meeting with the Russian daily *Izvestia*, Assad argued that the allegation of his use of chemical weapons was "politically motivated," while by contrast, Secretary of State Kerry said that Assad was trying to block investigation into chemical weapons use.[35] In March, UN Secretary-General Ban Ki-moon announced that the United Nations would conduct an investigation into chemical weapons use, together with the World Health Organization (WHO) and the Organization for the Prohibition of Chemical Weapons (OPCW). Evidence of the Assad regime's use of chemical weapons was gathered, and in August Assad allowed a UN team into Syria to investigate.

On August 21, a large-scale chemical attack occurred in Ghouta, a suburb of Damascus, a region from which the Assad regime had been trying to expel rebel forces. Over 1,000 people died as the result of the attack, the vast majority civilians, and many of them children. Assad said he would allow UN inspectors to investigate, but snipers attacked the convoy transporting them. No one was injured but inspectors could not personally visit all the sites that related to the attacks. US investigators however soon concluded that Assad was behind the attacks, and the British assessment concluded that he was "most likely" behind the attacks. The French government also concluded that Assad was responsible and that his actions violated the 1925 Geneva Protocol.

A military intervention appeared a real possibility, as the US military provided Obama with a range of strike options in Syria, and repositioned naval forces—a ship armed with cruised missiles had appeared in the Eastern Mediterranean.[36] Moscow, for its part, also deployed a missiles cruiser and an anti-submarine ship to the Eastern Mediterranean, while Russian military sources stressed that the deployment was part of the usual rotation.[37] Obama still hesitated, and on August 31 he announced his intention to seek authorization to use force for limited strikes, but opted not to call Congress in session immediately. It is difficult to imagine that Obama did not know the mood on the Hill. Even Ben Rhodes, then deputy national security advisor to Obama had noted after he left the administration that when Obama consulted with his Cabinet as to whether or not to go to Congress to seek authorization to use force against Assad, Susan Rice, who had recently become national security adviser, told Obama, "We needed to hold Assad accountable ... Congress is never going to give you this authority." Rhodes notes she was "the only person to make this prediction," and that Rice and Obama's lawyers insisted that Obama could reserve the right to use force if Congress refused. This indicates how congressional authorization for limited strikes may have been preferable, but legally unnecessary. And the administration knew that there was little appetite for another intervention domestically.[38] It is noteworthy that in his article, Rhodes also observes that in going to Congress, Obama had forced Rhodes to "let go of a part of himself" that wanted to "do something" after seeing the horrific images coming out of Syria.[39] Rhodes notes that by going to Congress, Obama tried to address the "dysfunction" and hypocrisy between accusations of his being too weak on Syria, but when push came to shove not authorizing action. These comments show that the Obama administration chose a more politically popular path and cloaked it in morality— perhaps out of guilt for turning away from Assad-perpetrated carnage in Syria.

On September 4, the Senate Foreign Relations committee, for its part, approved on a bipartisan basis, the use of force against Assad, but the House predictably did not. The same day the measure did not pass, Obama denied that he set the red line in the first place at another press conference, this time in Sweden:

> Q Thank you, Mr. President. Thank you, sir. Have you made up your mind whether to take action against Syria whether or not you have a congressional resolution approved? Is a strike needed in order to preserve your credibility for when you set these sort of red lines? And were you able to enlist the support of the Prime Minister here for support in Syria?
>
> **President Obama** Let me unpack the question. First of all, I didn't set a red line; the world set a red line. The world set a red line when governments representing 98 percent of the world's population said the use of chemical weapons are abhorrent and passed a treaty forbidding their use even when countries are engaged in war.[40]

Even if one accepts Obama going in one year from "that would be a red line for me" to "I didn't set a red line," at the end of the next, he was even more obligated to act by his own admission that "the world" required it—domestic politics aside. On this point, another comment from Ben Rhodes stands out, from the same article. Rhodes quoted Benjamin Netanyahu telling Obama that history would judge that Obama's decision to go to Congress "was right ... and history will be kinder than public opinion."[41] This comment suggests that, for all the "dysfunction" mentioned earlier, Netanyahu believed that the public would support pushing back against a human rights violator, but that he thought that military action would, nonetheless, be the wrong decision.

The Syrian crisis was incredibly complex, and internally, the administration struggled with its multitude of different aspects. All governments, even democratic ones, require narratives to work effectively—in other words, they require a vision that propels them forward towards a unifying goal. And in Syria, "we didn't have a narrative that was coherent and compelling," said Alexander Bick, who held the Syria portfolio at the US State Department state policy planning staff from 2013–14 before taking over as Syria director at the National Security Council in the Obama administration.[42] The definition of what the crisis was about kept changing over time—whether it was about anti-Assad protests, chemical weapons, Sunni terrorism, the European refugee crisis, or the Russian intervention. Still, for all the complexities and confusion of the crisis, a broader issue is that many, but crucially, Obama himself doubted that the United States could, or should be involved in the Middle East, whether American involvement could lead to a better outcome. As prominent journalist Jeffrey Goldberg concluded after a series of personal interviews with Obama:

> [T]he Middle East is no longer terribly important to American interests ... even if the Middle East were surpassingly important, there would still be little an American president could do to make it a better place ... [and] the innate American desire to fix the sorts of problems that manifest themselves most drastically in the Middle East inevitably leads to warfare, to the deaths of US soldiers, and to the eventual hemorrhaging of US credibility and power.[43]

Syria presented an incredibly difficult, and in many ways unprecedented challenge, with no easy options. This challenge also came at a time of serious Middle East fatigue in the West and broad public desire to disengage from the region. Syrian opposition for its part was bitterly divided. But perhaps it is this climate that arguably made the crisis so difficult to define in the first place. No one can lead without confidence in themselves, and at the heart of the Syria crisis stood the problem of doubt that America could play a positive role in Syria, that staying out would be a better option. Where did all of this leave Moscow? For one thing, it had a clear narrative on Syria. It also knew what it wanted to see in this country, and geo-strategically beyond the country itself. The Russian state remained focused on getting there.

For all the resolutions the Kremlin blocked on the UN Security Council, it did agree to several important ones. After the use of chemical weapons, the UN Security Council passed Resolution 2118[44] on chemical weapons which stipulated that "no party in Syria should use, develop, produce, acquire, stockpile, retain, or transfer chemical weapons." The resolution also noted "that Member States are obligated under Article 25 of the Charter of the United Nations to accept and carry out the Council's decisions," and that "defiance of the resolution" would bring about "sanctions or stronger coercive action" under Chapter VII. The idea that all Council decisions, not just Chapter VII, are legally binding, is "due to careful diplomacy between the United States and Russia, with the former wanting a legally binding instrument and the latter refusing to agree to a Chapter VII resolution," as one legal scholar noted. The reference to Article 25, was a compromise.[45] This point underscores the concern Moscow had for resorting to Chapter VII—which entailed coercive measures.

Here is how Moscow saw Resolution 2118. Vitaly Churkin said it "opened a window of opportunity for convening an international conference on Syria." He underscored that "Christians find themselves under threat" in Syria—another Kremlin theme that took prominence over the years—and that while the Syrian government "frequently said that it was ready to participate in the Geneva meeting," some members of the Syrian opposition were hindering peace efforts. "[T]here is a need for the armed opposition also to comply unswervingly with the requirements in resolution 2118 (2013) in terms of providing full assistance to the OPCW and United Nations support during the joint mission. It is clear that at least part of the opposition is trying to undermine the efforts to implement the resolution,"[46] he said. His comments again underscored Moscow's support for Assad.

At a press conference in London on September 9, 2013, John Kerry made an off-the-cuff remark: if Assad put his chemical weapons arsenal under international control "without delay," the United States would not strike.[47] The Kremlin saw an opening. Sergei Lavrov immediately came up with a proposal that would be hard for Obama to refuse: Syria would agree to dismantle its chemical weapons program and allow international monitoring, and in exchange, the United States would not conduct military strikes. (It is worth recalling here that decades earlier, Moscow had helped build Syria's chemical weapons arsenal in the first place.)

Syrian Foreign Minister Walid al-Moallem welcomed the proposal. Obama and European leaders began a discussion on how to implement the plan through the UN Security Council. Meanwhile, Obama also asked Congress to postpone the final vote on use of force.[48] On the anniversary of 9/11, Putin published an op-ed in *The New York Times*, warning against a US strike in Syria, as there were "few champions for democracy" in the country, and a strike could result in loss of innocent lives, spread conflict beyond Syria's borders, and "undermine multilateral efforts to resolve the Iranian nuclear problem and the Israeli–Palestinian conflict and further destabilize the Middle East and North Africa ... [and] throw the entire system of international law and order out of balance."[49] Putin also cast the proposal on chemical weapons removal as an opportunity to avoid use of force and build mutual trust, as well as "improve the atmosphere international affairs." In the end, the Kremlin position on chemical weapons removal prevailed. On September 14, Kerry and Lavrov reached an agreement—a "framework for elimination" of Syria's chemical weapons.[50] Assad avoided military strikes and Moscow played a key diplomatic role in the Syrian conflict, on par with the United States. Europe, for its part "was caught off guard" by US hesitation in Syria after use of chemical weapons, as one Western official put it, "and did not immediately understand what lessons Russia could draw from the new US restraint."[51] A key lesson, of course, was that Moscow could act largely with impunity—indeed the Crimean annexation followed the next year, and then came the Syria intervention. The EU for its part concluded that its leverage was limited to sanctions, while "European risk aversion prevented any move that could risk a military escalation with Moscow. The general consensus was that it was necessary to keep channels of dialog open even if they did not produce tangible outcomes immediately."[52] Russia, for its part, was simply not as risk averse as the Europeans.

Meanwhile, UN discussions continued to highlight the divergence in the Russian and Western views on Syria. An illustrative example was provided by a September 27, 2013 meeting, following adoption of the resolution on Syrian chemical weapons removal. Sergei Lavrov said, "The resolution does not fall under Chapter VII of the Charter of the United Nations and does not allow for any automatic use of coercive measures of enforcement ... Particular responsibility lies with those who back and sponsor the opposition; they have to ensure that chemical weapons do not fall into the hands of extremists."[53]

While Lavrov emphasized problems within the opposition and "extremism," and highlighted that Resolution 2118 does not fall under Chapter VII given Moscow's concerns about coercive action, Kerry for his part, emphasized that the bulk of responsibility lay with Assad, and the importance of eliminating Syria's chemical weapons arsenal. At the same time, Kerry's comments were positive on Russia. This is illustrative of the additional layer of confusion over Russia—while Western leaders over the years displayed outrage at Moscow's actions, they also frequently expressed support, if only perhaps in the hope that such language might coax Moscow to be more constructive. This may have been a fairly common diplomatic approach, but it was not the only option available to Western diplomats. As noted earlier, this situation highlights the posture of regarding Russia simultaneously as part of the problem and of the solution. Thus, in response to Lavrov, Kerry praised joint US–Russian efforts on the elimination of chemical weapons.[54]

Reports indicated that Russia and the United States might host a peace conference on Syria—while Lavrov later publicly berated the United States for not doing enough to bring opposition groups to the negotiating table, and questioned the thoroughness of the UN investigation into chemical weapons use in Syria in the context of claims by the Kremlin and Damascus of the opposition using chemical weapons.[55] Over the coming months, Moscow continued to reiterate the danger of Assad's regime falling and the radicalization of the Syrian opposition.[56]

For his part, throughout 2014—and under the supervision of countries that included Russia, Assad's closest ally aside from Iran—Assad had removed most of the Syrian regime's disclosed chemical weapons arsenal. But doubts lingered over remaining chemical weapons, and indeed, smaller scale chemical attacks continued.[57] Skipping ahead, major chemical attacks resulted in two military strikes against Assad by the Trump administration in April 2017 and 2018— further proof that Assad, under Russian supervision, did not remove all chemical weapons. As the Arms Control Association noted as late as September 2018, "The Syrian government has been found responsible for most chemical weapons attacks in Syria, and the Islamic State has also been found to have used chemical weapons on several occasions."[58]

Returning to 2014, the United States and Russia ultimately failed to reconcile their divergent positions on whether Assad should step down. Moscow also began insisting that Iran be included in peace talks.[59] "No-one has done more to make Syria a magnet for terrorists than Bashar al-Assad," Kerry said, for example in January 2014, "You cannot save Syria with Bashar al-Assad in power."[60] But it was obvious that Kerry could not credibly back his diplomacy with force, and his meetings with Lavrov ultimately only showed that the Kremlin ran rings around him; all he could do was buttress the perception of Moscow's indispensable role in Syria. And for Moscow, Assad had to stay, even as it continued to pay lip service to being committed to a "legitimate government" in Damascus, rather than Assad. One could argue that this ultimately was not necessarily a contradiction—for Moscow these were simply one and the same. Moscow always equated the "legitimate government" in Syria with Assad's regime.

In January 2014, Geneva II peace talks commenced under UN auspices, but unsurprisingly failed to reach an agreement. In this context, Moscow stepped up and, in December 2014, proposed its own peace talks between the Syrian government and the opposition.[61] Obama for his part remained proud of his decision to refrain from strikes against Assad after drawing a red line earlier. "I'm very proud of this moment," he told Jeffrey Goldberg, and continued, "the fact that I was able to pull back from the immediate pressures and think through in my own mind what was in America's interest, not only with respect to Syria but also with respect to our democracy, was as tough a decision as I've made—and I believe ultimately it was the right decision to make."[62]

Diplomacy with Military Action

At the time the United States was unwilling to match its diplomacy with military action, Russia had done just that to support its preferred outcome in Syria. Obama genuinely believed that the United States was not engaged in a geopolitical struggle with Russia overall, and certainly not in Syria. By 2014, the chief US objective in Syria was to fight ISIS. Moreover, as Alexander Bick explained, the Obama administration largely looked at Russia's intervention from the prism of what it might mean for US interests, not how it might enhance Russia's regional reputation.[1] Once Putin intervened, the thinking was, "If Russia could be helpful in defeating the Islamic State—great, but any cooperation with Russia would require them changing their approach."[2] And to be sure, the United States never cooperated militarily with Russia in Syria, which is why the US had a de-confliction mechanism on the ground—a very narrow focus on avoiding clashes. The belief that Russia would find itself stuck in Syria likely also added to the mix, as Obama's own comments suggest. On the whole, the administration did not treat the intervention with the seriousness it deserved—in terms of what it meant for Syria, the region, and broader Western interests that spanned far beyond the Middle East.

For its part, the Kremlin did believe it was engaged in a great-power struggle with the West, but too few in the West had understood this. This struggle always stood in the backdrop of repeated Russian calls for a multipolar world. In fact, by 2014, prior to the Russia's Syria intervention, the Obama administration knew about Russian disinformation efforts it could use to interfere in Western democracies but if anything, did not take this information seriously enough.[3] Moreover, the administration needed Russian cooperation on the nuclear deal with Iran that stood at the heart of Obama's broader designs for reducing American involvement in the Middle East. Contrary to the Kremlin's belief that the United States was out to destroy Russia, the Obama administration's error lay in its belief that Moscow could be a constructive, even if difficult partner. Syria emerged as the one arena where Americans and Russians not only de-conflicted to avoid military clashes, but also simply talked the most. This situation may have been a far cry from full-scale cooperation, but it allowed Moscow to gain ground—literally and politically.

Meanwhile, Putin engaged in a double game. While he had called for a coalition with the United States and Saudi Arabia against ISIS in spring 2015, he had secretly engaged in negotiations with Tehran and Damascus to save Assad. The rest was, as John Parker wrote, a "cover story."[4] Days after the Russian military intervention began, Lavrov said that the Russian side was ready to establish contacts with the moderate Syrian opposition—if only such a thing existed. "We are ready to establish contacts with it, but so far no one has told where they are," he said, "And if nothing is known about them, then the results of air strikes by the American coalition can be used by opposition forces."[5]

In addition, weeks after Moscow's military intervention in Syria began, another peace talks initiative began in Vienna, with US, Russian, Saudi, Turkish and other representatives in what came to be known as the Vienna process. And that is not all. At least in part due to Moscow's insistence, for the first time, Iran was included as a participant, only months after the conclusion of the Joint and Comprehensive Plan of Action, or the Iran nuclear deal as it became known. In this context, the West appeared to signal that Iran was now less of a pariah than it used to be, and that on Syria, diplomacy with Assad's two biggest supporters was the necessary course of action.[6] In the following months other rounds of Vienna peace talks took place. Riyadh also held meetings with anti-Assad factions, including Ahrar ash-Sham, which Assad and Moscow had rejected.

In early November 2015, as Moscow's military intervention continued, the Kremlin reportedly put forward a six-point plan to end the Syrian conflict, in preparation for an upcoming meeting in Vienna on Syria.[7] The same report suggested that Assad could take part in the transition process, and suggested that Moscow wanted to label all insurgents as terrorists. These two issues presented a clear problem for Western officials, but it was clear that the West hesitated to act, while Moscow at this point had already resorted to force to stand by its position.

In late December 2015, the UN Security Council met again. This time, the Council had been able to reach consensus, and on December 18, 2015, unanimously passed Resolution 2254, a critically important document which reiterated the 2012 Geneva communiqué, which did not say explicitly that Assad had to leave. The resolution called for a ceasefire, six months to create a transitional and unified Syrian government, and eighteen months for a new constitution and democratic elections. Vitally, it also included the Iranian four-point peace plan. The UN would administer the vote, and the vote would include the Syrian diaspora. At the time of this writing, in June 2020, the resolution remains the single international guiding legal document on settling the future of Syria.

Yet the resolution had major gaps. It made no mention of the future of Assad— in fact it did not use his name at all. Technically, nothing precluded Assad from participation in both the transitional government and elections; and Syria's electoral law at the time of this writing does not allow many in the diaspora to participate in elections.[8] Laws aside, a scenario where Assad runs for office is bound to be a farce. Thus the resolution legitimized Moscow's interpretation of Syria's future, and—knowingly or not—Western countries implicitly agreed to it. Although 2254 calls for inclusion of the diaspora, in effect, given the Syrian law, it could disenfranchise millions forced to flee Syria as refugees, many of them after facing barrel bombs, chemical weapons, or death squads targeted at their towns and neighborhoods because they were deemed disloyal to Assad. The gaps in the resolution, unless addressed, could allow Assad to head the transitional government and then potentially manipulate elections to ensure his victory.

The resolution also left questions about the relationship between Saudi Arabia and the Syrian opposition, and disagreement about which groups were considered to be terrorist organizations beyond ISIS and the al-Nusrah Front. Indeed, at the time of the document's signing, Moscow had been bombing groups in Syria that the West supported.[9] Assad for his part quickly violated the ceasefire in Resolution 2254 and Moscow at the very least did nothing to stop it.

The divergence in the Russian and Western interpretations of the resolution and the future of Syria were particularly glaring in the different remarks Kerry and Lavrov gave after the resolution passed. Kerry emphasized Assad's culpability; Assad "lost the ability and credibility to unite his country," he said. Lavrov by contrast got onto another Kremlin diplomatic hobbyhorse about a "Syrian-led, inclusive dialogue." Reading between the lines, this implied the inclusion of Assad. Lavrov also added that the passage of the resolution "was a response to the attempted imposition of an external solution on Syria,"[10] another favorite Kremlin narrative that implicitly accused the West and its allies of the Syrian tragedy, rather than Assad himself. In sum, clear differences remained between Russia and the United States. The resolution did nothing to change this. But once the document passed in its form, it further legitimized Moscow's interpretation.

UN special envoy Steffan de Mistura took charge of organizing the Syria peace talks. Moscow then accelerated its initiatives to host its own Syria peace talks. As mentioned earlier, it also engaged with faux Syrian opposition figures who supported Assad. For example, Moscow engaged with Randa Kassis, leader of the Movement for Pluralistic Society, who publicly supported[11] Putin's Syria policy and co-founded the pro-Kremlin Center of Political and Foreign Affairs.[12] Reportedly, in April 2015, then-president of Kazakhstan, Nursultan Nazarbayev, accepted Kassis' proposal to hold Syria peace talks in the country's capital, Astana. Despite criticism from Syrian opposition, the first talks commenced the following month, in May. No representatives from the Assad regime attended, but new rounds of discussions continued over the coming months and years.

Other Syria peace talks continued to take place, again highlighting the immense complexity of the situation. For example, meetings took place in Riyadh between some members of Syrian opposition, which excluded the Syrian Kurds. Eventually these meetings resulted in the creation of the High Negotiations Committee. France, Saudi Arabia, Turkey, and Qatar supported the committee. Moscow, however, felt the group was not in a position to speak on behalf of the Syrian opposition.

In January 2016 Geneva III talks took place, but again achieved nothing of substance and de Mistura suspended the talks the following month. Moscow for its part criticized the Syrian opposition for the failure. Lavrov said, "The goal of resuming the negotiation process, which was suspended in an atmosphere where part of the [Syrian] opposition took a completely unconstructive position and tried to put forward preconditions, was stressed [at the ISSG meeting].[13]

His comment also highlights the ambiguity of Resolution 2254, which allowed for different interpretations and enabled Moscow to use this uncertainty to its own ends. The same month as Geneva II commenced, Putin also made public mention of the need for a new Syrian constitution,[14] and by May that year reports suggested that Moscow had completed a draft, which the United States supported, though the Syrian regime denied having seen this draft.[15]

Syrian Chechenization?

By late December 2016, support for holding peace talks in Astana (subsequently renamed as Nursultan) gathered momentum between Moscow, Tehran, and Ankara. The same month, the Moscow Declaration laid out a peace plan for Syria, and representatives of these three governments agreed to implement it. The first round of talks commenced in January 2017. The parties involved in the talks described Astana as a neutral venue. This was the reason they chose the city. The problem was that calling Astana a neutral place was a stretch to say the least. Kazakhstan remained part of the Russia-led Customs Union, which differs in several key aspects from the European Union it claims to mirror. As one official German study had concluded in 2017, Russia dominated the Customs Union both in terms of GDP (87 percent) and population (80 percent), with living standards far superior to those of other member states—in other words, it is "no union among equals." By comparison, while Germany is the largest member of the European Union, it has a far more modest role: 27 percent of the EU's GDP and 16 percent of its population.[16] Living standards are also not as starkly high in Germany as compared to other member states. In addition to a high degree of control, Kremlin-dominated processes are also not transparent, unlike Western ones. Moreover, while some talks took place in Vienna, Geneva was the main venue, and Switzerland is not a member of the European Union, even it maintains strong links to the organization. Geneva was a more neutral venue than Astana.

Once the first Astana meeting began, as one BBC journalist put it, the ground began shifting.[17] Under the officially stated guise of Resolution 2254 and the Geneva communiqué, Moscow pushed its own vision. It marginalized the Gulf-led peace talks, and created an alternative diplomatic track that excluded the United States. To be sure, the group's organizers invited US diplomats—sometimes at the last minute, which made it difficult to accept the invitation. On occasion, Americans also participated as observers. It was obvious that this process aimed to marginalize the United States and the Geneva process under a patina of international legitimacy. Syrian writer and journalist Hassan Hassan said, "Russia wants a military solution disguised as a political one . . . This is the Astana-isation of Geneva."[18] His comment echoes Moscow's earlier diplomatic efforts decades earlier in Chechnya (discussed in more detail in earlier chapters).

The Middle Eastern landscape is far more complex that of Chechnya, and Moscow did not have the same degree of control. But it did apply similar templates to negotiations in Syria—it purposely helped marginalize genuine anti-Assad opposition that demanded his departure as a precondition for talks. The Kremlin also promoted those who would not oppose Assad remaining in power. Thus, over the years, Moscow engaged such faux opposition figures as Qadri Jamil (a Syrian politician who "always hovered on the outskirts of [Assad] regime politics"),[19] Khaled Mahamid (another member of "Syrian opposition" who openly supported Moscow's goals of restoring Assad's control across Syria), and Randa Kassis (mentioned earlier). The Astana/Sochi talks produced little of substance. But they did succeed in another goal—further marginalizing groups friendly to the United States—and diminished the importance of the Geneva talks. Often, during Astana talks, Assad regime's symbols decorated conference facilities.[20] Many members of the Syrian opposition boycotted the Astana/Sochi talks, not unlike Chechnya's genuine opposition decades earlier.

In Chechnya, the Kremlin was a nearly impossible negotiating partner when it came to bringing about a genuine resolution because Russian officials put appearances and process above all else. Thus, they stalled peace processes such as prisoner exchanges and ceasefires over linguistic matters of definitions. As Ilyas *Akhmadov*, who served as the Chechen Republic's foreign minister during the second Chechen War explained, when they took Chechen fighters prisoners, they considered them "criminals" or "bandits." They refused to call them "combatants," which made prisoner exchanges nearly impossible; and as these processes barely moved, fighting continued and innocent people died.[21] Even so, in Chechnya, Moscow was interested in putting an end to fighting under the rubric of restoring "constitutional order," within its distorted narrative of trying to end "a civil war."[22] In Syria, things grew even more complicated and while Moscow did want to see fighting end, it also had no real incentive nor desire to have Assad accept a real diplomatic process—rather it wanted to see Assad reach a settlement that would legitimate his regime and eliminate opposition that could threaten his rule. In doing so, it would thwart the Western vision of seeing Assad leave power and would expand Russian influence in Syria and the region—this was the bigger picture.

Assad for his part perhaps grew even more rigid. Over the years, Syrian security forces arrested several dissidents who planned to participate in Russia-sponsored talks, and envoys that did attend the talks entirely stonewalled any possibility of a political compromise. Syrian officials who met with Putin were often no better. As John Parker observed, in June 2015 Syrian foreign minister Walid Moallem in Moscow refused a proposed anti-ISIS coalition with Syria and Sunni regional partners.[23]

As part of the Astana/Sochi process, Moscow continued to push for a Syrian constitutional committee. It offered another version in January 2017, which among other things outlined decentralization or federalization of Syria. Moscow took the lead on this issue and worked with international partners—Turkey and Iran—to work towards this goal.[24] A fourth round of Geneva talks between February and March 2017 meanwhile predictably also produced few tangible results. For the first time, armed Syrian opposition met with Assad representatives, but even de Mistura himself did not expect a breakthrough.[25] A 2017 RAND report concluded, "The Syrian opposition negotiators in Geneva ... represent a diminishing constituency inside Syria. Their demand that Assad must step down as part of any settlement has little prospect of prevailing and prevents any realistic off-ramp to the conflict based on the parties' respective leverage."[26]

One might reasonably ask if the Geneva process mattered at all. It was doomed from the start in terms of achieving a genuine diplomatic breakthrough. Assad was intransigent and could rely on Russian support; he was under little pressure to compromise. The Syrian opposition was also unwilling to compromise, but had little leverage. Many involved knew that this was a mission impossible even if they did not say so publicly. There was simply little else that could be done other than these discussions. Still, this process did matter in some respects—it was about aspirations, going through the motions of a process in a hope that it might eventually turn into something real. It offered opportunities for small tactical wins, but perhaps more importantly, an internationally recognized political process, rather than a Russia-shaped alternative.

Yet, it also became painfully clear that in the context of Moscow's commitment to its alternative vision and Western hesitation, Geneva could not produce real results—if these were defined as advancing a real peace settlement. In the backdrop of diplomatic meetings, periodic cessations of hostilities took place in Syria. While the United States and Russia had brokered the ceasefires, it was Russia that served as their guarantor, while Assad had typically violated all terms. Moscow utilized de-escalation zones as tactical measures to allow Russian and Assad's forces to defeat their enemies. These zones served to keep military activity in certain areas at a low level until Moscow and the Assad regime were prepared to attack them. In time, the Assad regime, with Russian support, attacked and reconquered the majority of de-escalation zones. The real purpose of these zones was probably to weaken the Assad opposition.[27] This is how Russian diplomacy reinforced military action—diplomacy was about how Moscow could put others in a position where they had little choice but to accept its preferred terms. In the backdrop of this, Russian officials cried crocodile tears about the United States and their allies operating "only on the basis of dictates and ultimatums."[28]

By June 2018, the Syrian Democratic Council announced it was ready for "unconditional talks" with the Assad regime.[29] This was an important shift for members of the opposition who had been against such talks for years and signaled the increasing desperation in the face of the growing certainty that Assad was not leaving. It is all the more astonishing, given that on his own, Assad, according to the views of military figures and other analysts, remained unable to hold the territory he had conquered. Indeed, he resorted to the use of chemical weapons not only as a terrorist tactic to subdue the population into compliance, but also because he had little conventional weaponry. Nor had his forces been particularly competent. He remained in power solely due to his Russian and Iranian backers in the context of Western inaction.

As of 2019, Moscow had held twelve rounds of "Astana" peace talks.[30] The Kremlin continued to publicly trumpet its victories in Syria. Lavrov, for example, said in January 2019 that "international terrorism" is being defeated in Syria, which "allowed to preserve Syrian statehood," and observed that the Astana process created conditions for a political process in full compliance with UN Security Council Resolution 2254."[31] The more tangible victory, in addition to keeping Assad in power no matter the depths of his depravities, was that by June 2019, when the latest UN envoy on Syria, Geir Pedersen discussed in an interview his fairly modest attempts to arrange a committee to oversee Syrian constitution reform, he said the committee would include "the five permanent UN Security Council members and two groups of countries that have been politically active on Syria: the 'Astana Group' comprising Iran and Turkey as well as Russia, and the 'Small Group,' which includes Egypt, Germany, Jordan, Saudi Arabia, France, Britain and the United States."[32] The United States, not to mention its allies, were reduced to a "small group."

10

Moscow's Relationships with Regional Actors: Israel

Moscow's effort to keep the Syria intervention limited required reliance on regional actors to do much of the legwork. Putin maintained a balancing act between key regional actors with opposing interests—a balance that was reflective of his broader approach to the region. Moscow's military entry into the Syrian theater was new, but Putin had already developed key relationships and set up expectations in terms of Moscow's behavior after the intervention started. This is the broader context for Putin's balancing act in Syria with Sunni actors and Israel after September 2015. Moscow's position in Syria had earned him a perception of importance and regional leaders began to court Putin. This chapter focuses on Israel.

Putin's Early Pursuit of Good Ties with Israel

Putin had cultivated a relationship with Israel since he came to power. This context frames how Moscow pursued its relationship with Israel specifically on Syria. Indeed, his relationship with Israel post-Syria intervention was the logical extension of the earlier years.

As Mark N. Katz had written, Putin pursued good relations with Israel from the beginning of his tenure, as a result of his own pragmatic calculations about Russia's interests.[1] Both Putin and Primakov came to believe that among the mistakes that led to the Soviet Union's collapse were its anti-Jewish policies. These policies led to the refusenik movement that connected with Western elites and resulted in Western pressure, and led among other things, to the passage of the powerful Jackson-Vanik amendment that leveraged the Soviet Union to change its human right policy on immigration. More broadly, these efforts helped expose the true evil of the Soviet regime, and highlighted the fact that there was no moral equivalence between the West and Soviet ideology. The lesson Putin and Primakov drew is that the Kremlin would benefit more if it neutralized Jewish influence, which, as both men percieved it, was powerful in the West.

Israel's support for Putin's actions in Chechnya was another chief reason why Putin pursued improved ties with Israel. Indeed, Israel (and ironically, Iran) did not criticize Putin over Chechnya. Immigrants to Israel from Russia and the former Soviet Union at its peak reached one million,[2] a major proportion of Israel's population which hovered at just around 5 million at the end of the Cold War, and reached approximately 9 million at the end of 2018.[3] For Putin, any country with a large Russian-speaking minority matters in terms of soft power leverage. Over the years, he routinely emphasized that Russia and Israel have a "special relationship," primarily because of Israel's Russian-speaking immigrants, and went so far as to exaggerate the number of Russian speakers in Israel. For example, Putin told Netanyahu in March 2016 "Russia and Israel have developed a special relationship primarily because one and a half million Israeli citizens come from the former Soviet Union, they speak the Russian language, are the bearers of Russian culture, Russian mentality."[4]

Jerusalem mattered to Moscow historically, and with Putin's use of the Russian Orthodox Church as a state instrument it mattered all the more. Furthermore, good relations with Israel shielded Moscow to some extent from accusations of being pro-Shia and bolstered Putin's pragmatic approach to building ties with all major actors in the Middle East. Taking a more assertive role in the Middle East Quartet early into his tenure, Putin also signaled his desire to play a key role as a mediator. As Katz had noted in 2005, "Putin's decision not to attend or send Russian representatives to the October 2000 Sharm el-Sheikh summit had less to do with Russian disengagement than with a desire to avoid any process which the United States dominated."[5] Indeed, Moscow's desire for great-power recognition and refusal to play second fiddle to Washington is reflected in its approach in Syria to create parallel international talks that marginalized the United States.

Another driver in Putin's Israel policy involved his emphasis on developing economic ties. He has correspondingly pursued trade with Israel, including in high-tech areas such as nanotechnology. The two countries share visa-free travel. Overall, Russia–Israel trade grew to $1 billion annually by 2005 and was more than triple this amount by 2014, at approximately $3.5 billion. This figure is slightly higher than Russian–Egyptian trade in the same year—a year when the West imposed sanctions, including economic measures, on Russia in response to its annexation of Crimea from Ukraine. In 2018, Russia's exports to Israel had approached $2 billion and imports—close to $1 billion (figures based on IMF Direction of Trade Statistics, see appendices of Russia's trade with the Middle East).

In April 2005, Putin made a historic trip to Israel and the Palestinian territories, where he made a series of visits—from a meeting with the prime minister and president, to visiting Vad Vashem and meetings with World War II veterans living in Israel, as well as a meeting and press conference with the Palestinian leadership, and laying flowers on Yassir Arafat's grave.[6] While many over the years have noted the visit to Israel, fewer have paid attention to the Palestinian aspect of the visit. This was classic Putin in the Middle East, as he extended his hand to virtually everyone. Then Israeli President Moshe Katsav called Putin "a friend of the state of Israel," and Prime Minister Ariel Sharon said Putin was "among brothers." Putin and Katsav signed a joint statement which noted "the Red Army's decisive contribution" to defeating Nazism and reaffirmed the "inadmissibility of resolving international conflicts by military means."[7] This meeting did not stop Moscow's support for Iran, Hezbollah, and other entities that are of grave security concern to Israel, yet many observers hailed the visit as a milestone in improvement of bilateral relations. The fact that a Russian head of state had come to Israel was in itself unprecedented.

Thus, before entering the Syrian military theater, Putin appeared to have done more for the Jews in Russia than any other Russian head of state. For many, the image of the first Russian head of state—and one who also had a reputation for not being anti-Semitic—to visit Israel was powerful.

Fewer had realized that a degree of anti-Semitism always underpinned Putin's regime. In late 2005, the Russian Duma voted to condemn anti-Semitism after some nationalist and communist politicians demanded a ban on all Jewish organizations. However, as *The New York Times* reported about the episode, "the course of the State Duma's short debate Friday showed that the question [of anti-Semitism in Russia] was far from settled."[8] Over the coming years, senior members of Putin's United Russia party periodically made anti-Semitic comments. At Putin's invitation, Fatah, Hamas, and Hezbollah leaders have also visited Moscow—a reflection perhaps more than anything of Putin's pragmatic approach to the region.[9] Russian Foreign Affairs Ministry spokesperson Maria Zakharova— who ostensibly often wears the Star of David and has professed her love for Jerusalem—said in November 2016, "If you want to know what will happen in America, who do you have to talk to? You have to talk to the Jews, naturally."[10]

In that vein, in June 2012, Putin again traveled to Israel, nine months before Obama made his first visit as US president. During his visit, Putin participated in an inauguration of a monument to the Red Army's victory over the Nazis.

Meeting with Israeli president Shimon Peres in Jerusalem, Putin said, "It is in Russia's national interest to provide peace and tranquility in the Middle East, peace and tranquility to the Israeli people. It is not by accident that the Soviet Union was among the initiators and supported the creation of the state of Israel."[11] It is unclear what he meant by "initiators." Putin may have meant the idea for the creation of the state of Israel, and indirectly referenced the fact that Joseph Stalin publicly supported the idea before the United States did.[12] Importantly, Putin here conveniently left out Stalin's quick policy reversal after Israel aligned with the West, which is illustrative of Putin's broader diplomacy efforts. Indeed, the theme of a fight against the Nazis, of Russia and Jews suffering together at the hands of the Nazis had become central to the relationship Putin had cultivated with Israel. During his 2012 visit he praised the Red Army for "smash[ing] the head of the Nazi monster."[13]

The Kremlin has gone to ever-greater lengths under Putin to deny or mischaracterize Stalin's initial pact with Hitler. The pact arguably contributed to the start of the war in the first place, while the Nazis and the Bolsheviks had much in common, ideologically as totalitarian, and tactically. Indeed, the Nazis emulated the Bolsheviks. Preeminent Russia historian Richard Pipes had documented, for example, that it was the Bolsheviks who, in 1919, gave the world the concentration camp as we understand it today—an idea that the Nazis eagerly seized upon.[14]

The Soviet Union suffered the most profound losses during the war, an issue that remains a sore point in Russia. Yet these losses occurred on such a massive scale because of Stalin's utter disregard for how many people and resources he had to sacrifice to win—which Putin's Russia has also refused to recognize. The Red Army were not simply liberators, but also perpetrators of massive war crimes in Eastern and Central Europe which the Soviet Union then came to dominate after the war—one monster replaced another. Putin's astounding whitewashing of history that is so fundamental to Russia's current domestic internal struggles, and Russia's relationship with the Jewish people is a crucial element to the relationship with Israel that he has cultivated.

In April 2014, after the Crimea annexation and shortly before Putin's Syria intervention, former *Jerusalem Post* executive editor and author Amotz Asa-El wrote, "Not only are relations between Jerusalem and Moscow normal, in many ways they are even warm. Traffic between the two countries is free and hectic, Russia has become Israel's major oil supplier, it is a potentially deep destination for Israeli exports, and the two countries are in the process of finalizing a free-trade agreement."[15] Yet a number of issues remained problematic in the relationship.

Putin continued to support Israel's adversaries, and his Russia stood in opposition to Western democracies, to which Israel belonged. No matter the improvements in the Russia–Israel relationship, it still had a very different tone from Israel's deep and enduring relationship with the United States built on shared values. Putin could not (and likely did not seek to) replace the United States.

The inroads Putin had made, though, could not be separated from Israel's relationship with the United States especially in the Obama years, when Israeli leaders grew frustrated with US policies in the region. This added reasons for Israel to improve relations with Russia and regional Sunni powers. Amotz Asa-El, wrote in April 2014, "The past three years' upheaval across the Arab world has for now resulted in increased Russian presence and diminishing American prestige." He continued that confronted with "such a Russian comeback, Israel would be foolhardy to squander its hard-earned relations with post-Communist Russia."[16] And two years later, in June 2016, Netanyahu told reporters in Moscow, "There is no alternative to the United States [and] I am not looking for one … But my policy is to look for other partnerships with great powers such as China, India and Russia and other countries."[17]

The Shia Factor in Russian–Israeli Relations

When it came to the Syria intervention, Putin's approach to Israel has ultimately been about building leverage, in a purely pragmatic, realpolitik sense, but for which he also utilized elements of soft-power projection. Putin ensured that Moscow had leverage over Israel's freedom of action, signaled it could be helpful in reigning in Iran and its proxies, and emphasized bilateral ties between Russia and Israel on other fronts. Israel for its part also actively sought a constructive, if limited, relationship with Moscow. Again, from a pragmatic standpoint, Russia, which Israeli leaders considered a great power, now stood on their doorstep and they had to deal with it rather than antagonize it.

Immediately after Putin's Syria intervention, Israeli Prime Minister Benjamin Netanyahu came to Moscow and met with Putin in Novo-Ogaryovo.[18] The two leaders agreed to a military coordination mechanism to avoid accidental clashes—a mechanism which Putin would later emphasize was set up on Netanyahu's initiative.[19] Netanyahu also told Putin, "Our policy is to do everything to stop weapons from being sent to Hezbollah."[20] Netanyahu reportedly also informed the US government "on each and every detail," as it is in everyone's interest to avoid "an unnecessary clash."[21]

Netanyahu recognized that despite the good relations and the open communication channel that Russia and Israel had established, key differences remained. "In Syria, I've defined my goals. They're to protect the security of my people and my country. Russia has different goals. But they shouldn't clash,"[22] he said. Putin did not say it, but he too did not seek a clash with Israel.

When Moscow set up its A2AD layout in Syria (discussed in Chapter 3), Moscow gained control of western and central Syrian airspace. This made Israel dependent on Russia. Over the coming years Netanyahu continued to be a regular guest in Russia (Moscow and other locales) and spoke to Putin on the phone. Other high-level exchanges also continued. A key issue for Israel relating to its chief security concerns was freedom of action in Syria to strike Hezbollah and other Iranian-backed targets to prevent these groups from obtaining advanced weaponry, and help block Iran's continuous effort to put Israel in a state of strategic siege via Syria and Lebanon. The Israeli leadership seemed to hope that by cultivating good ties with Russia, Moscow would ensure Israel's freedom of action.

Netanyahu and other Israeli officials repeatedly made their country's interests clear to both Moscow and Washington as the Syria situation unfolded. There was no ambiguity. The encroachment of Iran and Iranian-backed proxies such as Hezbollah and Shia militias were a primary security threat for the Jewish state. Moscow's interests however appeared more ambiguous. On the one hand, Moscow was intent on maintaining good relations and allowing Israel its freedom of action. On the other, its position on Iran and its proxies—as well as more broadly its proximity to anti-Sunni forces in the region (this includes Assad) raised questions. A review of the Kremlin's official announcements and transcripts of Putin's meetings and phone calls with Netanyahu with respect to Syria and Iran in particular tends to focus on what Netanyahu said rather than what Putin said.

For example, in a July 2018 meeting with Putin, Netanyahu said, "Of course, our focus is what is happening in Syria, the presence of Iran. This is not a new thing for you. A few hours ago, an unmanned vehicle penetrated from Syria into Israel, was successfully shot down. I would like to emphasize that we will very strictly stop any attempts to violate both our air and land borders." Putin's posted response was limited to, "We know about your concerns. Let's talk about it in detail."[23] Yet no detail had been made public. In other instances, Putin's public remarks would focus on Russia's connections with Israel and the role of the Red Army during World War II, but not on Iran and its proxies.

In February 2019, Netanyahu went to Moscow on another visit. "Mr. President," he told Putin, "I counted that there have been 11 meetings between us since

December 2015. And I think that there is a direct connection between us, our contacts—this is a very important element, which ensured the absence of problems, some kind of collisions, and ensured stability and security in our region." Netanyahu went on to talk about World War II, the Red Army's important contribution, and transitioned into Israel's current chief concern about Iran and its allies being "the biggest threat to stability and security in the region . . . We will do everything that depends on us to prevent the fulfillment of this threat," he said. Putin meanwhile once again emphasized the "1.5 million" Russian speakers in Israel, but said nothing in public about Iran.[24]

That the Russia–Israel relationship was unequal, with Moscow holding greater leverage, was also evident in some of Netanyahu's remarks. For example, speaking in November 2015 in Moscow, Netanyhu could do little other than express hope that Moscow would be helpful. "I must say that today our countries are involved in a big battle: they are involved in the battle against global terrorism. This is a truly barbaric trend that does not spare anyone . . . I really hope that Russia and Israel can find and will find common points of view and will agree on all global strategic issues," he said.[25]

Over the years, Netanyahu would also reiterate the theme of the joint fight against terrorism in his meetings with Putin and highlight Moscow's contribution. "One of the things that unites us is our joint struggle against radical Islamic terror," he said in June 2017, for example. "Last year there was a very serious advance in the fight against radical Islamic Sunni terror under the leadership of ISIL and al-Qaeda, and Russia made a great contribution to this result, to this advancement. Of course, we would not want radical Islam, Sunni terror to be replaced by radical Islamic Shiite terror under the leadership of Iran," he said, once again highlighting Israel's chief concerns.[26]

Putin, though—like other senior Russian officials—was more circumspect in public about Iran. Moscow signaled that it could rein in Iran and its proxies on some level, and at least look the other way when the Israelis hit their targets in Syria. Yet Russian officials also tended to emphasize that Iran is an independent actor, and one with which Moscow cooperates on a number of issues.

Moscow did allow Israel freedom of action. Indeed, Russia's complicated history with Iran gave Israeli and Western leaders reason to believe that Moscow also saw Iran as a regional competitor and would prefer that it did not become too strong. Yet at the same time, it was unclear how much leverage Putin truly had, over Iran and more to the point, whether it wanted to exercise it.

During one of Netanyahu's trips to Moscow, in August 2017, several Russian publications highlighted that there was little Putin could do to respond to his concerns. Prominent Russian journalist Andrew Kolesnikov suggested in the influential business-oriented daily, *Kommersant*, that Putin could only offer "psychotherapeutic help," that is, he could intently listen to his colleague.[27] Mainstream Pravda.ru (separate from the Communist Party *Pravda* newspaper) wrote sarcastically, "[w]hile Netanyahu in a cold sweat was feverishly describing the sinister scenario [of Iran in the Middle East] to Putin, the latter was sighing with sympathy, as if to say, 'Unfortunately, we cannot help you.'"[28]

More to the point, Moscow's actual record of accomplishments in terms of reigning in Iranian proxies instilled little confidence. After Russia and rebel forces in south Syria agreed to a ceasefire in July 2018, Moscow promised that Iran would withdraw its forces and proxies at least eighty-five kilometers away from Israel's border.[29] Yet many Iran-allied militia elements remained near the frontier, reportedly switching into Syrian military uniforms in an apparent effort to avoid Israeli airstrikes. Moreover, the agreement was unclear as to whether any Iranian "advisors" would be compelled to leave. The resultant withdrawal was superficial at best, and ultimately failed to diminish Iran's presence—though importantly, it succeeded in making Moscow look as if it had tried.

Nor had it been clear that Moscow could accomplish a more specific task of limiting the forces Tehran deploys in Syria. An incident in June 2018 is illustrative: Russia tried to get Hezbollah to leave a checkpoint in al-Qusayr and move closer to the Lebanon border, but Russian forces had to retreat instead, and Hezbollah soon fortified its presence. Likewise, the August 2018 deployment of Russian military police to the Golan Heights did not stop Hezbollah and other Iranian militias from encroaching there.

Indeed, reports about Iranians and their proxies switching uniforms, Hezbollah flying under the Russian flag to avoid getting hit by Israel, coupled with Moscow's failure to prevent an Iranian presence within eighty-five kilometers of the Israeli border show that if anything Moscow only empowers Iran.[30]

Yet Moscow succeeded in setting up a position for itself as a powerbroker in the context of a US retreat from the region, and overall inconsistencies. As Israeli military analyst Dmitry (Dima) Adamsky wrote, "Israel's instinct is still to turn to the United States during crises. Yet the dysfunction that characterizes the current US administration and the Kremlin's regional connections could make Moscow, with which Israel has already established military-to-military and political exchanges, a more relevant party in Israeli eyes."[31]

Still, while Israel had found itself in a very difficult situation, one cannot help but wonder about a degree of naiveté on the Israeli side in terms of a perception of Russia's utility in getting Iran out of Syria. Even after the southern ceasefire failed to meet any of Israel's security interests, Netanyahu announced to his cabinet in March 2019, "President Putin and I also agreed on a common goal—the withdrawal of foreign forces that arrived in Syria after the outbreak of the civil war." (For Putin, Russia of course was not a foreign force, since it was in Syria upon the invitation of the "legitimate Syrian government.") Putin was also ambiguous about how he saw Iran's presence in Syria, though likely had also been signaling that in order for him to pull the Iranian forces out he either needed to be presented with a deal he would be happy with, and/or that he needed extra help, which meant working with other forces.

Still, if anything, more recent developments point to Moscow's growing ties with Iran. In May 2019, Putin said, "We are not a fire brigade and we cannot always save someone, especially where little depends on us."[32] Yet for a variety of reasons (which included domestic Israeli politics), Netanyahu continued to press on, and proposed a trilateral meeting in Jerusalem between American, Russian, and Israeli senior officials to discuss Syria. The meeting finally took place in June 2019. At the conclusion of the meeting, Russian representative Nikolai Patrushev went as far as to call Iran a Russian ally—something Russian officials had not done before, limiting their descriptions of Iran to that of a partner.[33] Patrushev said:

> In the context of assessments made by our partners regarding a major regional power, which is Iran, I would like to note the following: Iran has been and remains our ally and partner, with whom we are consistently developing relations both bilaterally and in multilateral formats. In this regard, any attempts to present Tehran as the main threat to regional security and even more so to put it on a par with ISIS or other terrorist groups are unacceptable to us.[34]

In this context, Putin's June 2019 interview with the *Financial Times* and his use of terms that included the word "ally," while more careful and circumspect than Petrushev's comment, is worth highlighting, "We really have built up very good, partner, and in many respects even with alliance elements relations with many countries of the region, including not only Iran and Turkey, but also other countries," Putin said.[35]

Soft-Power Projection

An important backdrop for Moscow's policy toward Israel with regard to Syria is Putin's soft-power efforts that continued to reinforce hard-power projection, building on the ties forged in earlier years. Putin personally sent condolences to Israel after major terrorist acts.[36] Moscow assisted Israel on a variety of fronts, for example helping to fight wildfires[37]—an especially ironic act that highlights the Kremlin's pragmatism rather than altruism, given that when it came to Russian territory, Moscow preferred to let its own wildfires burn to suppress independent attempts of private citizens to put extinguish the fires.[38] In the same vein, Moscow signed an agreement to pay $83 million in pensions to former Soviet citizens now living in Israel—even as Moscow had no money to adjust pensions for inflation for Russian citizens.[39] As Joshua Krasna wrote, the actual dollar value of the pensions is mostly symbolic (approximately $200 a month), yet Russian speakers in Israel were "delighted" by this announcement.[40]

Putin personally intervened to bring home the body of an Israeli serviceman, Zachary Baumel, who went missing in the Battle of Sultan Yacoub, Lebanon, in 1982, for which he received a lot of public praise in Israel.[41] Speaking about this event, Putin made a major splash in the Middle East when he said, "Russian Army soldiers found the body in coordination with the Syrian military," during a joint press conference with Netanyahu. It is hard to tell for certain whether Putin knew that publicly acknowledging Assad's role in retrieving the body of an Israeli soldier would cast him in an extremely poor light within the "Axis of resistance." Yet, ultimately, the most interesting aspect of this episode is how short-lived and irrelevant the region's anger at Putin was, and his position as a perceived powerbroker did not change. Perhaps more than anything it revealed just how much Putin mattered in the region, and in Syria in particular.

The theme of the Holocaust and the Red Army's role during World War II (as Putin defined it) continued to play a major role in the Russia–Israel relationship. This subject routinely came up during the two leaders' meetings and conversations, including on Syria, as quoted in the previous section. Israel had unveiled a monument to honor victims of the Leningrad siege, for which Netanyahu invited Putin to Israel.[42] Moscow opened Russia's first prominent Holocaust memorial in June 2019.[43] That said, Moscow sometimes grew dissatisfied with Israel on this front. In August 2017, Poland excluded Russia from a commemoration project for victims of the Sobibor Nazi extermination camp in eastern Poland. Israel said it supported Russia's participation, but Moscow, it appeared, expected Israel to pressure Warsaw to change its position. The Russian Foreign Ministry summoned Israel's ambassador, Gary Koren, for an explanation, while the ministry's spokeswoman Maria Zakharova said she considered Israel's position to be "absolutely unacceptable" and "bordering on historical betrayal."[44] It is doubtful she could have made such a statement without Putin's prior approval, and when

Netanyahu and Putin met in Sochi the same month to discuss the Iranian presence in Syria, Netanyahu first tried to smooth over the incident.

In 2018, Netanyahu importantly also attended the May 9 parade in Moscow to commemorate victory over the Nazis—the biggest, most important event of the year in Russia, and one that the Kremlin had used for political purposes to stoke militarism. Indeed, since 2014, Western leaders had stopped attending it. Moreover, while at the parade, Netanyahu put on the controversial St. George ribbon, outlawed in Ukraine after Moscow's Crimea annexation.[45] Award-winning *Wall Street Journal* correspondent Yaroslav Trofimov's description of these events highlighted Israel's ultimate dependence on Russia, "[T]here was little that Israel's Prime Minister Benjamin Netanyahu could do more to ingratiate himself with Mr. Putin than flying to Moscow to participate in Wednesday's Red Square military parade."[46] And in September 2019, Putin said, "We consider Israel a Russian-speaking state," after exaggerating again the number of Russian speakers residing in Israel to "almost two million."[47]

Points of Friction

The Russia–Israel relationship had its points of friction on Syria. Overall, the relationship had never been colored by the same high degree of trust as with the United States, despite the lofty pronouncements of Netanyahu and Putin. Several examples are illustrative of how Moscow tends to view partners as subjects, and once again highlighted the inequality in the Russia–Israel relationship.

On March 17, 2017, the Israeli air force struck several targets in Syria to prevent advanced weapons from reaching Hezbollah. Although Israel routinely carries out such attacks, in this particular incident the Russian Foreign Affairs Ministry demanded that Israeli Ambassador Gary Koren "clarify" Israel's unilateral actions. Details about the incident remain murky, and Netanyahu stressed that Israel would continue with its policy to prevent attempts to transfer advanced weapons to Hezbollah. However, Lavrov warned on March 22 in Moscow, "We will judge by deeds and not by statements in order to figure out if our Israeli counterparts abide by" Russian–Israeli agreements "concerning military cooperation" in Syria.[48]

Yet the largest incident to date came in late September 2018 when, following the latest in a series of Israeli airstrikes on Iranian targets in northern Syria, one of the Assad regime's S-200 missile batteries accidentally shot down a Russian Ilyushin 20 (Il-20) reconnaissance plane. All fifteen service members on board died as a result. Syrian air defenses proved (once again) incapable of stopping the strike. Instead, they belatedly launched dozens of SAMs in various directions, which, if anything, showed disregard for the Russian plane's safety and ignored the fact that Israel's jets were already back in their own airspace.

The Russian Defense Ministry called it an intentional Israeli provocation. Russian Defense Ministry Spokesman Igor Konashenkov said Israel's actions were "hostile," and that the ministry reserved the right to an "adequate"[49] response, which often translates as "tit for tat."[50] Some in the Duma went as far as to propose strikes against Israel.[51] Deputy defense committee chairman Alexander Sherin said, "I call on the systems Bastion, S-400, Iskander to show how they really work. Here we have the Vostok-2018 training ground, so the same thing has to be done with the platform from which airplanes take off—that's all,"[52] though he later tried to backtrack on his comments. On the face of it, Putin's own comments appeared more reasonable, but it is important to read his full statement, which came on September 18 at a press conference on the conclusion of Russian–Hungarian talks, when someone asked Putin if the situation with the Il-20 resembled the earlier episode when Turkey shot down a Russian jet:

> In this connection, of course, I offer first of all condolences to the relatives of the victims. As for your comparison with the well-known events, when our plane was shot down by a Turkish fighter, this is still a different situation. Then the Turkish fighter deliberately shot down our plane. Here, rather, it looks like a chain of tragic random circumstances, because an Israeli plane did not shoot down our plane. But, of course, we must seriously study this. And our attitude to this tragedy is set out in a statement by the Ministry of Defense of the Russian Federation, which is in full agreement with me. As for the responsive actions, they will be primarily aimed at providing additional security for our military personnel and our facilities in the Syrian Arab Republic. And these will be steps that everyone will notice.[53]

It was a carefully weighted answer, which on the one hand led many to note that Putin personally did not blame Israel (unlike the Russian Defense Ministry). Yet he also said that he agreed with the Defense Ministry's assessment. Moreover, he said that a response would be defensive, but one that would be hard to miss.

And the response came. Moscow provided the S-300 system to Syria the next month. Ultimately, it was more of a political statement of dominance than anything else, especially since Moscow already had the more advanced S-400 system in Syria. At the same time, the S-300 gave Assad (and therefore Moscow) options they did not previously have to undermine the US position in Syria. It would potentially enhance Syria's Integrated Air Defense System (IADS) capability and thus provide additional cover to the activities of Iran and Assad in Syria. It could also complicate US and coalition operations against ISIS. Ultimately, it showed how the Kremlin leveraged a situation that clearly exposed its incompetence (in addition to the incompetence of its ally) to assert dominance.

Israel temporarily halted its operations after the Il-20 incident. Although Israeli airstrikes eventually resumed, Israel has been careful, and more to the point, the incident demonstrated Israeli dependence on Moscow, even as both sides quickly took public and private steps to preserve their arrangement in Syria. In this context it should hardly be a surprise that more recently, in December 2020, Russian ambassador to Israel, Anatoly Viktorov, cast Israel rather than Iran and its proxies as a source of instability in the Middle East. He did so indirectly, and under the cover of UN resolutions—that is, he depicted Israel, not unlike the United States, as failing to uphold its international obligations. "The problem in the region is not Iranian activities," said Viktorov, "It's a lack of understanding between countries and noncompliance with UN resolutions in the Israel–Arab and Israel–Palestinian conflict," while, "Israel is attacking Hezbollah, Hezbollah is not attacking Israel,"[54] Viktorov said. Whatever hope Israeli officials continue to harbor that Moscow will limit Iranian activities in any meaningful way in the Middle East is misplaced. As time goes by, Russian officials show their preference for Iran and its proxies more openly, even as they try to maintain a veneer of balance and refuse to take sides outright.

11

Moscow's Relationships with Sunni Actors, Iran, and Assad

In addition to Israel, Moscow balanced other multiple and contradictory interests in Syria—Sunni states where the Turkish role in particular stood above others in importance, Shia Iran, and Assad himself. To one degree or another, most of these actors had a problem with Moscow, but in the end came to accept its presence as useful if not outright necessary. For Assad in particular of course Moscow became fundamental to his own survival, but beyond Assad himself Moscow worked to put other actors in a position where they needed Russia. Far from outright antagonizing the region, as was the Soviet experience in Afghanistan, Putin instead worked to gain acceptance by building pragmatic and hardnosed leverage. How Moscow accomplished this juggling act is the subject of this chapter.

Turkey

Russia–Turkey Relations Prior to the Syria Intervention

By the time Putin entered office, Russia–Turkey relations were already improving. Putin worked to improve them further. Like Israel and Iran, Turkey—most likely due to the loss of leverage over Russia in the 1990s mentioned earlier—did not criticize Putin's actions in Chechnya, which was especially important to Putin at the beginning of his tenure. Energy cooperation became very important in the bilateral relationship, including for construction of the Blue Stream pipeline, which would carry gas directly from Russia into Turkey. But cooperation also increased in trade, arms contracts, terrorism-related issues, and cooperation in the Eurasian region.[1] Turkey also came to be in a position to support Russia's aim to gain observer status in the Organization for Islamic Cooperation (OIC).[2] In addition, the downturn in US–Turkish relations in the context of the Iraq war helped Putin in his outreach to Erdogan.

In late 2004, Putin came to Ankara—the first such visit in thirty-two years for a Russian head of state; and the next year Erdogan went to Moscow. Russian–Turkish trade increased by 60 percent in 2004, as compared to the first half of 2003.[3] In 2005, Erdogan made the year's first official visit to Moscow, on January 10—a visit that further signaled improvements in the relationship.[4] Just months after, in July that year, the two met again in Sochi. "We gave a lot of attention to the problem of stabilizing the entire Caucasus and Black Sea basin region," Putin said upon the conclusion of the meeting, while Erdogan underscored the "common will" to combat terrorism, an important allusion to the Kurdish and Chechen issue.[5] The Russian press wondered whether Erdogan had obtained coveted Russian recognition of the PKK as a terrorist organization,[6] though over the years it became clear he did not. As many other visits followed over the years, on balance, it became clear that Russia benefited more from this relationship than Turkey, given Turkish increasing dependence on Russian energy—a precursor of things to come in Syria. Erdogan had probably failed to see that he was slowly walking into a trap; certainly as Putin had pacified Chechnya and installed a loyal warlord, Ramzan Kadyrov, Turkey lost leverage over Russia, but Russia retained the coveted Kurdish card over Turkey. Between 2004 and 2009, Putin and Erdogan met ten times.[7] By 2009, Turkish sources claimed Russia had emerged as Turkey's number one trading partner, and by 2014 bilateral trade reached approximately $33 billion.[8] IMF numbers show virtually the same level of bilateral trade for 2014. By 2018, Russia had appeared to downgrade slightly as Turkey's fifth largest trading partner according to official Turkish sources.[9] Even so, according to IMF statistics, bilateral trade hovered at slightly under $30 billion.[10] Turkey also become a top destination for Russian tourists—an important lever of influence for the Kremlin.[11]

Putin and Erdogan had a lot in common. They came to power at approximately the same time and took their countries further down an authoritarian path. Over time, Erdogan would even surpass Putin in the number of jailed journalists in his country.[12] Both sought to restore great-power status for their countries. Both presided over a degree of economic improvement early in their tenure that began to decline over time due to the corruption and mismanagement that was characteristic of their style of authoritarian governance. This led both of them to look for external enemies to blame for their problems. During their meetings, Putin and Erdogan often dismissed their aides to have private meetings.

That said, there were also clear differences between them. Turkey remained a more divided country than Russia and Erdogan could not control internal politics to the same extent as Putin has done in Russia. Putin was also arguably more calculated and cool-headed than Erdogan. Perhaps more importantly, Turkey remained a NATO member, and the Kremlin perceived NATO as a top threat. For all the improvements in relations, Putin benefited more from the relationship than the other way around. Tourism and other economic levers, especially on energy, became taps Putin could turn on and off; these were levers of control. Turkey grew especially dependent on Russian energy.

The year 2013 also marked an important change in US policy when it came to the Kurds. The State Department began refusing leaders of the Democratic Union Party(PYD) visas, even as the PYD and its military arm, the People's Protection Units YPG (which also constitute the largest proportion of the Syrian Democratic Forces), had proven the top fighting force against ISIS in Syria. Indeed, the most secure areas in Syria were those won by the Kurds. In this context, Moscow began to look especially attractive to the Kurds, and the Kremlin, unlike Washington, issued the PYD with visas.

In this context, Russia and Turkey began discussing a "strategic partnership" in 2014. Indeed, much of the discourse on Russia–Turkey relations had focused on how far the "strategic partnership" would go. In 2014, 3.3 million Russian tourists visited Turkey, and a million more came as non-tourists. To put the tourism numbers in perspective, approximately 10 million Russian citizens in total had traveled abroad annually, while the extra one million of non-tourists was telling in terms of the overall state of the bilateral relationship. In terms of trade in 2014, $6 billion worth of Turkish exports went to Russia.[13] By 2015, Russia was not only Turkey's main supplier of natural gas, but also a top trading partner and source of foreign investment.[14]

The First Years of Syria Intervention

The outbreak of the war in Syria originally did not damage Russo–Turkish relations—the two had found ways to compartmentalize the diametrically opposed positions of Ankara and Moscow on Assad. Indeed, initially, Erdogan demanded that Assad must go, but talks with Russia in 2014 focused on tripling trade by 2020.

However, the relationship changed dramatically with the start of Moscow's Syria intervention. Moscow had violated Turkish airspace twice in Hatay province—on October 3, 2015, when a Su-30 warplane crossed over, and again on October 4. In response, Erdogan referred to Article 5 of the NATO treaty.[15] As Ambassador James Jeffrey wrote, Hatay is populated in part by ethnic Arabs of the Alawite sect of Islam, which added a layer of complexity from Turkey's perspective toward Moscow's Syria intervention and violations of Turkey's airspace.[16]

Then came what would be the biggest standoff to date. Turkey downed a Russian Su-24 jet on November 24—Ankara claimed that the plane had briefly violated Turkish airspace and that the Turkish military had issued multiple warnings to the jet prior to the shooting down. Several days before the event, the Turkish foreign minister had reportedly warned Russia's ambassador to Turkey that Russia's "intensive" bombing of Syrian Turkmen villages in northern Latakia "could lead to serious consequences."[17] Putin angrily said that Turkey had "stabbed Russia in the back"[18] and demanded an apology from Erdogan, who refused to comply. Several days after the downing of the plane, Putin announced economic sanctions against Turkey "to ensure national security" and expanded these sanctions in late December 2015.[19] Russian tourists stopped coming to Turkey. Moscow also effectively kept the Turkish military out of northern Syria. Bilateral tensions continued into 2016.

The Kurdish Factor

Moscow's ties to the Kurds go back approximately two centuries.[20] Russian and Soviet leaders used the Kurds against Ottoman and Turkish leaders to assert control. The PKK is essentially a Kremlin-sponsored creation of the Cold War era.[21] With the Syrian civil war, Putin perceived an opportunity to improve ties with the PKK. Unlike the United States and many European countries, Russia had never designated the PKK as a terrorist organization. As the war raged on in Syria, Moscow began pushing for inclusion of the PYD in the Geneva peace talks and had an ongoing relationship with the YPG. In December 2013, on the Russian Defense Ministry's invitation, PYD leader Salih Muslim visited Moscow, where he stressed that the Geneva II talks could not succeed if the Kurds were excluded.[22] According to Russian press reports, as part of his visit, Muslim also attended a Kurdish-organized birthday celebration for Abdullah Ocalan in Moscow.

These moves fit Putin's plans to divide and weaken the West and prop up Assad. The inclusion of the PYD in the peace talks, from Moscow's perspective, would dilute the Syrian opposition with individuals who did not insist on Assad's departure as a precondition for negotiations. This move also reduced Turkey's— and therefore NATO's—influence in Syria and created broader leverage for Moscow against Turkey, while exacerbating tensions between Turkey and the United States. After the plane was shot down, Moscow also began arming the

PYD and providing it with air support against Turkey-supported rebels. When Moscow sent the S-400s to the Hmeimim Air Base in Syria, it created a de facto safe zone for the Kurds against Turkish operations. The S-400 also complicated any potential military operations Ankara (along with other powers supporting the Syrian opposition) may have considered.

In December 2015, shortly after the downing of the Russian jet, Selahattin Demirtas, leader of Turkey's Kurdish Opposition Peoples' Democratic Party (HDP), visited Moscow, where he criticized the shooting down. This move was a clear signal to Ergodan. Demirtas, an Erdogan critic, was the highest-level Turkish politician to see a Russian counterpart following the bilateral standoff. Moreover, Erdogan reportedly believes the HDP was connected to the PKK. Broadly speaking, the visit signaled to Erdogan that Moscow would leverage the Kurds within Turkey to weaken his rule. And this time, Erdogan had no equal card to play against Moscow, as he did with Chechnya in the 1990s.

In February 2016, the PYD formally opened a representative office in Moscow. At the opening ceremony, Merab Shamoyev, chair of the International Union of Kurdish Public Associations, reportedly described the event as a "historical moment for the Kurdish people."[23]

Meanwhile, the Russian economic restrictions and the travel ban began to take its toll on the Turkish economy and the military exclusion from northern Syria also mattered. Erdogan caved. In June 2016, he apologized to Putin for downing the Russian jet. Putin lifted the travel ban, and the two leaders began to mend and deepen ties. A joke began circulating in Turkey that Erdogan apologizes to no one except the tsar.

And Putin continued to let Erdogan know that he had leverage over him. After the apology, in response to Erdogan's request to close down the Moscow PYD office, Andrey Karlov, Russia's ambassador to Turkey, stated that Russia did not consider the PYD to be a terrorist organization and that the office would remain open. Simultaneously, Moscow's air support allowed the PYD to expand eastward and to cut off Aleppo from Turkey-based rebel groups. The Kurds became a key card Putin would play against Erdogan, who feared Kurdish nationalism in Syria. Furthermore, even after Erdogan apologized, Putin did not withdraw the S-400 from the Syrian theater.

It is partly because of fears of Kurdish nationalism in Syria that Erdogan has come to believe he has no choice than to edge closer to Putin's position on Assad, especially in the context of years of US absence in Syria; nor did he criticize Putin on his relationship with the Syrian Kurds, as he did the United States doing the same.

Putin Leverages Erdogan

For Putin, Aleppo became a challenge once he entered Syria. Prior to the outbreak of civil war in Syria, Aleppo was the country's largest city and vital to its industry and finance. Once fighting broke out it quickly reached Aleppo, and by the summer of 2012 it was divided between the regime and the rebels. The standoff continued for four years. Turkey had supported the rebels, and Syria's open borders had helped in these efforts. Some supply routes to the Syrian opposition ran through the Turkish border. The capture of Aleppo was a major stepping stone to ensuring Assad's survival.

There was a deal to be made with Erdogan on Aleppo. Erdogan's priority was to prevent the Kurds from gaining autonomy in Syria because he feared this would encourage Kurdish separatist aspirations in Turkey. To Erdogan, this issue mattered more than Assad's fate. Thus, as John Parker wrote, Moscow (and Tehran) closed their eyes to the Turkish campaign against the Kurds, while Ankara in exchange softened its position towards Assad and no longer called for his ouster.[24] Moreover, since the Obama administration was not going to act in Syria, "Turkey could thus now take over the Western lead from the United States."[25] In addition, Moscow also allowed the PYD to open a Syrian Kurdistan, or Rojava, "representative office" in February 2016 in Moscow. Still, the Kremlin played a balancing act here with Erdogan—this office had the status a "nongovernmental organization" and no Russian official attended the opening.[26]

These steps paid off. Ankara's policy in Syria shifted in early 2016, when Ankara turned its attention to Afrin, a majority-Kurdish region in northwest Syria. Ankara also focused its military campaign on the Kurdish militia, especially the YPG.[27] In August 2016, Turkey moved thousands of rebel fighters from Aleppo, which fell in December 2016 as a result of a brutal Assad offensive backed by Moscow. While extremist elements within the Syrian opposition committed atrocities in Aleppo, as usual, the lion's share were committed by the Assad regime. The UN High Commissioner for Human Rights described "crimes of historic proportion" in Aleppo during the Syrian government offensive in 2016, which Moscow aided.[28]

The Aleppo campaign, where the Syrian regime razed the city to the ground, was very much reminiscent of Putin's bloodletting in Chechnya's capital, Grozny. When John Kerry and Boris Johnson compared Aleppo to Chechnya, the Russian embassy tweeted in response, "Grozny today is a peaceful, modern, and thriving city. Ain't that a solution we're all looking for?"[29] Implicitly, therefore, Moscow said a brutal indiscriminate bombing campaign was worth it to achieve peace—and that such an approach would succeed in achieving genuine peace in the first place. Then, in September that year, Syrian and Russian forces bombed a humanitarian aid convoy outside Aleppo, which many had called a war crime. Despite the condemnations, the two regimes pressed on with the offensive.

As the Aleppo campaign was unfolding, another breakthrough in Russia–Turkey relations came after a failed coup attempt in Turkey in July 2016, which aimed to unseat Erdogan. Erdogan blamed the United States and the CIA, as well as Fatuleh Gulen, for the coup attempt. Coupled with Ergodan's growing authoritarianism, the failed coup and the crackdown on civil society that Erdogan unleashed only contributed to growing anti-Erdogan sentiment in the West. Putin saw another opportunity and immediately called Erdogan after the coup to offer words of support.

After Aleppo, Ankara and Moscow continued to cut deals as the need for them arose. One such example was Turkey's Operation Euphrates Shield, from August 2016 to March 2017. As a result of the operation, Turkey occupied northern Syria. In early 2018, Ankara went through with Operation Olive Branch, which resulted in Turkey capturing Afrin from the YPG. In return, Erdogan said nothing while Moscow helped Assad bomb civilians in East Ghouta, at the time one of the last remaining rebel-held de-escalation zones.[30]

Another flashpoint came in February 2016 in the town of Azaz, which lies on the road from Turkey to Aleppo—a brief but important episode that suggested the war could have escalated out of control, when Ankara began shelling US-backed Kurdish militia which, interestingly, aided by Russian airstrikes, advanced towards Azaz and Turkey. This incident received little coverage, but Turkey and Russia came very close to a major confrontation.[31] Putin and Erdogan managed to resolve the crisis, though it highlighted perhaps as few other incidents in Syria had done, just how easily these situations can spin out of control. The precarious balance Putin had maintained between all conflicting actors on the ground was by no means easy or guaranteed.

Putin also drew Turkey into the Astana peace process. In January 2017, on the conclusion of the latest round of these talks, Putin and Erdogan only moved closer by agreeing, together with Iran, to jointly fight ISIS and al-Qaeda affiliate, Jabhat Fatah al-Sham.[32] Reportedly, Turkey and Russia then launched joint strikes in Syria. After the latest ceasefire had collapsed, Putin was now effectively working with Erdogan in Syria. John Parker observed that because he had this partnership, he could ignore the political track with the Obama administration.[33] Thus, for Erdogan a good deal would be one that helped him defeat the YPG and the PKK. For Putin, Erdogan could reduce help to the Syrian rebels to keep

Assad in power, and provide support for the Astana process. After Aleppo, Idlib became the last rebel stronghold. Many had fled Aleppo for Idlib. Once Putin and Erdogan signed a buffer and ceasefire agreement on Idlib in September 2018, Erdogan was also essentially on the hook in Idlib. Putin even asked him to control the armed rebel groups in the region.

Then there was the issue of Western divisions over Turkey's authoritarianism and support for radical Sunni groups, including an al-Qaeda affiliate in Syria, along with at least passive support for ISIS. This was the major reason why the United States decided to work with Syria's Kurds in the first place.[34] Erdogan's support for Sunni terrorist groups and Putin's improvement of relations with him is another example of how Putin had no qualms in reaching out to actors that supported radical Sunni groups, despite professing to regard them as terrorists.

One might rightly say that the West also continued to work with Turkey despite its embrace of radical Sunni ideology and groups. Yet in the West, the situation has been more complex. As noted above, it is because of Erdogan that the United States chose to work with the Kurds in Syria. The debate in the West about Turkey had been fierce, and created sharp divisions within NATO and the West more broadly. Many felt the West had no substitute for the Incirlik Air Base for conducting anti-ISIS strikes, though some disagreed and also believed the West could not effectively fight Sunni extremism as long as Erdogan continued supporting it, regardless of the air base.

Turkey had been a part of NATO prior to Erdogan coming to power, and Turkey before Erdogan was a different country. NATO is a consensus-driven organization and Turkey would ultimately have to vote itself out to leave it. The situation that unfolded in this regard is unprecedented—no NATO member had been kicked out before. NATO is also technically a military alliance, though in recent decades only democracies had been a part of it.

The complexities of this debate aside, as far as Putin is concerned, divisions worked in his favor and he capitalized on them as much as he could. Arguably from both his and Erodgan's perspective, the most damage to NATO can be done as long as Turkey remains a member. Earlier, in September 2017 Erdogan also signed a deal with Putin to buy the Russian S-400, though some have suggested that one of the conditions of Putin's acceptance of Erdogan's apology in 2016 was his agreement to buy the S-400. Deliveries began in July 2019, which added to the already serious rift with the United States and the West more broadly. As Moscow began constructing Turkey's nuclear power plant, and Sputnik began to play a critical information operations role,[35] it appeared that Putin's influence over Turkey was growing.

Saudi Arabia, Jordan, and Qatar

Turkey was clearly the dominant Sunni actor in the region. Only Turkey and Iran were part of the Astana peace process with Russia. Still, other Sunni actors mattered. Sunni regional leaders in Jordan and the Gulf, especially Saudi Arabia and Qatar, despised Assad and, like Turkey, wanted him to go. Assad was part of the anti-Sunni block in the region and, similarly to Israel, Sunni powers—especially Saudi Arabia—were looking to block Tehran's regional expansion. Still, although these powers supported the Syrian opposition militarily and financially, Turkey was the most active player. Unlike Saudi Arabia and Qatar, Turkey was willing to put its own boots on the ground—and even then this was not to fight the Assad regime.

Jordan too conducted military strikes in Syria, but also against the Islamic State and as part of the US-led anti-ISIS coalition from September 2014 to January 2017, although the strikes decreased after December 2015. Jordan also supported select opposition groups within the so-called Southern Front, though in early 2017 it cut back, and focused mainly on targeting radical Islamist groups in Syria, rather than supporting efforts to topple Assad. Lastly, Amman was never as vocally anti-Assad as other regional Sunni actors.

Perhaps most importantly, the Sunni regional actors generally did not coordinate with each other (the support of Turkey and Qatar for the Muslim Brotherhood notwithstanding), and more to the point, often times, these states supported divergent actors, which fueled rivalry, especially between Saudi Arabia and Qatar.[36] These divisions benefited Putin.

Some suggested that by 2013, Qatar had emerged as the main arms supplier to the rebels, though it had more contacts with the Muslim Brotherhood and tended to align itself closer with the extreme elements of the opposition, while Saudi Arabia focused on the Free Syrian Army.[37] This divergence drove Qatar's rivalry with Saudi Arabia, although Saudi Arabia reportedly also supported hardline Islamist groups.[38] Then there were the broader goals of regional actors that spanned beyond Syria. For Qatar, it was regional leadership. As one Arab politician reportedly said in 2013, Hamad bin Khalifa al-Thani, Qatar's ruling emir, "wants to be the Arab world's Islamist (Gamal) Abdelnasser."[39] For Saudi Arabia, the main issue was the broader Iranian influence in the region that went beyond Syria alone. In the spring of 2015 Riyadh also focused on the fighting in Yemen and Iranian-backed Houthi rebels there. Syria was important, but not the only issue.

Saudi Arabia for its part worked hard to try to peel Russia away from Iran. As with other actors in the region, the groundwork Putin had laid out in terms of earlier efforts to build ties mattered. While Moscow's relationship with Riyadh had for the most been part colored by antagonism, the Kremlin understood the importance of the Saudi kingdom and tried to pull it closer into its orbit whenever opportunities presented themselves, however slightly. Indeed, Putin had invited Saudi King Salman to come to Moscow as early as April 2015, months before the Syria intervention.[40]

In June 2015, then-Deputy Crown Prince Mohammed bin Salman attended the annual St. Petersburg Economic Forum—the first time the prince became publicly involved in energy issues, according to press reports at the time. Here he met with Putin.[41] The following month, Saudi Arabia's sovereign wealth fund committed to invest $10 billion in Russia over five years, the largest ever foreign direct investment in the country according to the Russian Direct Investment Fund.[42] Meanwhile, during a visit to Moscow in spring 2017, Bin Salman said that "relations between Saudi Arabia and Russia are going through one of their best moments ever."[43] Moscow also worked on developing what essentially became a de facto membership role in OPEC. In early 2017, Riyadh and Moscow signed an unprecedented agreement to limit oil output—the OPEC-plus accord—a factor that contributed to oil prices doubling from approximately $30 a barrel to over $60.[44]

As events in Syria unfolded, Riyadh soon understood that Moscow was gaining a prominent role in the region, in Syria and also in Yemen. It seemed Riyadh hoped that closer cooperation with Moscow on other fronts would pull it away from Iran. Furthermore, Riyadh likely came to recognize that Assad was not about to relinquish power, and sought to open the door to reconciliation through Moscow.[45] Indeed, on October 5, 2017, King Salman made an unprecedented visit to Russia. After the summit, Salman and Putin signed a package of documents on energy, trade, and defense, and agreed to several billion dollars' worth of joint investment.[46] Reportedly, Riyadh agreed to purchase Russia's S-400 air defense system, making it the second US ally to do so after Turkey.[47] Saudi Arabia has not yet received the S-400, and ultimately deals with Russia are never final, but the agreement clearly matters.

Russia's relationship with Jordan had not been at the forefront of its Middle East strategy, though the Syrian crisis has certainly elevated Jordan's importance. After Moscow's intervention, the two countries began to operate a joint intelligence-sharing center in Amman,[48] specifically on southern Syria and to coordinate military activities. According to some reports, it is because of Jordan that the September 2017 de-escalation zone agreement was possible. According to some accounts, Jordan is useful for the Kremlin in stabilizing Syrian "safe zones."[49]

The West for its part has shown that it is unable, from Jordan's perspective, to fully acknowledge just how much Jordan has done in terms of Syrian refugees, and what a toll it took on the country. At the same time, the West did little in terms of pushing back militarily against Assad, including specifically in the south. Thus, Putin did what he always does very well—stepped into a vacuum created by absence of American leadership.

Another key area of cooperation both sides routinely touted publicly is anti-terrorism. Jordan has also come to see Russia as an essential neutral broker when it comes to resolving the Israel–Palestinian dispute. When it comes to Iran, Jordan—unlike Saudi Arabia—believed that diplomacy with Moscow can play a useful role. Lastly, Russia's large Muslim population is important to both sides, and they routinely talk about it. One example is Jordan's large Circassian community. Other areas of cooperation include various forms of energy, including nuclear energy, and natural resources, as well as military cooperation.

In sum, had the Sunni actors been unified both in rhetoric and effort to oust Assad, they would arguably have presented a greater challenge to Putin. But in a situation of disagreement and divergence, if not outright rivalry on a number of key issues, Putin could pull a balancing act and work with all actors on different issues, cut deals, build leverage, and use it without hesitation when it was necessary. Ultimately, these activities elevated his image as a neutral powerbroker who the United States had to treat at minimum as an equal. Importantly, this situation made it easier for Putin to outsource Syria and essentially control the region through proxies, and this contributed to keeping Russia's costs low and political dividends high.

Iran

With the start of Moscow's Syria campaign, Russia's relationship with Iran continued to develop even as occasional friction arose. In June 2016, Putin called for Iran's role in the Shanghai Cooperation Organization to be elevated to that of a full-fledged member, rather than an observer, which had hitherto been its status.[50] Just as with the Customs Union, he had never invited an Arab state into this organization. Iran for its part had tried to upgrade its status to full-fledged member in the previous eight years. Upon the conclusion of the JCPOA which provided some sanctions relief for Tehran, some SCO members reportedly expressed support for offering Iran full-fledged membership, and during the 2018 Qingsao summit, Putin renewed his call for Iran to be admitted as a full member[51] Discussion about Iran's membership continued into 2019. In March 2019, SCO Secretary General Vladimir Norov reportedly said that the SCO was interested in reaching an agreement with Tehran for its official membership.[52] At the time of this writing, the discussion is ongoing. China, rather than Russia, seems to have been the chief obstacle to Iran joining the SCO, despite official pronouncements from Beijing of support for Iran's membership.[53] A major issue is that Iran's membership in the SCO is likely to jeopardize China's relations with the GCC states, on which China is especially dependent for energy.

Another illustrative event occurred in August 2016. Moscow surprised the world—including, notably, many in Iran—when it used Iran's Hamadan airbase to bomb targets in Syria. The last time a foreign power had based itself in Iran was during World War II. Russian media gushed praise for Russia–Iran anti-terrorism cooperation. The Iranian public however was outraged, and in this context, Iranian Defense Minister Hossein Dehghan accused Moscow of "ungentlemanly" behavior—but specifically for publicizing its use of the base, rather than actually using it.[54] This situation highlighted the rift between the Iranian public, which continued to distrust Russia, and the Iranian regime which remained intent on working with Moscow, despite their own mistrust. The public spat may have signaled for some that Moscow and Tehran were not interested in cooperation, but the reality was more nuanced. Iranian Parliament Speaker Ali Larijani said only days afterwards that, "The flights [of Russian warplanes] haven't been suspended. Iran and Russia are allies in the fight against terrorism," though the Hamedan air base, he claimed, was only "used for refueling."[55]

Once the Astana/Sochi process on Syria officially took off in January 2017, Iran found itself in an interesting position. Moscow was in the driver's seat of international diplomacy on Syria, yet it was Tehran, not Moscow, that invested heavily in Syria at this point, both in terms of blood and treasure, and ensured that it had a strong military position on the ground. Tehran could not have been thrilled that Moscow took the lead when Tehran paid. Moscow and Tehran diverged in their broader goals in Syria—Moscow never appeared to care about the Shia Crescent that Tehran aimed to create—at least it was unwilling to invest resources to that same end, although with Moscow's preference for non-Shia forces it is reasonable to conclude that Moscow also would not object to Tehran's ambitions. Moscow's goals had always spanned beyond Syria alone, whereas for Tehran Syria was instrumental to its regional designs. Tehran appeared to be afraid that Moscow would make a deal with the West at Tehran's expense—a persistent Iranian fear.[56] This fear specifically included the issue of Assad's fate. Moscow, after all, signaled that it was not wedded to Assad and appeared most interested in brokering a deal that would primarily ensure Moscow's own interests. Tehran, however, threw its entire lot with Assad; there was no ambiguity. Thus, Moscow and Tehran both in their own different ways have goals beyond Syria, yet these interests do not necessarily clash either on a strategic scale.

It was Russia that pushed to include Iran in Syria peace talks to begin with, and ensure that Iran had a key seat at the table when it came to the Astana/Sochi peace talks. Over the coming years, Moscow continued to stick with Assad. Ultimately, Moscow's actions in Syria only empowered Iran's own plans there, or at the very least did not hamper Iranian interests. Despite Moscow's talk of not being wedded to Assad, its actions showed the opposite.

In addition, after Putin and Rouhani met in November 2015, the two leaders announced a package of signed agreements, which included trade deals, easing travel for citizens of both countries, and contracts on construction in Iran of the Garmsar–Incheh Borun railway electrification project, a thermal power plant, and a desalination plant, and an agreement on deep-groundwater reserves in Iran. Putin added that the two countries would continue to cooperate on nuclear energy.

In early 2019, disagreements surfaced publicly between Moscow and Tehran on Syria, and over the ensuing months these appeared to intensify. It seemed the issue was mostly over divisions of spheres of influence in Syria, as well as its natural resources.[57]

In addition, in January 2019, soon after Assad's military accidentally shot down a Russian plane—an incident for which Moscow, in what appeared to be an effort to save face, blamed Israel, Russian deputy foreign minister Sergei Ryabkov said in an interview with CNN that Russia and Iran are not allies: "I wouldn't use that type of word to describe what we are with Iran" and said the two countries are only cooperating in Syria.[58] He added that Moscow is also genuinely concerned about Israel's security. This comment came only days after Israel carried out strikes in Syria over Iranian targets and the head of Iranian Majlis's (Parliament's) foreign affairs and defense committee chairman Khashmatula Falakhat Pishe claimed angrily that Moscow turned off its S-300 during Israeli strikes. Russian Middle East expert and Putin critic Alexander Shumilin suggested that in this context Moscow was rethinking its policy in the Middle East.[59] Still, Ryabkov's comment, made to a US audience and widely recirculated in Israel, was not posted on the Russian foreign affairs website. Moreover, just days prior to Ryabkov's interview, Moscow also called on Israel to stop "arbitrary" strikes in Syria, a "sovereign country."[60] This episode is illustrative of broader tactical Russian–Iranian tensions over Syria in the first half of 2019 and of the complexity of the relationship that continued to endure, despite whatever tactical tensions may have surfaced. Syria appeared to be the primary arena of cooperation even as tensions arose.

Influence over Assad?

The issue of how much influence Putin has over Iran is a matter of debate among analysts. Still, there is more information on the topic, which provides a degree of clarity. But how much influence does Putin have over Assad?

In October 2015, less than a month after Putin's Syria intervention began, Assad came to Moscow. As Putin's military intervention in Syria commenced, Assad's supporters gave Putin an affectionate nickname, "Abu Ali Putin."[61] Pro-Assad forces sprayed graffiti on the buildings thanking Russia and China for their Security Council vetoes, and pictures of Putin, Assad, and at times Hezbollah leaders covered the streets. As the events in Syria unfolded, the Assad regime's own propaganda efforts grew more systematic and Sam Dagher noted that it had the elements of the Russian disinformation campaign that Moscow unleashed in the United States during the presidential election.[62] Furthermore, in August 2019, the Russian military launched a website "to combat fakes" in Syria.[63]

Unlike the Islamic Republic of Iran, by design, the Syrian state is entirely dependent on one family, essentially one person. There is no real state to speak of except for Assad and his very small, close-knit circle. Even the Russian system, which historically has been centered on one ruler since its inception, by comparison with Syria, has far more developed state institutions.

Assad owes Putin for saving him in 2015 and thus Putin has more influence over Assad, it would seem, than he does over Iran. There are indicators suggesting that this is correct, however questions still remain.

A Soviet ambassador once told a British diplomat about the Soviet Union's relationship with Hafez al-Assad, "They take everything from us, except advice."[64] The diplomat may have been exaggerating—after all, he was speaking to an envoy of an adversarial state. Making it look as if the Kremlin had tried but had not succeeded due to the failures of others would give it plausible deniability. With regard to Assad and Putin, such framing would allow Putin to keep the great-power status that he most covets. Still, given the nature of the Assad (as opposed to Iran's) regime, the Soviet diplomat's comment provides insight that was relevant during the Cold War, and remains relevant now.

When Assad came to Moscow in October 2015 to meet with Putin, one member of the Syrian opposition noted that it was the Kremlin that announced the visit, not Assad, which says that Syria "has turned into a scrap of paper, which Iran and Russia use at their discretion."[65] Indeed, over the coming years, Syria turned into a failed state, divided into zones of influence of outside actors. Assad's own conventional forces had not been enough to hold the territory he had inherited, and he continued to stay in power only thanks to Russian and Iranian backing.

Yet when it comes to how Assad views the situation, some suggest a very different picture. Professor David W. Lesch, Assad's biographer, said, "Putin apparently thinks Syria needs Russia more than the other way around. But Assad and his inner circle probably arrogantly think it is quite the reverse."[66] Putin's perspective is, if anything, more in touch with reality. But Assad is not, and that makes him a problematic client. *New York Times* journalist Anne Bernard wrote that over the course of many interviews with people close to the Assad regime, they paint a picture of someone who is "expert in playing allies off one another; often refuses compromise, even when the chips appear to be down; and, if forced to make deals, delays and complicates them, playing for time until Mr. Assad's situation improves."[67]

A deeper underlying issue is that because the entire Syrian political system is so dependent on Assad, Moscow sees no alternatives to him. Anne Bernard mentions how "brittle" the Syrian regime is—and Hafez al-Assad intended it that way to maintain a total grip on power. As far as the Kremlin is concerned, this issue may matter more than Assad's arrogance and skill at playing Russia and Iran against each other, though this issue is also a factor. One analyst at Chatham House observed in March 2019, "Assad constantly seeks to enlarge his own margin for maneuver by manipulating the interests of his allies."[68]

For all his arrogance, Assad does seem to recognize that he owes Putin, at least on some level. When Putin and Assad had a surprise meeting in Sochi in November 2017, Assad hugged the Russian strongman. Assad's admiration for Putin coupled with his arrogance suggests a more complicated picture when it comes to his relationship with Putin. When Putin came to Syria in December 2017, Assad stood waiting for Putin as he came down, and rushed to tell him how happy he was to see him. In a several-second exchange, Putin takes control of the conversation and says, "We will talk more," as he proceeds to make an announcement about another so-called "withdrawal" from Syria. As he walks to a podium, someone from the Russian military gently pulls Assad aside so that Putin can speak. Those brief seconds are revelatory in terms of who was actually in charge.[69]

There is not yet enough information to judge with complete certainty just how much influence Putin has over Assad. Still, the information available suggests that Putin does have influence. Speaking in 2017 at the UN, Ukraine's permanent representative Vladimir Yel'chenko said, "Russia has all means necessary to influence Damascus and its allied armed forces to abandon their militaristic approach and begin to support the political process and national reconciliation," but "for some reason" continues to refrain from utilizing this influence towards positive changes, to get Damascus to end its military approach and work towards a political settlement and reconciliation.[70] His comment does not take Iranian influence in Syria into account. Yet Putin clearly bet on the anti-American and anti-Sunni bloc in the region, regardless of the complexities of the Russia-Iran-Syria triangle.

12

Russia and Syria's Resources

The future political game in Syria is increasingly shifting towards reconstruction. This discussion implies a focus on Syria's resources. The way Moscow has handled the economic aspect of its relationship with Syria also shows why the costs of the intervention have been bearable for Russia. The commercial relationship between Russia and Syria has never been at the forefront of Moscow's priorities, but it is an important piece of the puzzle. Moreover, the economic element may become more important in the future. Indeed, the Eastern Mediterranean is important geostrategically not only because of its position, which of course is of primary importance, but also to some extent because of its resources.

Russia–Syria Trade Prior to the War

First, broader context is needed. Prior to the outbreak of protests in March 2011, Syria mattered little for Russia in terms of trade, but Russia mattered to Syria— Russia was a key trading partner for the country, especially as a supplier of industrial goods and commodities, such as steel, timber, and wheat. In the mid-2000s, several Russian oil companies received contracts in Syria to explore the country's oil assets. In 2005, Tatneft signed a production sharing agreement to explore block 27 on the border with Iraq, and in 2006 Soyuzneftegaz signed a similar agreement on block 12 in Syria's south east. In addition, Russian companies made fairly large investments in the Syrian tourism and real estate sector. As The Free Syria Report writes, in early 2011 "Intourist Sinara, a Russian consortium, was developing a four-star tourist resort in the coastal city of Latakia at a cost of $50 million."[1]

By 2008, Russia emerged as Syria's largest trade partner, providing $2.3 billion worth of exports to the country. In 2009, Russia–Syria trade dipped along with the decline of commodity prices; it rose again by 2010 to 1.1 billion and to

1.9 billion in 2011. By 2010, Russia was the fourth largest supplier of commodity goods to Syria, and climbed to second place by 2011—second only to China.[2] In late 2010, a Russian–Turkish company Renaissance Construction bought a 30 percent share in a $180 billion real-estate development in Aleppo.[3] Some Russian companies invested in Syria's industrial and technological sectors. Stroytransgaz received several contracts to build gas-processing plants near Palmyra and earned "several hundred millions of dollars from these contracts."[4]

By late 2010, Syria had approximately $17 billion in foreign reserves. After the West imposed sanctions in Syria in 2011, especially on Syria's banking sector, Damascus moved its foreign holdings from European banks to Russian ones. Western sanctions, among its provisions prohibited printing of the Syrian currency, but Moscow could—and did—print Syrian dinars.[5] A Reuters report from June 2012 noted that, "Four Damascus-based bankers told Reuters that new banknotes printed in Russia were circulating in trial amounts in the capital and Aleppo, the first such step since a popular revolt against President Bashar al-Assad began in 2011."[6]

As early as 2010, Damascus announced its interest in joining the Russia-led Customs Union, and in 2012 Syria's economic minister Qadri Jamil went as far as to suggest it would happen "very soon."[7] The Assad regime continued talking about it in the coming years. In 2013, Russian and Russian-language sources suggested Syria had agreed on the entry with Russia and was discussing the issue with Belarus and Kazakhstan.[8] Some pro-Kremlin Russian sources suggested that Syria should join the Customs Union but on Russian terms.[9]

Syria's Energy Resources and Overall Strategic Location

Syria possesses small amounts of energy reserves. Their primary importance is not quantity, but location. By 2011, Syria had important oil and gas pipeline networks connecting Syria with Egypt, Jordan, Turkey, Iran, and Iraq, and analysts expected this integration to grow.[10] The US Energy Information Administration (EIA) wrote in August 2011, several months after protests broke out in Syria, "Although Syria produces relatively modest quantities of oil and gas, its location is strategic in terms of regional security and prospective energy transit routes."[11] Similarly, the Syria Report wrote, "In international terms, Syria plays a small role as an oil producer but has strong potential as an energy transit hub. Syria has pipeline connections to Egypt, Jordan, Lebanon, and Iraq; additional pipeline projects have been stalled due to the conflict."[12]

Syria's largest oil accumulation is in Suwaidiyah, followed by al-Thayyem and Umar groups of fields of al-Furat according to EIA. Different sources estimated Syria's oil reserves to be anywhere between 1.8 and some 2.5 billion barrels. The *Oil & Gas Journal* estimated Syria's reserves to be at 2.5 billion barrels in 2012.[13] BP provides the same number—2.5 billion barrels by the end of 2018.[14] Based on independent sources, the EIA estimated in August 2011 that, "Syria's proven oil reserves [were] recoverable at costs not exceeding $8/b[arrel] at less than 1.8bn barrels. The SPC in pre-2011 years put the proven oil reserves at 3bn barrels, a figure it had maintained since end-1993."[15]

To put this estimated number in perspective, Syria's oil reserves hovered at around 2 percent of Saudi Arabia's oil reserves, which measured at 264.5 billion barrels in 2010–11.[16] Iran, with the fourth largest global oil reserves, had 137 billion in 2011 according to the *Guardian*.[17] Prior to the outbreak of the war in Syria, the country produced 380,000 barrels a day,[18] and output dropped drastically with the onset of fighting. According to the World Bank, Syrian oil revenue fell from $4.7 billion in 2011 to an estimated $0.22 billion in 2014.[19] Syria's gas reserves were also fairly minor. For comparison, Iran's proven gas reserves, according to OPEC, in 2018 were 33.899 billion cubic meters.[20] According to the IEA, in 2011, Syria had 6.599 million cubic meters.[21] To provide more detail, the IEA wrote:

The SPC [Syrian Petroleum Company] has been sticking to figures it first published in 1993, saying the recoverable reserves of associated and non-associated gas stood at 285 BCM [billion cubic meters]. This figure was again given in 2009 by the MPMR [Ministry of Petroleum and Mineral Resources], which said the size of recoverable gas was 285 BCM. It said its plan was to produce 160 BCM from 2009 to 2025. The MPMR said Syria had potential reserves of 6,500 MCM [million cubic meters], including 4,675 MCM of oil and 1,825 MCM of condensate, in 2010 describing the oil sector as pivotal and basic to the development of the economy. In 2010 it said domestic demand for clean sales gas was growing rapidly to reach 50 MCM/day by 2020 as it was a substitute for gasoil/diesel, gasoline and other liquid fuels.[22]

According to OilPrice.com, Syria's gas production has been hit less than its oil production with the onset of the fighting.[23] Regardless, the war certainly damaged all infrastructure to one degree or another, and the estimated costs of Syrian reconstruction are massive. The UN had put the number at $250 billion in March 2019, though other sources, including Assad himself, put the cost at $400 billion. The higher end of these estimates is nearly tenfold Syria's GDP prior to 2011, which measured approximately $40–55 billion between 2007 and 2009.[24]

Syria's location, in and of itself, also matters beyond energy resources alone—a point that many in Russia have understood very well. In an interview that took place as early as 2010, head of Soyuzneftegaz, Yuri Shafranik, underscored that Syria's central position as a hub attracts foreign business with more than energy resources. Because it neighbors Turkey, Iraq, Jordan, and Lebanon, in addition to its proximity to Egypt, "Syria plays and will play an important role in the development of transportation arteries of the region. And, I am sure, [Syria] will develop big projects in energy and many other spheres with Iraq if the situation there gets better. It would be a sin for Russia with its good political and economic reputation in both countries not to take part in the projects."[25]

The War and Moscow's Assistance to Assad

Moscow provided Assad with many forms of assistance. This included loans. According to flight manifests obtained by ProPublica, Moscow flew more than two hundred tons of "banknotes" to the Syrian regime in summer 2011, during periods when the fighting escalated.[26] In late 2014, reports suggested Damascus also tried and failed to borrow a $1 billion from Moscow, possibly due to Russian concerns about giving Assad too much without getting the money back. This was especially so because, in 2005, Moscow had already forgiven the majority of Syria's $13.4 billion debt. Tehran for its part provided a lot more to Assad than Moscow. Official Iranian figures indicate $6.6 billion according to The Syria Report of 2017,[27] while then-UN Syria representative for Syria Staffan de Mastura said in June 2015 that Iran spends $6 billion on Iran annually and other experts believed it was even higher.[28] Yet whatever Moscow's reservations, the key point is that they nonetheless provided Assad with critical financial support to keep him afloat.

With the outbreak of fighting in Syria, many Russian companies pulled out. Yet some got involved in Syria after the 2015 military intervention or provided investment, and others simply expressed interest in the Syrian market.[29] Indeed, as early as October 2015, only days after the military intervention, a Russian delegation descended on Damascus to talk about leading Syria's post-war reconstruction.[30] Over the years, Russian companies that came into Syria encompassed a variety of sectors, from energy to education, finance, and tourism, to manufacturing, and real estate, but most focused on energy, phosphates, and infrastructure. Much about the activities of these companies remains murky. Primarily, they involved those with an already tarnished reputation, such as those under Western sanctions, or those which simply did not see any danger in involvement in Syria. The overall involvement of these companies underscores the broader nature of Russian business, dominated by criminal or semi-criminal structures, the so-called "legalized bandits,"[31] those who gained their wealth by questionable means in the 1990s and then officially legalized it early 2000s but have never been able to follow transparent Western practices.

In the coming years, commercial interests hovered in the background of Syria's bloodletting. In November 2016 Syrian foreign minister, Walid al-Muallem, came to Moscow and promised priority to Russian companies. Though reportedly, Moscow warily declined the offer,[32] interest in Syrian business did not disappear. One small, unknown company that came to Syria is Adyg Yurag[33] from the province of Adygea in the North Caucasus, an enclave within Krasnodar Kray, bordering the Sea of Azov and the Black Sea. Adydea is home to a large Circassian community with connections to Syria; indeed, the province accepted over 1,000 Circassian refugees from Syria in 2013.[34] In 2016, Adyg Yurag signed an agreement to establish a permanent exhibition center for Syrian products in Russia, called "The Syrian house," based in Adygea. To date, it remains unclear as to whether the agreement has produced any tangible results. There is no indication that it was cancelled, still this episode suggests its relative unimportance, at least at the time of this writing.

Other bigger and better-known companies entered Syria later. In April 2016, Moscow signed contracts amounting to around $1 billion on reconstructing Syria's infrastructure, along with other contracts, according to Russia's Neftegaz.[35] In December 2016, the Syrian minister of communication and technology Ali Al-Zafir signed a $4.5 million contract with his Russian counterpart Nikolay Nikiforov to establish "an electronic government" in Syria.[36] According to Bloomberg, Russia's "fastest-growing" footwear chain Zenden was purchasing footwear, mainly sandals, from Latakia-based suppliers in late 2016, though the actual terms of Zenden's agreement with the Syrian government were unclear.[37] The founder of the company has been pushing the "made in Syria" along with "made in Crimea" labels in Russia. He pulled out his smartphone for a Bloomberg reporter in May 2017 to show a photo of the side-by-side Syria and Crimea displays that a Zenden customer had just posted on Instagram. The caption read: "Can't decide which would be more patriotic to buy."[38] Syrian tulle has also made its way in abundance into Russian stores (including online stores) in recent years.

At a February 2017 meeting with Russian deputies, Assad assured them that Syria will provide special conditions for Russian companies. "In the future, only Russian companies will work in the oil and gas industry in Syria. Indeed, now we do not have a single company, nor a country, nor China,"[39] he said—a point that did not get lost on Shafranik, who posted an article with his comments on his site.[40] In July 2017, Damascus awarded the infamous Evgeny Prigozhin's company, Evro Polis the right to "a quarter of all oil and gas from Syrian territory reclaimed from the regime."[41] Meanwhile, Stroytransgaz inked a deal on phosphate mining.[42] And in December 2017 another major business delegation came to Damascus. Ultra-nationalist then-Deputy Prime Minister Sergei Rogozin who headed the delegation said, "Syria is a country with unlimited riches."[43]

Wheat is important because bread is a key staple of Syrian households and indeed Hafez al-Assad, Bashar's father, understood the importance of control of the wheat infrastructure for retaining power. Bashar al-Assad also uses wheat as a weapon, starving his population into submission.[44] In September 2017, Damascus pledged to buy three million tons of wheat from Russia over the next three years.[45] This announcement came several months after Moscow said it would also give Syria wheat free of charge.[46] In September 2017, the deal was cancelled "due to difficulties in banking operations and execution."[47] Damascus also gave two Russian oil companies with reportedly longstanding ties to Prigozhin, Merkuriy (Mercury) and Vilada, geological exploration rights in December 2019.[48] Assad personally continued to push for entry into the Customs Union as late as 2017, and Syria remained on the list of interested countries in 2019.[49] At the time of this writing, the status Syria's entry into the Customs Union is unclear.

Securing Access to Resources

The year 2018 saw important developments in terms of Russian long-term access to Syria's natural resources. Russian (along with Iranian) companies dominated the Syrian trade fair that year.[50] Russian energy minister Alexander Novak reportedly signed a cooperation agreement with Syria in January 2018.[51] In February 2018, Moscow and Damascus signed a cooperation agreement on power industry development. That year, Moscow also received exclusive rights to produce oil and gas in Syria.[52] This included rights to construct infrastructure, provide advice, and train Syrian oilmen. This is important because although the SDF continued to control most of the oilfields in Syria, control of oilfields does not automatically translate into trade because oil needs to be transported to the relevant markets, and the existing Syrian infrastructure is designed to facilitate trade via the Mediterranean, through Syria's West, and this is where Russia has control.[53] More to the point, Moscow had worked to push for Assad's retaking of

Syria's north, a territory the Kurds controlled. And in an April 2018 interview, military journalist Yuriy Matsarskiy told Radio Free Europe, "there is information that in exchange for help of [Russian private military] contractors Russian oligarchs receive access to approximately a third of Syrian oil."[54] Two months later, Regnum had also claimed that the US presence in Syria is about oil "after all,"[55] as Washington had offered Damascus a deal: US troops leave al-Tanf and Eastern Euphrates on three conditions: complete Iranian withdrawal from Syria, a share in oil access in Syria's northeast, and information about terrorists who may pose a threat to the West in the future.[56] Basically, Regnum claimed that the United States wants access to Syria's oil resources.

In early 2018, Moscow and Damascus also held talks about rebuilding Syria's telecommunications infrastructure.[57] In March 2018, a number of Russian companies signed a package of contracts in Syria that included a railway between Damascus and Damascus International Airport, power generation projects in Homs, and a number of industrial plants, though it remained unclear where the investment funding would come from.[58] In June 2018, Moscow also gained majority access to Syria's phosphate industry when Stroytransgaz, already in charge of developing Syria's phosphate reserves by this point, secured the right to extract 2.2 million tons every year for the next fifty years and get 70 percent of the revenue, leaving the rest for the Syrian government. At the time, some believed that Moscow had pushed the Iranians out of this market, but this remains unclear. Some have suggested that it was simply the case that Damascus had decided to award the contracts to Russia over Iran, and it may not necessarily have been matter of rivalry.[59]

In June 2018, this company had signed a preliminary deal for the next forty-eight years to take over the development and management of Syria's large fertilizer complex near Homs. Stroytransgaz is run by another infamous Russian oligarch, Gennady Timchenko, who was an ally of Putin and also under US sanctions. Fertilizer is a key Syrian economic asset according to *The Syria Report* and the deal "means that the Syrian government is giving up on a key economic asset." Russia is already the world's fourth phosphate producer, and as one publication observed, the reasons for its interests in Syria's phosphates remain somewhat of a mystery. However, Russian interest in and of itself is clear: reportedly, Moscow had pushed Iran out of this market. One possibility raised by the publication is that Syrian phosphates have low cadmium (a type of carcinogen) rates. Russia already dominates the fertilizer trade, but the ability to sell Syrian phosphate on the European market would boost Russia's competitiveness there.

The Syrian Observer provides another possible reason—it has to do with uranium, fuel used in nuclear plants:

> During the process of transforming phosphates to fertilizer, a secondary component is radioactive uranium. Syrian phosphates, in theory, contain a rate of up to 300 grams per metric ton, according to Al-Modon's sources. This is a high rate compared to other types of phosphates, which do not exceed uranium rates of 200 grams per metric ton. Al-Modon's sources did not know how uranium is extracted from phosphate, but did know that before the revolution, the Syrians had managed to separate uranium from phosphates.[60]

Russian Forbes suggested that Syrian phosphates are a lucrative market because labor there is cheap, and while Timchenko is under US sanctions he is not under European sanctions; nor are Syrian phosphates covered by European sanctions, unlike Syrian oil and gas.[61] Publicly, Moscow claimed that its interest in Syrian phosphate was centered on a "desire to increase its phosphate reserve, estimated at 700 million tons, after its annual production in 2017 reached 12.5 million metric tons."[62] In January 2018, Russian energy and Syrian oil ministries signed a cooperation road map, and in December that year the Syrian regime said it was ready to supply Crimea with phosphates.[63]

If Moscow was so interested in Syrian phosphates, it is unclear why it did not push for access to this resource in Syria earlier. It may be possible that it simply did not have the opportunity to gain access on terms as favorable as the war in Syria had allowed, or perhaps more likely Syria simply presented opportunities that Moscow had not considered earlier. It is also unclear if the Kremlin's interests are necessarily aligned with that of oligarchs like Timchenko. Ultimately, more information is needed to fully access this issue. However, it is not difficult to see why Moscow would want Syria's oil and gas resources, and that interest likely remains a key priority.

In April 2018, Moscow held an international business forum in Crimea, where Moscow and Syria signed a number of economic cooperation deals worth $1 billion.[64] Latakia and Yalta also signed a twinning agreement, while the governors of Latakia and Crimea, Sergei Aksyonov signed a memorandum of cooperation between the two regions.[65] By the end of 2018, according to RIA Novosti, the road map included thirty projects.[66]

In December 2018, Lavrov claimed that Russia was helping Syria with reconstruction and blasted the West for not doing the same.[67] In August 2019, Russian companies sought to work with Lebanon on rebuilding Syria.[68] Lavrov's comment was another example of Moscow's interest in moving towards a political settlement in Syria on its own terms and trying to get someone else to ultimately foot the bill. By 2019, Russian construction companies began discussion about collaboration with the Syrian government. Notably Stroytransgaz signed a contract to manage Tartus for the next forty-nine years.[69] In August 2019, at the Damascus International Fair, Crimea and Damascus signed an agreement on economic and trade cooperation.[70] In addition, Damascus reportedly signed three contracts with Russian energy companies, "in the domains of surveying, drilling and production in the oil and gas sectors in the central and eastern regions of Syria," according to Syrian Minister of Petroleum, Ali Ghanem.[71]

A Kremlin narrative soon emerged that the United States was trying steal Syria's resources. Indeed, The Russian Defense Ministry accused US contractors of doing just that and claimed that in territories not controlled by the Assad regime ongoing oil extraction was "illegal."[72] Sergei Lavrov also stressed the importance of Assad taking over northern Syria,[73] while Prigozhin's news outlet also accused the United States of "stealing" Syria's oil, which underscored his own interests in Syria's energy resources.[74]

Many analysts had rightly expressed doubts about the implementation of a number of economic projects between Moscow and Damascus, since previous agreements had often amounted to little if anything, often as a result of the Syrian government's failure to provide the necessary resources or other support.[75] Ultimately, Moscow's major obstacle in Syria is its own lack of financial resources to invest. This is why it has worked so hard to get others to foot the bill. Moreover, when push comes to shove, Moscow appears unlikely to be willing to guarantee security on a large scale, as that would entail a greater military commitment than Moscow is prepared to make, even as the Russian government promised Assad publicly in late 2018 to offer "protection" against "terrorists" in exchange for developing Syria's energy resources.[76] Yet, ironically, this unwillingness points to another safeguard that Moscow has implemented to guard against becoming overly committed to Syria to the point of serious overstretch.

In the absence of other alternatives, Moscow is also well positioned to control the direction of Syria's reconstruction, even if it lacks the necessary investment funds. Since it is clear that Damascus is unlikely to repay loans, it is instead giving Moscow access to Syria's resources on a long-term basis. Just as Assad had slowly given control of part of his country to Iran earlier, he is also slowly giving away part of it to Russia. The Kremlin is likely, in part, looking to the future, and sooner or later, would be interested in exploring what lies on the shelf of the Western Mediterranean—after all, it is the same shelf as that of Lebanon, Israel and Cyprus.[77] Thus, there is an uncertain element of playing a game for the future. Certainly, it will be important to watch the entry of Russian companies into Lebanon in this regard. To some extent, Moscow's Lebanon policy has been an extension of its Syria policy, and Lebanon offers the ideal entry way into Syria. At the same time, some elements of Russian business will be able to make a small profit there. Some Russian analysts suggest this access is also the Kremlin's way to reward actors such as Prigozhin, who have been useful to the Kremlin. Ultimately, economic interests have been the "garnish" of Russia's interests in Syria. For all the companies that have entered, the absence of Gazprom and Rosneft—two major state-owned energy giants that the Kremlin uses as foreign policy tools—is also notable. If Moscow's priorities lay with the economy, we would be seeing these companies in Syria, but to date, they are absent. To be sure, the December 2019 Caesar Syria Civilian Protection Act (known as the "Caesar Act"), which sanctions the Syrian regime and those doing business with it[78] added an extra complication for Russian companies who were interested in investing in Syria, and remains a source of pressure on, and isolation of, the regime. But sanctions alone have never been able to bring it down entirely.

To some extent, Iran and China, will compete over Syria with Russia. These events are going to unfold in the years ahead, and in this regard Moscow faces a lot of uncertainty. Still, access to natural resources of a county on a long-term basis is not something to dismiss as entirely inconsequential. Securing long-term access without large-scale commitment from key Russian state industries such as Gazprom also suggests a degree of long-term thinking on the part of the Kremlin and casts doubt on the argument that Moscow will find itself severely overstretched in Syria.

Conclusion

Despite their many differences with Obama, Donald Trump came into office with a broadly similar interest of disengagement from the Middle East. The rhetoric on Syria took a tougher tone under Trump. Moreover, Trump ordered two limited strikes against Assad. Still, Trump himself cared little about Syria, the land of "blood, sand and death," as he called it. He unilaterally ordered a withdrawal of approximately 2,000–2,500 US troops from Syria in December 2018, a decision that led Jim Mattis to resign as Secretary of Defense while Brett McGurk, US special envoy for the anti-ISIS coalition forwarded his departure from February to December in protest. The withdrawal order drew widespread condemnation and strong pushback within the government and ultimately the troops did not leave. But Trump had not given up—he had promised to bring US troops home from "endless" wars. In October 2019, he abruptly ordered another withdrawal from Northeast Syria that threw Kurdish allies under the bus and laid the groundwork for another resurgence of ISIS in the future. As US troops withdrew in haste from Manbij, Russian soldiers and reporters entered their base and began posting photos and videos of themselves going through the dining hall still stocked with food and drinks—an image that could not have been easy even for Trump to watch. In the end, approximately 700 US troops officially remained in eastern Syria, with a mission to continue fighting what remains of ISIS and prevent the Assad regime from gaining control of oilfields. But the damage was done, both literal in terms of Kurdish lives lost as a result of the Turkish offensive, and political in terms of US credibility and standing in the region. For its part, Moscow mostly worried that the US withdrawal was not real—which showed just how much Russian officials wanted to push the United States out of Syria. After the first withdrawal did not materialize and the second was not complete, they could perhaps be forgiven. Wasting no time, Moscow began working to establish a new Kurdish-majority military force in northeast Syria to replace US-backed Kurdish groups.[1] After the United States threw the Kurds under the bus they had little choice but to think about moving closer to Putin and Assad out of self-preservation.

The northern province of Idlib, the last rebel stronghold and home to the largest single displacement in Syria since 2011,[2] remains a major point of contention at the time of this writing. It stands in Assad's, Moscow's, and Tehran's shared desire to destroy the remnants of anti-Assad opposition. For Putin, this is ultimately about ending the war in Syria on his terms, which includes Assad gaining control of the strategically important M4 highway that runs across the province and connects Syria to the region. Reopening of the highway can help revive commercial activity. Although Russia and Turkey support opposing forces in this area, both want economic activity to resume, so Turkey is unlikely to oppose the reopening of strategically vital Syrian highways.

Idlib is home to approximately four million people, one million of them children. Almost half of its population fled from other previous opposition-controlled areas. The vast majority are peaceful civilians, though some are members of radical jihadist groups such as Hizb ut-Tahrir (HTS). Moscow's professed priority is the elimination of terrorist cells in Idlib, but a real solution would require a scalpel rather than a sledgehammer. The only place where Idlib refugees can flee is into Turkey, but the last thing Erdogan wants is more Syrian refugees—a prospect that also worries the European Union. Erdogan has been working on carving out a buffer zone on the border to push refugees back into Syria instead, and thus prevent Syrian Kurds from establishing links with Turkey's Kurds, especially the YPG, the People's Protection Unit, which Turkey has designated as a terrorist group. Since late 2019, Russia and Turkey have been conducting periodic joint patrols in the area, including along a carved-out security corridor near the M4 highway, but none of the ceasefires have held. The situation has ultimately required more direct Erdogan–Putin talks to calm down, but these have changed little because both sides want different things, and Moscow will work to limit Turkish military operations. Still, neither Erdogan nor Putin want a serious fight that gets out of control, and continue schizophrenically cooperating in other areas of their bilateral relationship as they disagree on Idlib. As always, the broader context matters—the West is largely absent. It has done next to nothing about massive humanitarian catastrophe in Idlib, nor has it been interested in a confrontation there with Russia or Assad. Turkey is still a NATO ally in name but Erdogan's authoritarianism and support for radical Sunni extremism has severely strained his relationship with the West, and diminished good will beyond treaty obligations. In the context of divergent interests and Western absence, Idlib is poised to become a long-term if not permanent refugee settlement."[3] Similarly to how Moscow manages so-called "frozen conflicts" in the post-Soviet space, Syria is headed for a frozen conflict scenario. This is not an ideal situation for Moscow in Syria but one it can regrettably manage for awhile, especially absent a serious US effort to pressure Russia. Moscow excels at creating frozen conflicts in the post-Soviet space—conflicts that, if solved, do not require a Russian presence. Therefore Moscow has no interest in resolving them. In Syria, Moscow did not start a conflict but has positioned itself as a manager, similar to a role it plays in other frozen conflicts.

With its Syria intervention, the Kremlin has come full circle in pushing back against the perceived chaos of US interventionism in the Middle East that began, in Putin's tenure, with Iraq. But more broadly, Moscow pushed back against the danger it perceived from US supremacy in world affairs, and against the universality of liberal principles such as human rights. And at a time when this liberal, US-built post World War II order finds itself increasingly challenged by authoritarian actors, the United States continues to doubt itself. Calls for selective disengagement from places such as the Middle East and Afghanistan, for admitting failure of military efforts, contine to grow. The Kremlin meanwhile views the world through the lense of external geopolitics, and thus, unlike the United States, never took its eyes off great-power competition. Covington notes, "The West is witnessing a deliberate, strategic recoupling of the military to Russia's core geo-strategic interests and Putin's core political aims," which "represents a remilitarization of Russia's overall security policy."[4] Thus, while the United States is more concerned with China, a peer competitor, it is underestimating the threat from the Kremlin.

For its part, Russia is now positioned to direct much of Syria's future, with all the difficulties that entails for the Kremlin. Russia now has permanent bases in the Eastern Mediterranean—a goal that eluded even the Russian tsars. Moscow is using this position to project power further into the region and deeper into Africa. With Putin's eastward shift (not only to the Middle East but also towards China), Russia is also experiencing another iteration of its internal identity struggles and shifting away from the West, as its traditional concerns about the vulnerable south remain a constant.

Some might argue that the Russian government will face many of the same problems that the United States, or anyone else would have faced in Syria. But the crux of the issue is precisely that Moscow does not aim to resolve anything in the way Western countries would approach the issue, and thus the challenges it will face by definition are different. Moscow accepted from the start, perhaps in a kind of Russian fatalism, that it ultimately could do little to truly affect change—Moscow could not conceive of a better alternative to Assad, at least not in the foreseeable future, nor a better vision for Syria. Thus, Moscow will not necessarily have to face the same struggles of nation-building that the West had faced in the Middle East. It saw no need to invest massive resources to achieve more ambitious goals. Rightly or wrongly, the United States went into Iraq not only to end the appeasement of states that sponsor terrorism, but also guided by a belief that America could help Iraq, in what Fouad Ajami, one of the world's leading authorities on Middle Eastern politics called the "foreigner's gift"—a consensual government.[5] For all its myriad mistakes, the 2003 Iraq War brought a degree of freedom to the country, and a level of free public debate that no country in the Middle East except Israel and perhaps Tunisia enjoy. This freedom is fragile and will be easily be lost with American disengagement. Moscow's influence brings corruption, and a broader vision of authoritarianism. Putin's Russia brought to Syria carpet bombings, repression, and support of a brutal dictator—a recipe for instability and suffering.

Moscow derived a key lesson from the Soviet experience in Afghanistan— that it could not affect real change in the country. Therefore, it never even tried to attempt it in Syria. Rather, Moscow threw a direct challenge to the United States and the West more broadly, out of a paranoid need to boost its own image, and because the Middle East mattered in its own right to the Russian state. The West never truly challenged the Russian position in Syria. It gave Syria to Moscow without much of a fight—perhaps partly due to an acceptance that the West, just like Russia, can do little to stabilize the country or the region.

Contrary to official Russian pronouncements and hopes, the world is not multipolar. In a multipolar world, several states would possess roughly equal material capabilities, such as GDP, population size, and military. By such definition, the United States still holds more cards in this system; even Russian analysts tend to acknowledge this. But the United States is not alone in the sandbox, and the Middle East matters in great-power competition, as well as in Russia's perceptions of its security. The West had missed this point and therefore missed the Syria intervention and what it was ultimately about. Russia could not accept a junior position in an international system, and it chose to compete with the West for the Middle East. It made great strides, primarily because the West did not oppose it, but also because Moscow incorporated lessons learned from previous experiences.

For years Westerners consoled themselves with the idea that Putin is merely an opportunist, rather than a strategist, but such a dichotomous view failed to take into account Russia's commitment to undermining the West, historic longstanding interests in the Middle East, and the fact that in order to be able simply to take advantage of an opportunity one has to be prepared, as Moscow was. To do that it could not be entirely devoid of strategic thinking—the way Moscow defined strategy. Ironically, it is the West that failed to think strategically about Russia and what its involvement in Syria and the Middle East would do to Syria, the Middle East, and broader Western interests and values globally. Western officials talked of Moscow getting stuck in Syria but did not work to create such a situation for Russia, with any strategic whole government and long-term consistency, which was regardless easier to do earlier into the Russian intervention.

Certainly, Moscow's Syria adventure is not over. Lack of economic development prevents it from delivering a public message of a victory in Syria, and this adds to reasons why Russian officials are so angry about the Caesar Act and promote a narrative that it harms Syrians. Still, Moscow created certain safeguards to reduce the possibility of getting "stuck" in Syria, and has already made considerable gains at the expense of the West and the Syrian people.

With an accelerated American retreat, Moscow may risk getting itself more bogged down in Syria than it would have wanted; it may require a greater commitment of resources than Moscow has available or wants to expend on Syria. This could also put more pressure on Moscow to do what it has avoided for so long—openly taking sides in the region beyond Syria, rather than superficially maintaining its coveted position of a peacemaker and leaning closer to anti-Western forces. Since Moscow is closer to Assad and Iran, that leaves Iran as the more likely candidate that Moscow would choose. Syria is a failed state after Assad murdered over half a million people, and turned millions into refugees. Assad's control remains tenuous, while Syria's economy is in shambles.

Certainly maintaining a balance between divergent actors in the Middle East has never been easy for the Kremlin, especially since Moscow simply strong-armed some of them into agreement, such as Turkey, whose aggression in the Mediterranean also grows. Distrust continues to underlie the Russia–Iran relationship. Nonetheless, during almost five years of Russia's involvement in Syria, coupled with Putin's earlier approach to the Middle East, Moscow has demonstrated a degree of awareness of its limitations. Putin established a strategic position on the Mediterranean. He was also accurate in his reading of Western intentions in Syria. He capitalized on, and arguably encouraged US retreat which the United States was already predisposed towards. The West simply handed Syria to Putin—it never attempted to compete for it.

Critically, Putin leveraged other actors, rather than going it alone—an element of his success was the ability to co-opt others to support his vision. Iran did much of the heavy lifting in Syria. Putin built pragmatic partnerships with all key actors there. He was careful not to expend too many resources, and where possible sought practical gain, such as with arms sales and training for the military. Regardless of how Assad feels about it, Moscow's stake in directing Syria's future is growing not only because of its bolstered political role, but also because, as the last chapter shows, it is increasingly taking long-term ownership of its natural resources. That Syria's future remains highly problematic is important, but the Kremlin has experience living with—and perpetuating—low-level conflict. The Kremlin does not define success the same way as the West does when it comes to conflict resolution and reconstruction. To be sure, Moscow needs someone else to foot the reconstruction bill and is working to that end with China and the Gulf states. The Trump administration's approach towards Syria was to put long-term pressure on the Assad regime and his supporters, primarily through sanctions, including the Caesar Act, so that Assad would be forced to change his behavior from the use of violence to participation in the UN-led conflict resolution mechanism. The administration also tried to counter the efforts of other Arab states to normalize relations with the Assad regime. In addition, Trump ordered two limited airstrikes after Assad's use of chemical weapons. These showed that the select use of military force would not inevitably lead to war with Russia as some had feared, and might indeed send the right message—at least briefly.

The resultant situation was contradictory—Trump's personal lack of interest in Syria, general Middle East fatigue that had set in long before he came into office, and the inability of sanctions alone to change behavior even as they caused pain cast doubt on whether this pressure alone was enough. Trump's announced withdrawal from northern Syria in late 2019 both shamefully betrayed the Kurdish allies and undercut these gains, including his own team's successful fight against ISIS—to say nothing of giving more reasons for others to think twice now about partnering with the United States in the region. And yet, ironically, for the decade of bad and ultimately disjointed policies on Syria, the Trump administration still showed itself to be stronger than Obama's, but Trump repeatedly undermined his own administration.

At the time of this writing, Biden's Syria policy remains unclear, but no one realistically expects Syria to be a priority, both because of overriding domestic priorities, chiefly the pandemic, and the persistent and misleading narrative of ending "forever wars." Perhaps most importantly, because the view that the US retains crucial security and strategic interests in Syria is a minority one. Moscow, for its part, is very likely to remain strongly engaged in pushing for its preferred outcome in Syria. And, as the United States is expected to continue to disengage from the Middle East as it pivots to China, Moscow can also be counted on to stay engaged and vie for influence in this region.

On March 16, 2021, Biden gave an exclusive interview to George Stephanopoulos of ABC News who asked him, "So you know Vladimir Putin. You think he's a killer?" to which Biden said, "Mmm hmm, I do." This was not a prepared speech or statement of policy to be sure, merely a response to a question. But after more than two decades of US officials, Democrat and Republican alike, who were all too willing to give Putin a free pass, Biden's comment stood out.

Having made this comment, Biden cannot now walk away. From the mysterious apartment bombings that propelled Putin into power, to the murder of opposition critics at home, and support for murderers abroad—Assad being the worst of them all—the United States has a responsibility to uncover and speak the truth. The Kremlin seeks to erode the US-led liberal global order grounded in human rights and individual liberty, so it can do whatever it wants with impunity, because in the Kremlin's vision individuals do not matter as the state reigns supreme. It is this line of thinking that led Putin to support Assad.

It is too early to say if the Biden will back up his talk with action with regard to Putin. And to be sure, for Syria, there are no easy or quick solutions. But the worst thing he can do is acquiesce to Putin's vision of Assad coming back into the fold of legitimacy, ignore Iraq, and rush to return to the Iran deal before ensuring Tehran's compliance with its nuclear obligations.

And given the Kremlin's history of fomenting and maintaining frozen conflicts, it can muddle through for a long time. Moscow has been pushing for a resolution to the Syrian crisis on its terms through a constitutional committee, with a patina of international legitimacy through the UN.[6] This shows that Moscow clearly wants a resolution on its terms. This would not be a successful resolution by a Western definition of the term, but the Kremlin primarily cares that its own position is secured and the scale of fighting is down to manageable levels.

In addition, as Moscow proceeds with the construction of its Nord Stream-2 pipeline together with TurkStream gas pipeline that already runs from Russia into Turkey, it is now in a position to control Syrian gas. As discussed in the chapter on natural resources, the issue is not Syria's own meager energy resources, but Moscow's control of transit routes. This position will allow Moscow to further control routes through which Europe obtains its gas and ensure that Europe would have to deal with Russia one way or another, whether directly or indirectly. Furthermore, these pipelines would allow Moscow to circumvent Eastern Europe.

Russians may prefer that their government spends resources on its own citizens, but the Russian public has too many other, more immediate problems to put Syria at the forefront of its concerns. Indeed, the Syria intervention did not spark significant protests to end involvement there, nor has a call for withdrawal taken front and center in the anti-Putin opposition, as Syria is only one subset of broader issues with the Putin regime itself, and domestic issues take precedence. The Russian public also remains unaware of the true scope of Moscow's activities in Syria. And in the backdrop of massive anti-Putin protests the restoration of Russia's image as a great power still appeals to a sizable segment of the Russian population, especially as government-driven rehabilitation of Joseph Stalin grows at an alarming rate.

Finally, in addition to bases in Tartus and Khmeimim, Moscow most recently moved into Qamishli and other parts of eastern Syria, as mentioned earlier.[7] Together with the Russian base in Gyumri and its fleet stationed in Crimea, Moscow is attempting to encircle Turkey. The A2AD laydown Moscow set up in Syria, with all its flaws, shows how much NATO's southern flank continues to matter to the Kremlin and deterrence of the West remains a key priority for Moscow. And its military position in Syria increases Moscow's influence in the Eastern Mediterranean. Together with Moscow's influence in the Black Sea and the Caspian, this is a significant development that goes beyond Syria. Assad has never been an easy partner for Moscow, and his intransigence has no doubt caused frustration. But with or without Assad, Russia has cemented its presence in Syria and ensured for itself a seat at the table in terms of controlling Syria's future. Ultimately, this was Syria's bigger prize for Moscow.

Moscow's intervention has compounded the immense suffering of the Syrian people, while Russia's newly achieved strategic position provided a useful springboard for low-cost expansion, including into Libya and deeper into Africa. This position matters in its own right, not simply in the light of Kremlin demands for Western acceptance of its sphere of influence in Ukraine and other parts of the former Soviet Union. Far from giving up, or waiting for Moscow to eventually get stuck somewhere in the Middle East, the West should engage in broader competition with Russia rather than de-prioritize the region. Ambassador James F. Jeffrey, who served as the special representative for Syria engagement and special envoy to the global coalition to defeat ISIS from August 2018 to

November 2020, said in May 2020 that his job was to make Syria into a "quagmire" for the Russians.[8] But the United States, including the new Biden administration, is prioritizing peer-to-peer competition with China, and while at the time of this writing the administration has yet to flesh out its overall approach to Russia beyond rhetoric about pushing back, it does not appear interested making a serious and comprehensive effort to compete with Russia for the Middle East.

To that end, the administration should first and foremost resist calls for another reset with Russia, or to increase engagement to fix the relationship—calls that came in late 2020 from senior experts both Democrat and Republican.[9]

The problem is not a lack of understanding between the United States, and more broadly, the West and Russia. Rather, the core issue is that the Kremlin is not a good-faith negotiator and its interests do not align with those of the West. Of course, the United States can still talk to the Kremlin when necessary, but it should do so insofar as it establishes a position of strength, builds leverage, and names and shames Kremlin corruption and abuses the United States should look beyond sanctions alone—a tool that can be effective when used as part of a strategy, but one that cannot be a substitute for strategy.

Even if the administration is broadly intent on pivoting away from the Middle East, it can still stand by allies big or small in pushing back against the Kremlin influence, including not only in Europe but also in the South Caucasus and the conflict over Nagorno-Karabakh, a region that sits within the Kremlin's perceived "vulnerable underbelly." As mentioned earlier, the Middle East is a critical arena of great-power competition with both Russia and China, not a distraction from it. Moscow knows this. To that end, the Biden administration should take Russian PMC activity seriously and look for ways to push back. As the administration looks to revive the Iran deal it should avoid the mistake of the Obama administration in thinking that Russia can be helpful in such diplomacy, and avoid concessions to the Kremlin (not to mention Tehran) in exchange for perceived cooperation. In Syria in particular it would be a mistake to rely more heavily on Russia (and Turkey), as it would only hurt US interests and the Syrian people. It would also be a mistake to lift sanctions against Assad regime.

In sum, the broader Russia policy matters as much as the policy specifically on Russia in Syria and the Middle East; it is all connected in the Kremlin mind that seeks Western accommodation. The West rarely gets Russia right—it either outright dismisses it as weak, declining, and inconsequential, or acts shocked when another Kremlin-created crisis erupts, and elevates Putin to the position of a genius. The new US administration, and the West more broadly, need to dispense with these unhelpful extremes, and design a comprehensive and patient long-term strategy that acknowledges Russia's ability to erode the post-World War II liberal world order and works towards building hardnosed leverage to push back against the Kremlin on multiple fronts. Such an approach would only complement the important long-term challenge of pushing back against China, with which the Kremlin has also increasingly forged closer ties. This approach would entail taking calculated risks when necessary—indeed Moscow has understood better than the West that risk can be mitigated, but cannot be eliminated entirely, and it has often achieved gains simply by being less risk averse than the West.

Historically, Russia retreated from the Middle East due to constraints largely separate from the region, such as internal problems, and those may yet come to the fore in the future; but its desire for a strategic position in the Middle East that puts a check on the West has by and large been a constant. It is far more than a fleeting search for relevance. Until the United States chooses to compete with Russia seriously, Moscow is unlikely to find itself in a quagmire in Syria. Moreover, Moscow will continue empowering anti-Western actors in the region. A more explicit Russia–Iran–Assad nexus will only hurt Western interests beyond the Middle East. And Syria will remain a driver of regional and international instability for the foreseeable future.

A truly free Russia, one that holds a fundamental reckoning with itself where individual freedom, liberal market reform, and rule of law emerge victorious, would be a partner to the West. It is unclear when such a Russia might emerge but historically the United States—and the West more broadly—was unafraid to profess its values and support those who for fought for their freedom, who understood that real change comes from within. This approach was rooted in the optimistic liberalism that served as the backbone of the post-World War II order. Liberalism is increasingly coming under assault in the West from multiple internal and external fonts, not only from Vladimir Putin. The United States needs to remember its longstanding and bipartisan tradition of helping those who wish to help themselves, and serving as a model of freedom that inspired others across the globe. Revisiting these lessons would not only help push back against the Kremlin, but position the United States and the West more broadly on the right side of history, especially given the uncertain future of where Russia goes.

Appendix: TIV of Arms Exports from Russia, 1981–2018

Figures are SIPRI Trend Indicator Values (TIVs) expressed in millions.

Figures may not add up due to the conventions of rounding.

A "0" indicates that the value of deliveries is less than 0.5m.

www.sipri.org/databases/armstransfers/sources-and-methods/

Source: SIPRI Arms Transfers Database, retrieved August 5, 2019.

	1993	1994	1995	1996	1997	1998	1999	2000	2001	2002	2003	2004	2005	
Egypt	8	16	11	5	140		47			60	60	60	135	
Iran	559	83	47	289	119	256	258	341	298	92	85	15	15	
Iraq														
Jordan									8					
Kuwait		6	134	73	96									
Libya													1	
Morocco									6				69	
Palestine			1	7										
Qatar														
Syria	10					20	23	9	8	25	25	5	15	
Turkey	24	7	44	95										
UAE	138	196	202	36	99	133	68	44	14					
Yemen		4						53		524	22	229	245	
Total	3439	1477	3888	3571	3347	2040	4264	4503	5291	5746	5169	6279	5229	

	2006	2007	2008	2009	2010	2011	2012	2013	2014	2015	2016	2017	2018	Total between 1993–2018
Egypt	60	75		8	367	416	68	27	110	6	178	1111	813	3782
Iran	368	283	15	15	41	33	15	22	4	4	413	4	4	3894
Iraq	68	27	95		68	81		51	304	440	319	140	556	2147
Jordan				60	80	40	44						60	292
Kuwait					36	65				48				459
Libya	13	13	13		15			36						90
Morocco	27	27	27											156
Palestine		2		14	6									29
Qatar												4	4	8
Syria	26		44	72	348	392	461	461	2	16	3	25	181	2184
Turkey				16	16									201
UAE			1	113	288	90	90	90						1783
Yemen					90								80	1180
Total	5159	5535	6235	4970	6208	8690	8414	7932	5387	5842	6685	5741	6409	140057

Notes

Introduction

1 "Press Conference by the President," The White House, President Barak Obama archives, October 2, 2015 https://obamawhitehouse.archives.gov/the-press-office/2015/10/02/press-conference-president.
2 Alan Yuhas with Julian Borger, Spencer Ackerman, and Shaun Walker, "Russian airstrikes in Syria: Pentagon says strategy 'doomed to failure'—as it happened," September 30, 2015, *The Guardian* www.theguardian.com/world/live/2015/sep/30/russia-syria-air-strikes-us-isis-live-updates.
3 Mark Lander, "What Quagmire? Even in Withdrawal, Russia Stays a Step Ahead," March 15, 2016, *The New York Times*, www.nytimes.com/2016/03/16/us/politics/what-quagmire-even-in-withdrawal-russia-stays-a-step-ahead.html.
4 Joel Gehrke "John Bolton: 'The Russians are stuck' in Syria," August 22, 2018, *The Washington Examiner* www.washingtonexaminer.com/policy/defense-national-security/john-bolton-the-russians-are-stuck-in-syria.
5 National Commission on Terrorist Attacks Upon the United States, https://govinfo.library.unt.edu/911/about/index.htm.

1 Tsarist Russia's History in the Middle East and North Africa

1 Nikolay Berdyaev, *The Russian Idea*, Hudson, NY: Lindisfarne Press, 1992, p. 20.
2 Geoffrey Hosking, Russia, *People and Empire, 1552–1917*, Enlarged Edition. Cambridge University Press: Cambridge, MA 1997.
3 Sergii Plokhy, *Lost Kingdom: The Quest for Empire and the Making of the Russian Nation, from 1470 to the Present*, Basic Books: New York, 2017 p. X.
4 Janet Martin, *Medieval Russia, 980–1584* (Cambridge Medieval Textbooks). Cambridge: Cambridge University Press, 2007, p. 23.
5 Sergii Plokhy, *Lost Kingdom*, Introduction.
6 Ibid.
7 Ibid.
8 As cited in Anders Åslund and Andrew Kuchins, *The Russia Balance Sheet,* Peterson Institute for International Economics: Washington, DC, 2009.

9   Michael Khodarkovsky, *Russia's Steppe Frontier: The Making of a Colonial Empire, 1500–1800*, Indiana University Press: Bloomington and Indianapolis, 2002, p. 40.

10 Ibid.

11 Orlando Figes, *The Crimean War, A History*, Metropolitan Books: New York, February 2012, chapter 1.

12 Stephen Kotkin, "Russia's Perpetual Geopolitics. Putin Returns to the Historical Pattern," *Foreign Affairs*, May/June 2016 www.foreignaffairs.com/articles/ukraine/2016-04-18/russias-perpetual-geopolitics.

13 Barbara Jelavich, *A Century of Russian Foreign Policy, 1814–1914*, K.B. Lippincott Company, Philadelphia and New York, 1964, p. 7.

14 Peter I, Biography, Accomplishments, Reforms, Facts, Significance, & Death, *Encyclopedia Britannica*; Edward J. Phillips *The Founding of Russia's Navy: Peter the Great and the Azov Fleet, 1688–1714*, Greenwood Press, Westport, CT: 1995, pp. 127–9. Lindsey Hughes, *Peter the Great: A Biography*, Yale University Press, New Haven, CT 2008, pp. 44–6.

15 Orlando Figes, *The Crimean War,* chapter 1.

16 Paul du Quenoy, "Arabs under Tsarist Rule: The Russian Occupation of Beirut, 1773–1774," *Russian History,* 41 2014, pp. 128–41.

17 Ibid.

18 Ibid., p. 141.

19 Ibid.

20 Orlando Figes, *The Crimean War,* chapter 1.

21 Paul du Quenoy, p. 139.

22 Stephen Kotkin, "Russia's Perpetual Geopolitics."

23 Michael A. Reynolds, "Vladimir Putin, the Godfather of Kurdistan?" *National Interest*, March 1, 2016. https://nationalinterest.org/feature/vladimir-putin-godfather-kurdistan-15358.

24 Eileen Kane, *Russian Hajj, Empire and the Pilgrimage to Mecca*, Cornell University Press: Connecticut, 2015.

25 Ishaan Tharoor, "A Russian Ambassador was Murdered. The Apology Came in a Huge Diamond," *The Washington Post*, December 22, 2016. www.washingtonpost.com/news/worldviews/wp/2016/12/22/a-russian-ambassador-was-murdered-the-apology-came-in-the-shape-of-a-huge-diamond/?noredirect=on&utm_term=.5ab39ed0f0aa.

26 Orlando Figes, *The Crimean War,* chapter 1.

27 Ibid.

28 Ibid.

29 Ibid., chapter 2.

30 As cited in Orlando Figes, *The Crimean War,* Epilogue.

31 Sean McMeekin, *The Russian Origins of the First World War*, Harvard University Press, 2011.

32 Mark N. Katz, "Iran and Russia," Iran Primer, United States Institute of Peace, October 11, 2010 https://iranprimer.usip.org/resource/iran-and-russia.

33 Fritz Ermarth, "The Soviet Union and the third world: purpose in search of power," RAND Corporation, April 1969 https://apps.dtic.mil/dtic/tr/fulltext/u2/687024.pdf.

34 Peter Hopkirk, *Setting the East Ablaze: Lenin's Dream of an Empire in Asia*, John Murray; Reprint edition 2006.

35 Andrei Snesarev, translated and edited by Lester W. Grau and Michael Gress *Afghanistan: Preparing for the Bolshevik Incursion into Afghanistan and Attack on India, 1919–20* (Helion Studies in Military History).

2 The Soviet Union in the Middle East and the Afghanistan Intervention

1 Eileen Kane, *Russian Hajj*, pp. 157–9.

2 Robert O. Freedman, *Moscow and the Middle East, Soviet Policy since the Invasion of Afghanistan*, Cambridge University Press: Cambridge, 2009 edition, p. 15. See also James Phillips, "Moscow's Thriving Libyan Connection," The Heritage Foundation, June 26, 1984 https://www.heritage.org/middle-east/report/moscows-thriving-libyan-connection.

3 Speech of United States President Truman at a symbolic raising of the American flag in Berlin, Germany, July 21, 1945, available from: www.officialgazette.gov.ph/1945/07/21/speech-of-united-state-president-truman-at-a-symbolic-raising-of-the-american-flag-in-berlin-germany-july-21-1945/.

4 "Declarations of Cold War," US Department of Interior, www.nps.gov/articles/cworigins-declarationsofcw.htm. Page last updated October 20, 2020.

5 "February 9, 1946, Speech Delivered by Stalin at a Meeting of Voters of the Stalin Electoral District, Moscow," Wilson Center Archives, https://digitalarchive.wilsoncenter.org/document/116179.pdf?v=a831b5c6a9ff133d9da25b37c013d691.

6 Elizabeth Edwards Spalding, *The First Cold Warrior: Harry Truman, Containment, and the Remaking of Liberal Internationalism*, p. 33.

7 Martin Kramer, "Who Saved Israel in 1947?" Mosaic November 6, 2017 https://mosaicmagazine.com/essay/israel-zionism/2017/11/who-saved-israel-in-1947/.

8 Robert O. Freedman, *Moscow and the Middle East*, p. 15.

9 Ibid., p. 16.

10 Ibid., pp. 25–8.

11 Fritz Ermarth, "The Soviet Union and the Third World: Purpose in Search of Power," RAND Corporation, April 1969 https://apps.dtic.mil/dtic/tr/fulltext/u2/687024.pdf.

12 Rod Thornton, "Countering Prompt Global Strike: The Russian Military Presence in Syria and the Eastern Mediterranean and Its Strategic Deterrence Role," *Journal of Slavic Military Studies* 32, No. 1 (2019): pp. 1–24.

13 *Time*, "Russia: Power Play on the Oceans," February 23, 1968.

14 Marquis de Custine, *Letters from Russia*, translated by Robin Buss, Penguin Classics, p. 116.

15 Tim Weiner, *The Folly and the Glory: America, Russia, and Political Warfare 1945–2020*, Henry Holt and Company: New York, 2020 p. 57.

16 Ion Mihai Pacepa, "Russian Footprints," National Review Online, August 24, 2006, www.nationalreview.com/2006/08/russian-footprints-ion-mihai-pacepa/.

17 Craig R. Whitney, "Havel Says Predecessor Sent Libya Explosives," *The New York Times*, March 23, 1990, www.nytimes.com/1990/03/23/world/havel-says-his-predecessors-sent-libya-explosives.html?mtrref=undefined&gwh=E6E2F46F3B27A 95637687B2CD4B0F329&gwt=pay.

18 Robert O. Freedman, *Moscow and the Middle East*, p. 328.

19 Sam Dagher, *Assad or we Burn the Country. How One Family's Lust for Power Destroyed Syria*, Little, Brown and Company: New York, 2019, p. 40.

20 Raymond L. Garthoff, *Détente and Confrontation, American–Soviet Relations from Nixon to Reagan*, The Brookings Institution: Washington, DC, 1985, p. 914.

21 Artemy M. Kalinovsky, *A Long Goodbye: The Soviet Withdrawal from Afghanistan*, Harvard University Press, 2011.

22 Raymond L. Garthoff, *Détente and Confrontation*, p. 1018.

23 Ibid., p. 912.

24 James Phillips, "The Soviet Invasion of Afghanistan," January 9, 1980, The Heritage Foundation, www.heritage.org/europe/report/the-soviet-invasion-afghanistan.

25 Antony Austin, "Soviet says Afghans Asked for Help," *The New York Times*, December 29, 1979 www.nytimes.com/1979/12/29/archives/soviet-says-afghans-asked-for-its-help-charges-provocations-of.html.

26 Douglas MacEachin, "Predicting the Soviet Invasion of Afghanistan: The Intelligence Community's Record," Federation of American Scientists, May 2002. See https://fas.org/irp/cia/product/afghanistan/index.html.

27 Denis Kamenshchikov, "'Полная версия': вывод советских войск из Афганистана," Yeltsin Center, February 15, 2019. https://yeltsin.ru/news/polnaya-versiya-vyvod-sovetskih-vojsk-iz-afganistana/.

28 "The Brzezinski Interview with *Le Nouvel Observateur* (1998)," Translated from French by William Blum and David N. Gibbs. This translation was published in Gibbs, "Afghanistan: The Soviet Invasion in Retrospect," *International Politics* 37, No. 2, 2000, pp. 241–2. Available from University of Arizona https://dgibbs.faculty.arizona.edu/brzezinski_interview.

29 "Entry of Soviet Troops—Overthrow of President Amin," Keesing's Record of World Events (formerly Keesing's Contemporary Archives), Vol. 26, May, 1980 Afghanistan,

p. 30229. Available from: http://web.stanford.edu/group/tomzgroup/pmwiki/
uploads/2053-1980-05-KS-a-EYJ.pdf.

30 Raymond L. Garthoff, *Détente and Confrontation*, p. 914.

31 Christopher Andrew and Vasili Mitrokhin, *The Sword and the Shield* (New York, NY:
Basic Books, 1999).

32 "Entry of Soviet Troops – Overthrow of President Amin," Keesing's Record of World
Events (formerly Keesing's Contemporary Archives), Volume 26, May, 1980
Afghanistan, Page 30229. Available from: http://web.stanford.edu/group/tomzgroup/
pmwiki/uploads/2053-1980-05-KS-a-EYJ.pdf

33 Alexey *Vasiliev, Russia's Middle East Policy: From Lenin to Putin*," Routledge: Oxford,
2018, p. 213.

34 Tim Weiner, "History to Trump: CIA was aiding Afghan rebels before the Soviets
invaded in '79," The Washington Post, January 7, 2019. See www.washingtonpost.
com/outlook/2019/01/07/history-trump-cia-was-arming-afghan-rebels-before-
soviets-invaded/.

35 As quoted in "Entry of Soviet Troops—Overthrow of President Amin," p. 30229.

36 James Phillips, "The Soviet Invasion of Afghanistan."

37 Joseph J. Collins, "Afghanistan the Empire Strikes Out," *Parameters*, Journal of the
US Army War College, 1982.

38 "Population Afghanistan 1979," CountryEconomy.com, Accessed January 5, 2019,
https://countryeconomy.com/demography/population/afghanistan?year=1979.

39 Author email exchanges with Akhmad Khalid Majidyar, December 2019.

40 "US Sanctions over Soviet Invasion of Afghanistan. Soviet, Polish, and
Romanian Reactions," CIA Document approved for release, November 2, 2005,
April 11, 1980, www.cia.gov/library/readingroom/docs/CIA-
RDP81B00401R000600200023-2.pdf.

41 "The Soviet Invasion of Afghanistan and the US Response, 1978–1980," US
Department of State, Office of the Historian, https://history.state.gov/
milestones/1977-1980/soviet-invasion-afghanistan, pp. 2–4.

42 Douglas MacEachin, "Predicting the Soviet Invasion of Afghanistan: The Intelligence
Community's Record," Federation of American Scientists, May 2002, https://fas.org/
irp/cia/product/afghanistan/index.html.

43 See, for example, Don Oberdorfer, "Making Sense of a Soviet Coup," *The Washington
Post*, January 2, 1980 www.washingtonpost.com/archive/politics/1980/01/02/
the-making-of-a-soviet-coup/175c9707-dddb-4052-87be-9bf4f048bf56/.

44 "The Costs of Soviet Involvement in Afghanistan," CIA Special Collections
Release as Sanitized, 2000 www.cia.gov/library/readingroom/docs/
DOC_0000499320.pdf.

45 Wayne P. Limberg, "Soviet Military Support for Third-World Marxist Regimes," in
Mark N. Katz, ed, *The USSR and Marxist Revolutions in the Third World*, Cambridge
University Press: New York, 1990, p. 64.

46 "The Validity of Soviet Economic Statistics," Approved for Release, CIA Historical Review program, September 18, 1995. www.cia.gov/library/center-for-the-study-of-intelligence/kent-csi/vol4no3/html/v04i3a01p_0001.htm.

47 Народное хозяйство СССР в 1989 г.: Статистический ИЗО ежегодник / Госкомстат СССР.—М.: Финансы и статистика, 1990. 766c. c.11 (The National Economy of the USSR in 1989: Statistical Yearbook / Goskomstat of the USSR.— Ministry of : Finance and Statistics, p. 11), http://istmat.info/files/uploads/17055/narhoz_sssr_1989_ekonomicheskie_pokazateli.pdf. Entire publication available from: http://istmat.info/node/17055.

48 Andrew Rosenthal, "Gorbachev Announces First Withdrawal from Afghanistan," Reuters, July 28, 1986 www.apnews.com/ac8961700e64e98fcb764c6c1c8ca049 www.apnews.com/ac8961700e64e98fcb764c6c1c8ca049.

49 Review & Outlook (Editorial): "Stung in Afghanistan" (1987, December 8), *Wall Street Journal*, p. 1. Retrieved from http://search.proquest.com/docview/398040690/.

50 "The Soviet Presence in Afghanistan: Implications for the Regional Powers and the United States," National Intelligence Estimate, Director of Central Intelligence, information available as of March 26, 1986 was used to compile the estimate, approved for release December 16, 2010, available from www.cia.gov/library/readingroom/docs/DOC_0005445963.pdf p. 16.

51 Leon Aron, "Everything You Think You Know About the Collapse of the Soviet Union Is Wrong. and Why it Matters Today in a New Age of Revolution," *Foreign Policy*, June 20, 2011, https://foreignpolicy.com/2011/06/20/everything-you-think-you-know-about-the-collapse-of-the-soviet-union-is-wrong/

52 Artemy M. Kalinovsky, *A Long Goodbye*, p. 2.

53 Richard M Weintraub, "Agreement on Afghanistan Signed in Geneva," *The Washington Post*, April 15, 1988 www.washingtonpost.com/archive/politics/1988/04/15/agreement-on-afghanistan-signed-in-geneva/8657921a-b592-4c9c-a302-623c62b0e8f3/?utm_term=.ddad027c1234. Rosanne Klass, "Afghanistan: The Accords" *Foreign Affairs*, Summer 1988, www.foreignaffairs.com/articles/asia/1988-06-01/afghanistan-accords.

54 Sarah E. Mendelson, "Internal Battles and External Wars: Politics, Learning, and the Soviet Withdrawal from Afghanistan," 45 World Pol. 327 (1993).

3 Russia in the 1990s

1 Graham E. Fuller, "Moscow and the Gulf War," *Foreign Affairs*, Summer 1991, www.foreignaffairs.com/articles/russia-fsu/1991-06-01/moscow-and-gulf-war.

2 Ibid.

3   Vladimir Shlapentokh and Anna Arutunyanm, *Freedom, Repression, and Private Property in Russia*, Cambridge University Press, 2013, pp. 128–9; "The Making of a Neo-KGB State," *The Economist*, August 23, 2007 www.economist.com/briefing/2007/08/23/the-making-of-a-neo-kgb-state.

4   Dennis Ross, *The Missing Peace: The Inside Story of the Fight for Middle East Peace*, Farrar, Straus and Giroux; First edition, June 2005, p. 65.

5   Ibid., pp. 80–1.

6   "Developments Related to the Middle East Peace Process," Issue 2, April–September 1994, United Nations, New York, October 1994 www.un.org/unispal/document/auto-insert-193676/.

7   Sergei Plokhy, *The Last Empire: The Final Days of the Soviet Union*, p. 239.

8   Interfax, September 23, 1997, TASS, September 24, 1997.

9   Rodric Braithwaite, *Afgantsy: The Russians in Afghanistan 1979–1989*.

10 Artemy M. Kalinovsky, *A Long Goodbye*, pp. 200–5.

11 "Как Ельцин повлиял на судьбу Афганистана, Sputnik, February 12, 2019 https://ru.sputnik.kz/afghan/20190212/9262765/afganistan-eltsin-klincevich.html "Франц Клинцевич: американцы застряли в Афганистане всерьёз и надолго," Parliamentskaya Gazeta, February 15, 2019, www.pnp.ru/top/site/franc-klincevich-amerikancy-zastryali-v-afganistane-vseryoz-i-nadolgo.html.

12 "Асад не дал Западу и наркоторговцам превратить Сирию в Афганистан," May 4, 2020, https://riafan.ru/1273730-asad-ne-dal-zapadu-i-narkotorgovcam-prevratit-siriyu-v-afganistan, "США потворствуют наращиванию производства наркотиков в Афганистане," November 12, 2014 https://iz.ru/news/579340. "'Пропагандистский приём': как США способствуют росту производства наркотиков в Афганистане," RT, August 4, 2018 https://russian.rt.com/world/article/542230-ssha-afganistan-narkotiki-usaid, "Афганский наркотрафик без границ," April 4, 2018 https://topwar.ru/139375-afganskiy-narkotrafik-bez-granic.html.

13 "The Russians rethink democracy," Times Mirror Center for the People and the Press, Pew Research Center, January 27, 1993, www.pewresearch.org/wp-content/uploads/sites/4/legacy-pdf/the-Russians-Rethink-Democracy-1.27.93.pdf.

14 Reuters, *Excerpts from Yeltsin's Speech: "There Will Be No More Lies,"* June 18, 1992, *The New York Times*, www.nytimes.com/1992/06/18/world/summit-in-washington-excerpts-from-yeltsin-s-speech-there-will-be-no-more-lies.html.

15 "For Many Russians, Yeltsin Was No Hero," NPR interview with Lilia Shevtsova, April 24, 2007 www.npr.org/templates/story/story.php?storyId=9794098.

16 Robert O. Freedman, "Russia in the Middle East under Yeltsin," in The Middle East and the Peace Process: The Impact of the Oslo Accords, ed. Robert O. Freedman (Gainesville: University Press of Florida, 1998), p. 391.

17 Robert O. Freedman, "Russian Policy toward the Middle East under Yeltsin and Putin," Jerusalem Letter/Viewpoints 461 (Jerusalem Center for Public Affairs, September 2, 2001), www.jcpa.org/jl/vp461.htm.

18 Robert Olson, "Turkish and Russian foreign policies, 1991–1997: the Kurdish and Chechnya questions," March 20, 2007 pp. 209–27 https://doi.org/10.1080/13602009808716407.

19 Ibid.

20 Soli Özel and Gökçe Uçar, *The Economics of Turkey–Russia Relations*, Centre for Economic and Foreign Policy Studies (EDAM) July 2019 http://edam.org.tr/wp-content/uploads/2019/07/The-Economics-of-Turkey-Russia-Relations_compressed.pdf.

21 In later years, other sources cited higher figures.

22 Meeting on April 4, 1993, Pan Pacific Hotel, Vancouver, Canada, National Security Council and NSC Records Management System, "Declassified Documents Concerning Russian President Boris Yeltsin," *Clinton Digital Library*, https://clinton.presidentiallibraries.us/items/show/57568.

23 Andrei Kozyrev, *The Firebird: The Elusive Fate of Russian Democracy* (Russian and East European Studies) University of Pittsburgh Press; First edition (September 24, 2019), p. 250.

24 Robert O. Freedman, "Russia in the Middle East under Yeltsin."

25 James Brooke, "Russia Helped Build Syria's Chemical Weapons," *Moscow Times*, September 11, 2013, www.themoscowtimes.com/opinion/ar-ticle/russia-helped-build-syrias-chemical-weapons/485870.html.

26 Lilia Shevtsova, *Yeltsin's Russia, Myths and Reality*, Carnegie Endowment for International Peace: Washington, DC, 1999, pp. 262–6.

27 Evgeniy Primakov, "International Relations on the Eve of the 21st Century: Problems and Prospects," in Andrei Melville and Tatiana Shakleina (eds.) *Russian Foreign Policy in Transition, Concepts and Realities. International Affairs*, 1996 (10), p. 207.

28 Valeriya Sycheva, Sergei Zhikhar, "В Индии противников сближения с Россией нет," Kommersant April 2, 1996 www.kommersant.ru/doc/130009.

29 Boris Volkhonsky, "Пекин подвел Примакова," December 24, 1998, p. 4 www.kommersant.ru/doc/211101.

30 Evgeniy Primakov, *Russia and the Arabs: Behind the Scenes in the Middle East from the Cold War to the Present*, Basic Books: New York, 2009, p. 384.

31 National Security Council and NSC Records Management System, "Declassified Documents Concerning Russian President Boris Yeltsin," *Clinton Digital Library*, https://clinton.presidentiallibraries.us/items/show/57568. James Goldgeier, "Bill and Boris: A Window Into a Most Important Post-Cold War Relationship," Texas National Security Review, August 2018, https://tnsr.org/2018/08/bill-and-boris-a-window-into-a-most-important-post-cold-war-relationship/.

32 POTUS-Yeltsin One-on-One, April 21, 1996, Kremlin, Moscow, National Security Council and NSC Records Management System, "Declassified Documents Concerning Russian President Boris Yeltsin," *Clinton Digital Library*, https://clinton.presidentiallibraries.us/items/show/57568.

33 As quoted in Helena Belopolsky, "Russia and Saddam's Iraq: The Road to Nowhere," In *Russia and the Challengers*. Palgrave Macmillan-St Antony's Series, London, 2009.

34 Helena Belopolsky, "Russia and Saddam's Iraq: The Road to Nowhere."

35 Andrei Tikhomirov, *Президентство Бориса Ельцина: 1991–1999 гг. Хроника событий*, p. 323.

36 "Долг Ирака перед кредиторами Парижского клуба составил 20 миллиардов долларов," Rosbalt, July 11, 2003. www.rosbalt.ru/main/2003/07/11/107319.html, Oliver Burkeman, "Russia Spied for Saddam in war—Pentagon Report," *The Guardian*, March 24, 2006, www.theguardian.com/world/2006/mar/25/usa. russia.

37 "Кому Россия прощала долги," Kommerstant, December 10, 2013 www. kommersant.ru/doc/2364889.

38 Helena Belopolsky, "Russia and Saddam's Iraq: The Road to Nowhere," in *Russia and the Challengers*, Palgrave Macmillan-St Antony's Series, London, 2009, p. 139.

39 Daniel Williams, "Yeltsin says Bombing Iraq Might Bring 'World War,'" *The Washington Post*, February 5, 1998 www.washingtonpost.com/archive/politics/1998/02/05/yeltsin-says-bombing-iraq-might-bring-world-war/0807cf31-417e-44e8-882e-bbc7c7f65192/.

40 As quoted in Helena Belopolsky, "Russia and Saddam's Iraq: The Road to Nowhere."

41 "Russia maintains breakthrough reached with Iraq," Correspondent Peter Arnett and Reuters contributed to this report. CNN, February 3, 1998 www.cnn.com/WORLD/9802/03/un.iraq.on/index.html.

42 Bruce W. Nelan, "How the Attack on Iraq is Planned. The Bombs will Hit Saddam Hard, but they Probably Won't Kill Him or End his Drive for Bioweapons," CNN, February 23, 1998. www.cnn.com/ALLPOLITICS/1998/02/16/time/nelan.html.

43 Ibid.

44 Jim Nichol, *Kosovo Conflict: Russian Responses and Implications for the United States, Congressional Research Service*, Report for Congress, updated June 2, 1999, www.everycrsreport.com/files/19990602_RL30130_c7eb5305009da4ef114a673cfa 123cb658cc0b06.pdf.

4 Putin Returns Russia to the Middle East

1 Vladimir Kara-Murza, "Putin's Dark Cult of the Secret Police," *The Washington Post*, December 28, 2017 www.washingtonpost.com/news/democracy-post/wp/2017/12/28/putins-dark-cult-of-the-secret-police/?utm_term=.aefaecfe2873.

2 "The Making of a Neo-KGB State," *The Economist*.

3 A number of prominent scholars covered these events in great detail. See for example John B. Dunlop (2014). *The Moscow Bombings of September 1999 :*

Examinations of Russian Terrorist Attacks at the Onset of Vladimir Putin's Rule (Second, revised and expanded edition). Stuttgart: Ibidem-Verlag.

4   Full quote: Мы будем преследовать террористов везде. В аэропорту—в аэропорту. Значит, вы уж меня извините, в туалете поймаем, мы и в сортире их замочим, в конце концов. Всё, вопрос закрыт окончательно Quote is available from: Путин- Мочить в сортире !! penekvideo, Published on June 6, 2011. www. youtube.com/watch?v=KqBu0UK8bAg.

5   Arkady Ostrovsky, *The Invention of Russia: From Gorbachev's Freedom to Putin's War.* New York: Viking, 2016, p. 6.

6   PutinCon conference, organized by the Human Rights Foundation, chaired by Garry Kasparov, New York, NY, March 2017. Babchenko's remarks available from: www.youtube.com/watch?v=C04HkDhOr14 (Russian), www.youtube.com/ watch?v=nfw1SHiEQfI (English).

7   Karen Dawisha, *Putin's Kleptocracy. Who Owns Russia?* Simon & Schuster, New York, 2014, p. 220.

8   David Satter, *The Less You Know, the Better You Sleep: Russia's Road to Terror and Dictatorship under Yeltsin and Putin,* Yale University Press, 2016. John B. Dunlop, *The Moscow Bombings of September 1999 : Examinations of Russian Terrorist Attacks at the Onset of Vladimir Putin's Rule* (Second, revised and expanded edition). Stuttgart: Ibidem-Verlag. 2014.

9   Lester Grau and Charles Bartles, "Lessons Learned from the Battles of Grozny," chapter in *Russia's War in Syria: Assessing Russian Military Capabilities and Lessons Learned,* Edited by Robert E. Hamilton, Chris Miller, and Aaron Stein, Foreign Policy Research Initiative, September 2020, pp. 67–89.

10 Ibid.

11 S. I. Pasichnik, A.V. Gavrdt, and S.A. Sychev "Перспективы развития способов боевых действий общевойсковых формирований тактического звена" in the January 2020 *Вестник Академии Военных Наук*. http://www.avnrf.ru/index.php/ zhurnal-qvoennyj-vestnikq/arkhiv-nomerov/1228-vkstnik-avn-1-2020

12 Joint Publication of the International Helsinki Federation for Human Rights (IHF), International Federation for Human Rights (FIDH), Norwegian Helsinki Committee, Center "Demos," Human Rights Center "Memorial," Joint Publication of the International Helsinki Federation for Human Rights (IHF), International Federation for Human Rights (FIDH), Norwegian Helsinki Committee, Center "Demos," Human Rights Center "Memorial" *In a Climate of Fear "Political Process" and Parliamentary Elections in Chechnya,* January 2006. www.refworld.org/pdfid/46963aff0.pdf?__cf_chl_ jschl_tk__=0ddf62bf1d64523d875d8d817ce1d060a022b158-1581019072-0- AVMjEzdxoRbFyAgR-LD0n2zB12GitMO-9FVVPECAy73VzleODbM5yUvTxf7O54f ZJVb-TlFaDHEJqvH1d_HJK9gijdiNSz4CVnoIr1LRdF4uu4BkaDS4xvgX0tuTm 9iLTWOuDTtYI_fkaGGB-wI_ltMO15SwcYAbc2nL3DwNvylvcM9I0pPh5bwtNu0nr2 oCYOoijc5Rnjg9OQuLukMHN0CUD926POlNcySgMAX4IlsQ5ehEXD5vtTXO4RSi PZnomFbY8236Xpd01Srs5UY-bbMlN4_DcICTrhj-oglC5t2K p. 16.

13 Ibid, p. 16.

14 Ibid.

15 J. Y., "Chechnya and the Bombs of Boston," *The Economist*, April 20, 2013 www. economist.com/eastern-approaches/2013/04/20/chechnya-and-the-bombs-in-boston.

16 Stephen Blank, "Russia's Unending Quest for Security," Chapter 10 in Mark Galeotti, *The Politics of Security in Modern Russia* (Post-Soviet Politics). Taylor and Francis. Kindle Edition, p. 171.

17 Vladimir Putin, "Россия на рубеже тысячелетий," Nezavisimaya Gazeta, December 30, 1999 www.ng.ru/politics/1999-12-30/4_millenium.html.

18 Lester W. Grau and Charles K Bartles, The Russian Way of War, p. 29, www.gfsis.org/maps/view/russian-military-forces. Also conversation with Lester W. Grau, May 11, 2020.

19 Vladimir Putin, Annual Address to the Federal Assembly of the Russian Federation April 25, 2005, The Kremlin, Moscow. Video available from: www.youtube.com/watch?v=nTvswwU5Eco.

20 Vladimir Putin, with Nataliya Gevorkyan, Natalya Timakova, and Andrei Kolesnikov, translated by Catherine A. Fitzpatrick, *First Person: An Astonishingly Frank Self Portrait by Russia's President*, New York: Public Affairs, 2000, p. 140.

21 "Beslan School Siege Fast Facts," CNN, August 26, 2018 www.cnn.com/2013/09/09/world/europe/beslan-school-siege-fast-facts/.

22 Ilyas Akhmadov and Miriam Lanskoy (2010). *The Chechen Struggle: Independence Won and Lost* (1st ed.). New York: Palgrave Macmillan, p. 225.

23 Adrian Blomfield, "Mothers of Beslan Condemn 'Cover-up,'" *Telegraph*, December 29, 2005. www.telegraph.co.uk/news/worldnews/europe/russia/1506559/Mothers-of-Beslan-condemn-cover-up.html. "Decade after Beslan, Questions Remain Unanswered," *Moscow Times*, August 31, 2014 https://themoscowtimes.com/articles/decade-after-beslan-questions-remain-unanswered-38895.

24 "Putin Tells the Russians, 'We Shall be Stronger,'" September 5, 2004, *The New York Times*, www.nytimes.com/2004/09/05/world/europe/putin-tells-the-russians-we-shall-be-stronger.html?mtrref=www.google.com&mtrref=www.nytimes.com&gwh=8FBD8F7B06A7E25979D83558443D1E9B&gwt=pay.

25 "Address by President Vladimir Putin," September 4, 2004, http://archive. kremlin.ru/eng/text/speeches/2004/09/04/1958_type82912_76332.shtml.

26 Janet Reitman, "Putin Clamps Down: a Chilling Report from Moscow," *The Rolling Stone*, April 30, 2014. www.rollingstone.com/politics/politics-news/putin-clamps-down-a-chilling-report-from-moscow-96577/.

27 Vladimir Putin, "Speech and the Following Discussion at the Munich Conference on Security Policy," Kremli.ru February 10, 2007, http://en.kremlin.ru/events/president/transcripts/24034.

28 Stephen Blank, "Russia's Unending Quest for Security," chapter in Mark Galeotti. *The Politics of Security in Modern Russia (Post-Soviet Politics)*. Taylor and Francis. Kindle Edition.

29 Mark Galeotti. *The Politics of Security in Modern Russia (Post-Soviet Politics)* (p. 172). Taylor and Francis. Kindle Edition.

30 Mark Galeotti. *The Politics of Security in Modern Russia (Post-Soviet Politics)* (p. 173).

31 "Putin Rips 'Medieval Crusade' in Libya," *Moscow Times*, March 22, 2011, www. themoscowtimes.com/news/article/putin-rips-medieval-crusade-in-libya/433447. html; "Security Council Approves 'No-Fly Zone' over Libya, Authorizing 'All Necessary Measures' to Protect Civilians, by Vote of 10 in Favour with 5 Abstentions," meetings coverage, March 17, 2011, www.un.org/press/en/2011/ sc10200.doc.htm; UN Security Council Resolution 1973, March 17, 2011, www.un. org/en/ga/ search/view_doc.asp?symbol=S/RES/1973%20(2011).

32 Fiona Hill and Cliff Gaddy, *Mr. Putin Operative in the Kremlin,* Washington, DC: Brookings Institution Press, Introduction, p. 19.

33 "Putin: We Won Russian Election Honestly and Fairly—Video," *The Guardian*, March 5, 2012 www.theguardian.com/world/video/2012/mar/05/putin-we-won-russian-election-video.

34 Leon Aron, "Why Putin says Russia is Exceptional," *The Wall Street Journal*, May 30, 2014, www.wsj.com/articles/why-putin-says-russia-is-exceptional-1401473667.

35 Address by President of the Russian Federation, Kremlin.ru, March 18, 2014, http:// en.kremlin.ru/events/president/news/20603.

36 Robert O. Freedman, "Russian Policy toward the Middle East under Yeltsin and Putin," Jerusalem Letter/Viewpoints 461 (Jerusalem Center for Public Affairs, September 2, 2001), www.jcpa.org/jl/vp461.htm.

37 "Foreign Policy Concept of the Russian Federation," January 10, 2000, https://fas.org/ nuke/guide/russia/doctrine/econcept.htm.

38 Foreign Policy Concept of the Russian Federation, approved by President of the Russian Federation Vladimir Putin on November 30, 2016, December 2016, www. mid.ru/en/foreign_policy/official_documents/-/asset_publisher/CptICkB6BZ29/ content/id/2542248.

39 Evgeniy Primakov, *Russia and the Arabs, Behind the Scenes in the Middle East from the Cold War to the Present,* Basic Books: New York, 2009, p. 358.

40 Evgeniy Primakov, *Russia and the Arabs,* pp. 359–60.

41 "Exclusive Interview with Russia's Foreign Minister Igor Ivanov by RIA Novosti Political Analyst Dmitry Kosyrev," Ministry of Foreign Affairs of the Russian Federation, December 27, 2002, http://washin.st/1TmEpy9.

42 Ibid.

43 Alexander Yakovenko, "Without Russia—Nowhither," Ministry of Foreign Affairs of the Russian Federation, December 31, 2003, http://archive.mid. ru//bdomp/

brp_4.nsf/e78a48070f128a7b43256999005bcbb3/de9b66af1 0c96117c3256e0d00413 008!OpenDocument, originally published in the official *Kremlin Rossiyskaya Gazeta.*

44 Alexey Malashenko, Russia and the Arab Spring (Moscow: Carnegie Moscow Center, 2013), p. 7, http://carnegieendowment.org/files/russia_arab_ spring2013.pdf.

45 Putin increasingly relied on this rhetoric after assuming a third presidential term in 2012, following December 2011 anti-government protests that were the largest in Russia's post-Soviet history.

46 Wade Boese, "US Halts Arms Sales to Zimbabwe, Lifts Ban on Armenia, Azerbaijan," Arms Control Association, May 2002.

47 "Senior US diplomat says arms sales to Azerbaijan not for use against Armenia," ARMENPRESS Armenian News Agency June 13, 2014.

48 Lynn Berry, "Russia Defends Selling Arms to both Azerbaijan and Armenia," Associated Press, April 9, 2016.

49 President of Russia (2012), "Meeting of the Commission for Military Technology Cooperation with Foreign States," 2 July 2012, http://en.kremlin.ru/events/president/news/15865.

50 "Rogozin: Russia Ranks Second in the World on Export Supply of Military Goods," Daily News Light, December 11, 2013, http://dailynewslight. ru/?u= 11122013868.

51 Robert O. Freedman, (2018). "From Khrushchev and Brezhnev to Putin: Has Moscow's Policy in the Middle East Come Full Circle?" *Contemporary Review of the Middle East.* 5. 234779891876219. 10.1177/2347798918762197.

52 Mark N. Katz, "Moscow and the Middle East: Repeat Performance?" Russia in Global Affairs, October 7, 2012, http://eng.globalaffairs.ru/number/Moscow-and-the-Middle-East-Repeat-Performance-15690.

53 "Сергей Караганов: Русская отчаянность оседлала волну истории," Совет по внешней и оборонной политике December 5, 2017 http://svop.ru/main/25563/.

54 Vladimir Mukhin, "Станет ли Сирия вторым Афганистаном для России" Nezavisimaya Gazeta, October 17, 2019 www.ng.ru/politics/2019-10-17/1_7705_ syria.html.

55 "Черногория отказала России в размещении военной базы в Баре," Balkan Pro ru, December 18, 2013 https://balkanpro.ru/news/montenegro/11664/. "Военная база на Кипре,"https://kipros.ru/voennaia-baza-na-kipre.php.

5 The Russia-Iran-Syria Triangle

1 Lionel Beehner, "Russia–Iran Arms Trade," Council on Foreign Relations, November 1, 2006 www.cfr.org/backgrounder/russia-iran-arms-trade.

2   Mark N. Katz, "Russia and Iran," The Iran Primer, United States Institute of Peace, originally published in 2010, and is updated as of August 2015. https://iranprimer. usip.org/resource/iran-and-russia.

3   "Gore's Secret Pact," *The Wall Street Journal*, October 1, 2000 www.wsj.com/articles/ SB971819748452949326.

4   John M. Broder, "Despite a Secret Pact by Gore, Russian Arms Sales to Iran Go On," October 13, 2000, *The New York Times*, www.nytimes.com/2000/10/13/world/ despite-a-secret-pact-by-gore-in-95-russian-arms-sales-to-iran-go-on.html. Wade Boese, "Congress Levies Accusations on Gore–Chernomyrdin Deal," Arms Control Association, November 2000, www.armscontrol.org/taxonomy/term/15/about/ about/kingston_reif?page=56.

5   Mark N. Katz, "Russia and Iran," The Iran Primer, United States Institute of Peace, originally published in 2010, and is updated as of August 2015, https://iranprimer. usip.org/resource/iran-and-russia.

6   Georgiy Mirsky, "Iranian Atom, Arab Blood," *Echo Moskvy*, April 5, 2015, https:// echo.msk.ru/blog/georgy_mirsky/1524898-echo/.

7   Ariel Cohen and James A. Phillips, "Countering Russian–Iranian Military Cooperation," Backgrounder 1425 on Russia (Heritage Foundation, April 5, 2001), www.heritage.org/research/reports/2001/04/counteringrussian-iranian-military-cooperation.

8   Alla Kassianova, "Russian Weapons Sales to Iran Why They Are Unlikely to Stop," December 2006; PONARS Policy Memo No. 427 www.ponarseurasia.org/sites/ default/files/policy-memos-pdf/pm_0427.pdf.

9   Nader Habibi, "The Cost of Economic Sanctions on Major Exporters to Iran," Payvand, May 5, 2006, www.payvand.com/news/06/may/1046.html.

10 "Tehran, Moscow talk trade," *Tehran Times*, February 4, 2010 www.tehrantimes.com/ news/213679/Tehran-Moscow-talk-trade.

11 "Iran Exports to Russia Grow 36%," *Financial Tribune*, February 16, 2019 https:// financialtribune.com/articles/domestic-economy/96712/iran-exports-to-russia-grow-36.

12 Victor Mizin, "The Russian View," in Richard Speier, Rober Gallucci, Robbie Sabel, Viktor Mizin, *Iran–Russia Missile Cooperation*, Carnegie Endowment for International Peace, Proliferation Brief, Vol. 3, No. 22, July 25, 2000, pp. 8–9 http:// carnegieendowment.org/files/Repairing_12.pdf.

13 As quoted in Stephen Blank, "Resets, Russia, and Iranian Proliferation," *Mediterranean Quarterly* 23, No. 1 (Winter 2012), pp. 14–38.

14 "'Don't Exaggerate Case against Iran'—Russia," RT, January 11, 2012, www.rt.com/ politics/iran-russia-us-israel-missile-nuclear-535/.

15 "С.Лавров: Санкции превратят Иран во вторую КНДР," RBC, May 18, 2006 www.rbc.ru/politics/18/05/2006/5703bc259a7947afa08c9f5d.

16 Michael Shmulovich, "Russia: US Sanctions on Syria, Iran are Hurting our Businesses," *Times of Israel*, September 8, 2012 www.timesofisrael.com/russia-us-sanctions-in-syria-iran-are-hurting-our-businesses/.

17 "Владимир Путин дал интервью Би-би-си," BBC, June 22, 2003 http://news.bbc.co.uk/hi/russian/russia/newsid_3009000/3009738.stm#6.

18 "Лавров: РФ поддерживает МАГАТЭ в прояснении иранской ядерной программы," April 15, 2009, https://ria.ru/20090415/168225636.html.

19 Viktor Vladimiro, "Иран: страна-террорист или партнер по борьбе с терроризмом?," Voice of America, February 6, 2017 www.golos-ameriki.ru/a/vv-us-iran-russia-relations/3708118.html.

20 "Ахмадинеджад одобрил 'план Лаврова' по иранской ядерной программе," Lenta.ru, August 17, 2011, https://lenta.ru/news/2011/08/17/situation/.

21 "Лавров: иранский вопрос нельзя решить силой," Moscow State Institute of International Relations (MGIMO), September 2, 2010 https://mgimo.ru/about/news/smi/162475/.

22 *Партнерство России и Ирана: текущее состояние и перспективы развития*, Russian International Affairs Council (RIAC) and The Institute for Iran-Eurasia Studies (IRAS), p. 151 https://russiancouncil.ru/projects/bilaterial/russia-iran/.

23 Bulent Aras, Fatih Ozbay, "Dances with Wolves, Russia, Iran and the Nuclear Issues," *Middle East Policy*, Vol. XIII, No. 4, Winter 2006.

24 As quoted in Stephen Blank, "Resets, Russia, and Iranian Proliferation," *Mediterranean Quarterly* 23, No. 1 (Winter 2012), pp. 14–38.

25 Jean-Christophe Peuch, "Russia: Moscow Confirms Missile-Systems Deal with Iran," RFE/RL, February 10, 2006 www.rferl.org/a/1065656.html.

26 Richard F. Grimmett, *Conventional Arms Transfers to Developing Nations, 1998–2005*, Congressional Research Service, October 23, 2006 https://fas.org/sgp/crs/weapons/RL33696.pdf; Richard F. Grimmett, *Conventional Arms Transfers to Developing Nations, 2001–2008*, September 4, 2009, https://fas.org/sgp/crs/weapons/R40796.pdf.

27 Lionel Beehner, "Russia–Iran Arms Trade," Council on Foreign Relations, November 1, 2006 www.cfr.org/backgrounder/russia-iran-arms-trade.

28 Federal Register /Vol. 71, No. 150/Friday, August 4, 2006/Notices www.govinfo.gov/content/pkg/FR-2006-08-04/pdf/E6-12641.pdf.

29 "US slaps 'WMD' sanctions on firms," BBC, August 4, 2006 http://news.bbc.co.uk/2/hi/middle_east/5247350.stm.

30 Ibid.

31 Ibid.

32 "Timeline of Nuclear Diplomacy with Iran," Arms Control Association, updated July 2019 www.armscontrol.org/factsheet/Timeline-of-Nuclear-Diplomacy-With-Iran.

33 Robert Tait, Mark Tran, and agencies, "Putin Warns US against Military Action on Iran," *The Guardian*, October 16, 2007, www.theguardian.com/world/2007/oct/16/

russia.iran; Nazila Fathi and C. J. Chivers, "In Iran, Putin Warns against Military Action," *The New York Times*, October 17, 2007, www.nytimes.com/2007/10/17/world/middleeast/17iran.html?hp.

34 Talal Nizameddin, *Putin's New Order in the Middle East* (London: C. Hurst & Co., 2013), p. 266.

35 Peter Baker and David Sanger, "US Makes Concessions to Russia for Iran Sanctions," May 21 2010, *The New York Times*, www.nytimes.com/2010/05/22/world/22sanctions.html.

36 Ibid.

37 Визит членов "Хезболлы" в Россию окружен завесой тайны," BBC, October 20, 2011 www.bbc.com/russian/international/2011/10/111020_hezbollah_moscow_talks.

38 "Putin lashes out at Clinton over protests," Euronews, December 8, 2011, www.youtube.com/watch?v=TxmUFTTF9MQ.

39 "Восточной Европе, в Центральной Европе—масса фактов, когда американское посольство буквально руководит процессами, в том числе действиями оппозиции".

40 "Лавров заявил, что США в некоторых странах руководят оппозицией," RIA Novosti, August 11 2017, https://ria.ru/20170811/1500209550.html.

41 Nikolai Bobkin, "Сирийский конфликт: Иран—союзник России Syrian Conflict: Iran—Russia's Ally," Mir-politika, January 4, 2013, http://mir-politika.ru/2971-siriiskiy-konflikt-iran-soyuznik-rossii.html.

42 Russia and Iran also shared a concern about the resurgence of the Taliban in Afghanistan following President Obama's plans to draw down US troops by 2014. Ironically, Putin wanted the US to remain in Afghanistan more than the US wanted to—albeit on Putin's terms. Russia and Iran were impacted by narcotrafficking coming out of Afghanistan and viewed the Taliban, which is traditionally both anti-Shia and anti-Russian, as a potential enemy.

43 Oren Dorell, "Canceled Syria Talks May Get New Start in Moscow," *USA Today*, November 7, 2013 www.usatoday.com/story/news/world/2013/11/07/syria-peace-talks-chemical-weapons/3464091/.

44 "Иран просится в Евразийский союз, но его созданию 'мешают прозападные бюрократии России и Казахстана,'" Nakanune.ru. March 20, 2013 www.nakanune.ru/articles/17576.

45 Sean McMeekin, *The Russian Origins of the First World War*, Cambridge, Mass.: Belknap Press of Harvard University Press, 2011.

46 Yuri Roks, "Армения свяжет Иран с ЕАЭС," Nezavisimaya Gazeta, December 21, 2016, www.ng.ru/cis/2016-12-21/7_6890_armenia.html.

47 "ЕАЭС и Иран подписали временное соглашение о зоне свободной торговли," RIA Novosti May 17, 2018 https://ria.ru/20180517/1520730534.html.

48 Dr. Ricardo Giucci, Anne Mdinaradze, "The Eurasian Economic Union. Analysis from a trade policy perspective," Financed by the Federal Ministry for Economic Affairs and Energy—Second version: 8 September 2017 p.6 https://berlin-economics.com/wp-content/uploads/Eurasian-Economic-Union-trade-policy-perspective.pdf.

49 Bozorgmehr Sharafedin, "Iran Leader Hosts Putin, Says US Policies Threaten Tehran, Moscow," Reuters, November 23, 2015 www.reuters.com/article/us-mideast-crisis-iran-russia-idUSKBN0TC1M520151123.

50 "Putin in Tehran to Discuss Syria, Boost Ties," The Iran Primer, United States Institute of Peace, November 23, 2015 https://iranprimer.usip.org/blog/2015/nov/23/putin-tehran-discuss-syria-boost-ties.

51 "Заявление президента России Владимира Путина по завершении переговоров по ядерной программе Ирана," Kremlin.ru, July 14, 2015 http://kremlin.ru/events/president/news/49957.

52 Official twitter-account of the Ministry of Foreign Affairs of Russia, July 14, 2015, https://twitter.com/mfa_russia/status/620906964080422912.

53 Nikolai Bobkin, "Россия—Иран: альтернативы Асаду в Сирии сегодня нет," Fond Strategicheskoi Kultury (Fund of Strategic Culture), September 14 2015, www.fondsk.ru/news/2015/09/14/rossija-iran-alternativy-asadu-v-sirii-segodnja-net-35379.html.

54 MFA Russia, "The deal on #Irannuclearprogram is based on the approach articulated by President Vladimir Putin," Twitter post, July 15, 2015, https://twitter.com/mfa_russia/status/620906964080422912.

55 "Заявление президента России Владимира Путина по завершении переговоров по ядерной программе," Ирана," Kremlin.ru, July 14, 2015 http://kremlin.ru/events/president/news/49957.

56 "Russia to Open $5 Billion Credit Line for Iran to Finance Projects," Radio Free Europe/Radio Liberty, October 23, 2015, www.rferl.org/ content/russia-open-5-billion-credit-line-for-iran-finance-infrastructureprojects/27321777.html.

57 "Путин: справедливо, если Иран достигнет досанкционного уровня добычи нефти," RIA Novosti, September 5, 2016 https://ria.ru/20160905/1476118270 .html.

58 Sam Dagher, *Assad or We Burn the Country*, p. 127.

59 Ibid.

60 "А.Кудрин: Россия простила Сирии $9,6 млрд долгов," RBC, January 25, 2005, www.rbc.ru/politics/25/01/2005/5703ba5b9a7947afa08c75be.

61 Lyudmila Aleksandrova, "Why Russia Forgives Debts," TASS, May 22, 2014,. https://tass.com/opinions/763287.

62 Sam Dagher, *Assad or We Burn the Country. How one Family's Lust for Power Destroyed Syria*, Little, Brown and Company: New York, 201, p. 126.

63 "Syria Completely Supports Russia in the Georgia-Ossetia Conflict—Bashar Assad,"
    Regnum News Agency, August 20, 2008, www.regnum.ru/news/polit/1043940.html.

64 Khaled Yacoub Oweis, "Russia Plans to Raise Navy Presence in Syria: Diplomat,"
    Reuters, August 27, 2008, www.reuters.com/article/us-syriarussia-
    idUSLR39985220080827.

65 Howard Amos, "Billions of Dollars of Russian Business Suffers Along With Syria".
    The Moscow Times, September 1, 2011 www.themoscowtimes.com/2011/09/01/
    billions-of-dollars-of-russian-business-suffers-along-with-syria-a9298.

66 Richard F. Grimmett, "Conventional Arms Transfers to Developing Nations,
    2003–2010," Congressional Research Service, September 22, 2011, www.fas.org/sgp/
    crs/weapons/R42017.pdf. See also reference in David M. Herszenhorn, "For Syria,
    Reliant on Russia for Weapons and Food, Old Bonds Run Deep," *The New York
    Times*, February 18, 2012, www.nytimes.com/2012/02/19/world/middleeast/
    for-russia-and-syriabonds-are-old-and-deep.html.

67 Ibid.

68 Stockholm International Peace Research Institute (SIPRI) "TIV of arms
    exports from Russia, 1981–2018," retrieved August 5, 2019. www.sipri.org/
    databases/armstransfers/sources-and-methods/. See the full chart in the
    Appendix.

69 "The West 'prays' Russia and China will continue blocking Syria action," December
    22, 2012, RT, www.rt.com/news/syria-intervention-chemical-lavrov-651/.

70 Sam Dagher, *Assad or We Burn the Country*, p. 386.

71 Carol J. Williams, "New UN Probe of Syrian Chemical Weapons Use to Name
    Perpetrators," *Los Angeles Times*, September 10, 2015, www.latimes.com/world/
    middleeast/la-fg-syria-chemical-weapons-un-probe20150910-story.html. See also
    the following sources: "Despite UN Investigation, Lavrov Claims Syria's Chemical
    Weapons 'Resolved,'" National, August 9, 2015, www.thenational.ae/world/middle-
    east/despiteun-investigation-lavrov-claims-syrias-chemical-weapons-resolved;
    "Lavrov Urges US to Include Syria in Countering IS," Radio Free Europe/Radio
    Liberty, August 9, 2015, www.rferl.org/content/lavrovurges-us-syria-islamic-
    state/27179598.html; "Lavrov Urges to Refrain from Groundless Claims of Syrian
    Chemical Weapons," Sputnik, August 9, 2015, http://sputniknews.com/
    politics/20150809/1025548616.html#ixzz3jkymNmVV.

72 "A Ship Comes Loaded with Timber . . . or Weapons?" Utrikesperspektiv, December
    12, 2013, http://utrikesperspektiv.se/?p=348.

73 "Russia Denies Hijacked Ship Was Carrying Missiles," CNN, September 8, 2009,
    www.cnn.com/2009/WORLD/europe/09/08/russia.missing.ship/index.
    html?iref=nextin; Luke Harding, "Was the Cargo Ship Arctic Sea Really Hijacked by
    Pirates?" *The Guardian*, September 23, 2009, www.theguardian.com/world/2009/
    sep/24/arctic-sea-russia-pirates; Michael Schwirtz, "More Questions about a

Hijacked Ship," *The New York Times*, October 10, 2009, www.nytimes.com/2009/10/11/world/europe/11arctic.html?_r=0.

74 "US Embassy Cables: Russia Is Virtual 'Mafia State,' Says Spanish Investigator," *The Guardian*, December 2, 2010, www.theguardian.com/world/us-embassy-cables-documents/247712.

75 Luke Harding, "Cyprus Stops Syria-Bound Russian Ammunition Ship," *The Guardian*, January 11, 2012, www.theguardian.com/world/2012/jan/11/cyprus-stops-syria-russian-ship.

76 Oliver Carmichael, "Russia Confirms Cargo Ship Was Carrying Weapons to Syria," *Telegraph*, June 21, 2012, www.telegraph.co.uk/news/worldnews/middleeast/syria/9347014/Russia-confirms-cargo-ship-wascarrying-weapons-to-Syria.html.

77 "Finland Probes 'Syria Arms Smuggling Attempt,'" Al Jazeera, February 16, 2013, www.aljazeera.com/news/americas/2013/02/20132152 24954763885.html.

78 "A Ship Comes Loaded with Timber . . . or Weapons?" Utrikesperspektiv, December 12, 2013, http://utrikesperspektiv.se/?p=348.

79 Dafna Linzer, Michael Grabell, and Jeff Larson, "Flight Records Say Russia Sent Syria Tons of Cash," ProPublica, November 26, 2012, www.propublica.org/article/flight-records-list-russia-sending-tons-of-cash-to-syria.

80 Organization for Economic Cooperation and Development (OECD), accessed June 3, 2020 from OECD.Stat. https://stats.oecd.org/

6 The Military Campaign

1 Laila Bassam, Tom Perry, "How Iranian general plotted out Syrian assault in Moscow," Reuters, October 6, 2015, www.reuters.com/article/us-mideast-crisis-syria-soleimani-insigh/how-iranian-general-plotted-out-syrian-assault-in-moscow-idUSKCN0S02BV20151006.

2 John Parker, *Putin's Syrian Gambit: Sharper Elbows, Bigger Footprint, Stickier Wicket*, Center for Strategic Research Institute for National Strategic Studies National Defense University, No. 25, July 2017, https://inss.ndu.edu/Portals/68/Documents/stratperspective/inss/Strategic-Perspectives-25.pdf.

3 Ivan Buvaltsev, Oleg Falichev, "Ближний Восток на Южном Урале На учениях «Центр-2015» российские войска изучили тактику формирований террористов," November 2, 2015, Voyenno-promyshlenny Kurier, https://vpk-news.ru/articles/27827.

4 Laila Bassam, Tom Perry, "How Iranian General Plotted out Syrian Assault in Moscow."

5 Michael R. Gordon and Eric Schmitt, "Russian Moves in Syria Pose Concerns for US," *The New York Times*, September 4, 2015, www.nytimes.com/2015/09/05/world/

middleeast/russian-moves-in-syria-pose-concerns-for-us.html?_r=0. Previous reports indicated Russian troops were on the ground in Syria earlier: see Ruslan Leviev, a Russian blogger connected to the Conflict Intelligence Team (CTI), which follows Russia's military involvement in Syria and Ukraine, "Are There Russian Troops in Syria?" September 5, 2015, http://ruslanleviev.livejournal.com/38649.html.

6 "Read Putin's UN General Assembly speech," *The Washington Post*, September 28, 2015, www.washingtonpost.com/news/worldviews/wp/2015/09/28/read-putins-u-n-general-assembly-speech/?utm_term=.d4841dc12bd3.

7 Alexander Shumilin, "Российская дипломатия на ближнем востоке: возврат к геополитике," Russie.Nei.Visions N. 93 May 2016, www.ifri.org/sites/default/files/atoms/files/rnv93_version_ru_final_protege.pdf.

8 Stephen R. Covington, *The Culture of Strategic Thought Behind Russia's Modern Approaches to Warfare*, Defense and Intelligence Projects Belfer Center for Science and International Affairs Harvard Kennedy School, p. 29. See www.belfercenter.org/sites/default/files/legacy/files/Culture%20of%20Strategic%20Thought%203.pdf.

9 Ibid.

10 Ibid.

11 In part, this is based on author interview with anonymous US military source, September 2020.

12 February 2020, The Geneva Centre for Security Policy US-Russia Dialogue on Syria.

13 Ibid.

14 Guillaume Lasconjarias and Alessandro Marrone, How to Respond to Anti-Access/Area Denial (A2/AD)? Towards a NATO Counter-A2/AD Strategy; Conference Report n 01/16—March 2016, available from: www.ndc.nato.int/research/research.php?icode=0.

15 Luis Simon, "Demystifying the A2/AD Buzz," War on the Rocks, January 4, 2017, https://warontherocks.com/2017/01/demystifying-the-a2ad-buzz/.

16 Michael Kofman, "Russian A2/AD: It is not overrated, just poorly understood," Russian Military Analysis, January 25, 2020, https://russianmilitaryanalysis.wordpress.com/2020/01/25/russian-a2-ad-it-is-not-overrated-just-poorly-understood/.

17 Michael Kofman, "It's time to talk about Russian A2AD: Rethinking the Russian Military Challenge," War on the Rocks, September 25, 2019, https://warontherocks.com/2019/09/its-time-to-talk-about-a2-ad-rethinking-the-russian-military-challenge/.

18 Stephen R. Covington, *The Culture of Strategic Thought behind Russia's Moderl Approaches to Warfare*..

19 For a map of Russian A2AD, see Ian Williams, "The Russia—NATO A2AD Environment," CSIS, January 3, 2017, https://missilethreat.csis.org/russia-nato-a2ad-environment/.

20 Lester Grau and Charles Bartles, "The Russian Ground-Based Contingent in Syria" in Robert E. Hamilton, Chris Miller, and Aaron Stein (eds.), *Russia's Way of War in Syria: Assessing Russian Military Capabilities and Lessons Learned*, pp. 67–89, www.fpri.org/wp-content/uploads/2020/09/russias-war-in-syria.pdf.

21 Roger N. McDermott, *Russia's Electronic Warfare Capabilities to 2025, Challenging NATO in the Electromagnetic Spectrum*, Republic of Estonia, Ministry of Defense, September 2017. Available from: https://icds.ee/wp-content/uploads/2018/ICDS_Report_Russias_Electronic_Warfare_to_2025.pdf.

22 Ibid., p. 23.

23 Sergei Lavrov, "Выступление на конференции 'Средиземноморье: римский диалог,'" Russian International Affairs Council (RIAC) November 23, 2018, https://russiancouncil.ru/analytics-and-comments/comments/vystuplenie-na-konferentsii-sredizemnomore-rimskiy-dialog/?sphrase_id=31559967.

24 Author telephone interview with Robert E. Hamilton, September 4, 2020.

25 Dmitry Adamsky, "Lessons Learned from the Operation in Syria: A Preliminary Assessment," in Glen E. Howard and Matthew Czekaj, eds., *Russia's Military Strategy and Doctrine*, The Jamestown Foundation: Washington, DC, 2019, p. 381.

26 Ibid.

27 Specifically it was the policy of Chechenization. See Ilyas Akhmadov and Miriam Lanskoy, *The Chechen Struggle: Independence Won and Lost* (1st ed.). New York: Palgrave Macmillan, 2010.

28 Margarita Antidze, Jack Stubbs, "Before Syria, Russia Struggled to Land Air Strikes on Target," Reuters, October 25, 2015, www.reuters.com/article/us-mideast-crisis-syria-russia-bombing-idUSKCN0SK1WF20151026.

29 Ralph Shield, "Russian Airpower's Success in Syria: Assessing Evolution in Kinetic Counterinsurgency," *The Journal of Slavic Military Studies*, April 3, 2018, Vol. 31(2), pp. 214–39.

30 C. Hayes Wong and Christine Yen-Ting Chen, *Ambulances under Siege in Syria, BMG Global Health 2018,* https://gh.bmj.com/content/3/6/e001003.

31 "The UN Made a List of Hospitals in Syria. Now They're Being Bombed," The Century Foundation https://tcf.org/content/report/un-made-list-hospitals-syria-now-theyre-bombed/.

32 Evan Hill "UN Inquiry into Syria Bombings is Silent on Russia's Role Experts say a 'mealy-mouthed' United Nations Report Failed to Blame Russia for Bombing Hospitals and a School, for Fear of Alienating Moscow," *The New York Times*, April 6, 2020.

33 Tom O'Connor, "How Many Russian Troops in Syria? Military Reveals Full Count as told US to Leave," *Newsweek*, August 23, 2018, www.newsweek.com/how-many-russia-troops-syria-military-reveals-full-count-us-told-leave-1088409.

34 Another section will discuss Russia's military personnel in more detail.

35 Andrew S. Weiss, Nicole Ng, *Collision Avoidance: The Lessons of US and Russian Operations in Syria,* Carnegie Endowment for International Peace, March 20, 2019, https://carnegieendowment.org/2019/03/20/collision-avoidance-lessons-of-u.s.-and-russian-operations-in-syria-pub-78571.

36 Yossi Mansharof, "Implications of the Emergent Russian-Hezbollah Coordination in Syria," The Begin–Sadat Center for Strategic Studies, December 2, 2016, https://besacenter.org/perspectives-papers/383-mansharof-closer-collaboration-between-russia-and-hezbollah-in-aleppo/.

37 Alexander Corbeil, "Hezbollah is learning Russian," Carnegie Endowment for International Peace, February 26, 2016, https://carnegieendowment.org/sada/62896.

38 Alex Fishman, "'Hezbollah evades Israeli bombs in Syria by flying Russian flag,'" December 15, 2018, www.ynetnews.com/articles/0,7340,L-5425367,00.html.

39 Times of Israel Staff, "Praising Hezbollah, Russian envoy claims US could spark new Israel-Lebanon war," February 9, 2019, www.timesofisrael.com/praising-hezbollah-russian-envoy-claims-us-could-spark-new-israel-lebanon-war/.

40 See, for example, photos with the Russians and the Liwa al-Imam al-Baqir (Syrian Hezbollah group) in Philip Smyth, "The Shia militia mapping project," The Washington Institute for Near East Policy, May 2019, www.washingtoninstitute.org/policy-analysis/view/the-shia-militia-mapping-project.

41 Raja Abdulrahim, "Iran-Backed Fighters Switch to Syrian Uniforms to Avoid Israeli Strikes, Rebels Say," *The Wall Street Journal*, June 8, 2018, www.wsj.com/articles/iran-backed-fighters-switch-to-syrian-uniforms-to-avoid-israeli-strikes-rebels-say-1528478351.

42 Roger McDermott, "Gerasimov Unveils Russia's 'Strategy of Limited Actions,'" Eurasia Daily Monitor 16, No. 31, Jamestown Foundation, March 6, 2019, https://jamestown.org/program/gerasimov-unveils-russias-strategyof-limited-actions/.

43 Glen E. Howard and Matthew Czekaj, eds., introduction to Russia's Military Strategy and Doctrine (Washington DC: Jamestown Foundation, 2019), pp. xiv–xv.

44 "Moscow Close to Finalizing Deal to Lease Syria's Tartus Port For 49 Years," RFE/RL, April 21, 2019, www.rferl.org/a/moscow-damascus-near-deal-on-lease-syrian-port-tartus/29894114.html.

45 Yuliya Talmazan, "Russia establishing permanent presence at its Syrian bases: minister of defense," NBC News, December 27, 2017, www.nbcnews.com/news/world/russia-establishing-permanent-presence-its-syrian-bases-minister-defense-n832596.

46 Nora Kelly, "What is Al-Shayrat Military Arfield?" The Atlantic, April 6, 2017, www.theatlantic.com/international/archive/2017/04/what-is-al-shayrat-military-airfield/522249/.

47 Jamie Ross, "Russia Takes Over Vacated US Air Base in Northern Syria," The Daily Beast, November 15, 2019, www.thedailybeast.com/russia-takes-over-vacated-us-air-base-in-northern-syria.

48 Shwan Snow, "Russia Establishes Helicopter Base in Syrian City as US Pulls Out," *Military Times*, November 15, 2019, www.militarytimes.com/flashpoints/2019/11/15/russia-establishes-helicopter-base-in-syrian-city-as-us-pulls-out/.

49 Seth J. Frantzman, "Report: Iranians Build New Military Base in Syria," *Jerusalem Post*, November 11, 2013, https://m.jpost.com/Middle-East/Report-Iranians-built-a-new-military-base-in-Syria-513973.

50 Vladimir Putin, Decree, "Realization of the Plans for the Development of the Armed Forces and the Modernization of the Defense Industry," May 7, 2012, http://kremlin.ru/events/president/news/15242.

51 President of Russia, Meeting of the Commission for military technology cooperation with foreign states," Kremlin.ru, July 2, 2012, http://en.kremlin.ru/events/president/news/15865.

52 "Глава 'Ростеха' сообщил о росте продаж: 'Чем больше конфликтов, тем больше у нас покупают вооружения' " Newsru.com, February 23, 2015, www.newsru.com/russia/23feb2015/chemezov.html.

53 President of Russia, Meeting of the Commission for military technology cooperation with foreign states," Kremlin.ru, July 2, 2012, http://en.kremlin.ru/events/president/news/15865.

54 "Рогозин: ФСВТС сегодня является вторым внешнеполитическим ведомством," RIA Novosti, December 11 2013, https://ria.ru/20131211/983472868.html.

55 Thomas Gibbons-Neff, "Pentagon: Some Russian Cruise Missiles Crashed in Iran," *The Washington Post*, October 8, 2015, www.washingtonpost.com/news/checkpoint/wp/2015/10/07/these-are-the-cruise-missiles-russia-just-sent-into-syria/.

56 Russia's use of Syria to test weaponry has been well covered. Here are just a few examples:
"Putin Using Syrian Civil War as Testing Ground for New Weapons," *Washington Times*, February 28, 2016, www.washingtontimes.com/news/2016/feb/28/russia-using-syria-as-testing-ground-for-new-weapo/. Dave Majumdar, "How The Russian Military Turned War-Torn Syria Into A Testing Playground," The National Interest, July 31, 2018. https://taskandpurpose.com/russian-military-syria-weapons-testing. Associated Press, "Putin says Russia Perfected Weapons Based on Syria Campaign," September 19, 2018, www.defensenews.com/global/europe/2018/09/19/putin-says-russia-perfected-weapons-based-on-syria-campaign/.

57 Lara Siligman, "Russian Jamming Poses a Growing Threat to US Troops," *Foreign Policy*, July 30, 2018, https://foreignpolicy.com/2018/07/30/russian-jamming-poses-a-growing-threat-to-u-s-troops-in-syria/. Ben Brimelow "General reveals that US aircraft are being 'disabled' in Syria—the 'most aggressive' electronic warfare environment on Earth," Business Insider, April 26, 2018, www.businessinsider.com/syria-electronic-warfare-us-planes-disabled-2018-4. Anna Varfolomeeva, "Signaling strength: Russia's real Syria success is electronic warfare against the US," The Defense Post, May 1, 2018, https://thedefensepost.com/2018/05/01/russia-syria-electronic-warfare/.

58 Roger N. McDermott, *Russia's Electronic Warfare Capabilities to 2025*. Roger McDermott, "Russia's Network-Centric Warfare Capability: Tried and Tested in Syria," *Eurasia Daily Monitor* 15, No. 154 (October 30, 2018), https://jamestown.org/program/russias-network-centric-warfare-capability-tried-and-tested-in-syria.

59 Vladimir Putin, "Annual Presidential Addresses to the Federal Assembly," Kremlin.ru, December 1, 2016, http://en.kremlin.ru/events/president/news/53379. Vladimir Putin, "Annual Presidential Addresses to the Federal Assembly," Kremlin.ru, March 1, 2018, http://en.kremlin.ru/events/president/news/56957. Vladimir Putin, "Annual Presidential Addresses to the Federal Assembly," Kremlin.ru, February 20, 2019, http://en.kremlin.ru/events/president/news/59863 (there was no address in 2017). Vladimir Putin, "Annual Presidential Addresses to the Federal Assembly," Kremlin.ru, http://en.kremlin.ru/events/president/news/53379.

60 Vladimir Putin, "Annual Presidential Addresses to the Federal Assembly," Kremlin.ru, March 1, 2018, http://en.kremlin.ru/events/president/news/56957.

61 Associated Press, "Putin says Russia Perfected Weapons Based on Syria Campaign," September 19, 2018, www.defensenews.com/global/europe/2018/09/19/putin-says-russia-perfected-weapons-based-on-syria-campaign/. Vladimir Putin, "Annual Presidential Addresses to the Federal Assembly," Kremlin.ru, February 20, 2019, http://en.kremlin.ru/events/president/news/59863.

62 "Direct line with Vladimir Putin," Kremlin.ru, June 7, 2018, http://en.kremlin.ru/events/president/news/page/55.

63 Kimberly Marten, "Russia's use of semi-state security forces: The case of the Wagner Group," *Post-Soviet Affairs*, DOI: 10.1080/1060586X.2019.1591142, 2019.

64 Тютюнников, Н.Н., Том 1. Вооруженные Силы Российской Федерации р. 68.

65 "Славянский корпус: что он делал в Сирии Об этом сообщает Рамблер," Rambler, 4 May 2019, https://news.rambler.ru/middleeast/42132857/?utm_content=rnews&utm_medium=read_more&utm_source=copylink; and Mikhail Bushuev, "ЧВКВагнера: все, чтоонейизвестно," Deutsche Welle, August 1, 2018, www.dw.com/ru/чвк-вагнера-все-что-о-ней-известно/a-42596738www.dw.com/ru/чвк-вагнера-все-что-о-ней-известно/a-42596738.34.

66 Østensen and Bukkvoll, *Russian Use of Private Military and Security Companies—The Implications for European and Norwegian Security*, p. 25.

67 Author anonymous interview with US military source, September 17, 2020.

68 Dmitry (Dima) Adamsky, "Moscow's Syria Campaign: Russian Lessons for the Art of Strategy", *Russie.Nei.Visions*, No. 109, Ifri, July 2018. www.armyupress.army.mil/Portals/7/Hot-Spots/docs/Russia/Adamsky-Moscow-Syria.pdf.

69 Kimberly Marten, "Russia's use of semi-state security forces: the case of the Wagner Group."

70 Ibid.

71 Ibid.

72 Natalia Kantovich, chief legal adviser on Russian tax legislation at Yukos group companies at the time of the Russian Syria intervention. She was also watching the Russian Syrian campaign while studying for an LLM in International Peace and Security at King's College, London; author interview May 14, 2020.

73 Anna Borshchevskaya, "The Role of Private Russian Military Contractors in Africa," FPRI, August 21, 2020, www.fpri.org/article/2020/08/the-role-of-russian-private-military-contractors-in-africa/.

74 Author interview with anonymous US military source, September 17, 2020.

7 The Domestic Campaign

1 "Владимир Путин: Россия не собирается воевать в Сирии," the BBC Russian Service, September 28, 2015, www.bbc.com/russian/international/2015/09/150927_putin_cbs_interview. "Путин: Россия пока не будет участвовать в войсковых операциях на территории Сирии," Vedomosti, September 28, 2015, www.vedomosti.ru/politics/news/2015/09/28/610423-putin-rossiya-sirii.

2 "Putin Rules Out Russian Ground War Against IS; Air Strikes Possible," RFE/RL, September 29, 2015, www.rferl.org/a/putin-rules-out-russian-ground-war-against-islamic-state-air-strikes-possible/27276375.html.

3 Upper house of the Federal Assembly, the Russian parliament.

4 "Совещание с членами Правительства," Kremlin.ru, September 30, 2015, www.kremlin.ru/events/president/news/50401.

5 "Полный текст заявления Владимира Путина об использовании ВС РФ в Сирии," September 30, 2015, https://russian.rt.com/article/120245.

6 "Решение миротворца": реакция на согласие Совфеда использовать ВС РФ в Сирии," September 30, 2015, https://tass.ru/politika/2303457.

7 "Полный текст заявления Владимира Путина об использовании ВС РФ в Сирии."
Video of the announcement: Путин о применении ВС России в Сирии (Video of Putin's announcement) October 1, 2015, www.youtube.com/watch?v=VPh6B07EK40.

8 "Полный текст заявления Владимира Путина об использовании ВС РФ в Сирии," September 30, 2015, https://russian.rt.com/article/120245.

9 Ibid.

10 Putin uses a Russian expression here, "не собираемся погружаться в конфликт, что называется, с головой."

11 "Песков: Только Россия будет использовать войска в Сирии на легитимной основе," Vedomosti (byline says Interfax), September 30, 2015, www.vedomosti.ru/politics/news/2015/09/30/610852-peskov-sirii.

12 Bill Chappell, "Russia Begins Airstrikes in Syria After Assad's Request," NPR, September 30, 2015, www.npr.org/sections/thetwo-way/2015/09/30/444679327/ russia-begins-conducting-airstrikes-in-syria-at-assads-request. "Russia joins war in Syria: Five key points," BBC, October 1, 2015, www.bbc.com/news/world-middle-east-34416519.

13 Alexander Lenin, "Асад: Присутствие РФ в Сирии является долгосрочным," Rossiyskaya Gazeta, July 26, 2018, https://rg.ru/2018/07/26/asad-prisutstvie-rf-v-sirii-iavliaetsia-dolgosrochnym.html.

14 Giorgy Mirsky, "«Исламское государство» и российские СМИ," *Echo Moskvy, June 3, 2015,* https://echo.msk.ru/blog/georgy_mirsky/1560354-echo/. Shamsail Saraliyev, "За созданием ИГИЛ и майдана стоят одни и те же силы," *Izvestiya*, November 21, 2014, https://iz.ru/news/579709.

15 *Сирийский дневник project*, Корреспондент: Анастасия Попова Оператор: Михаил Виткин Режиссер: Евгений Лебедев, appeared in late October 2015, http://russia.tv/brand/show/brand_id/36945/.

16 Author Interview with Natalia Kantovich, May 14, 2020.

17 "Die Welt: Российская пропаганда наслаждается войной в Сирии," Unian, October 19, 2015, www.unian.net/world/1156749-die-welt-rossiyskaya-propaganda-naslajdaetsya-voynoy-v-sirii.www.unian.net/world/1156749-die-welt-rossiyskaya-propaganda-naslajdaetsya-voynoy-v-sirii.html.

18 "Как живут российские летчики на базе Латакия в Сирии," Gazeta.ru October 22, 2015, www.gazeta.ru/social/video/social2015/10/22/kak_zhivut_rossiiskie_letchiki_na_baze_latakiya_v_sirii.shtml.

19 Указ Президента Российской Федерации от 28.05.2015 № 273 "О внесении изменений в перечень сведений, отнесенных к государственной тайне, утвержденный Указом Президента Российской Федерации от 30 ноября 1995 г. № 1203" http://publication.pravo.gov.ru/Document/View/0001201505280001?index =0&rangeSize=1.

20 "Сирия, сестра моя, твой русский брат защитит тебя," Song performed by Russian schoolgirl in September 2013, posted November 21, 2015, www.youtube. com/watch?v=mnNwEKs3_kY.

21 "Из Сирии с любовью: русские жены Асадов", http://russia.tv/video/show/ brand_id/5169/episode_id/972224/. The show aired on March 7, 2014 on one of the main state TV channels, Rossiya1.

22 Andrei Piontkovsky, "Ночной портье Земного шара," RFE/RL October 19, 2015, www.svoboda.org/a/27318281.html.

23 "Всеволод Чаплин об операции ВВС РФ в Сирии: Борьба с терроризмом— священна," Ren.TV, September 30, 2015, https://ren.tv/news/v-mire/50886-vsevolod-chaplin-ob-operatsii-vvs-rf-v-sirii-borba-s-terrorizmom-sviashchenna.

24 Central Muslim Spiritual Board of Russia homepage, www.cdum.ru/en/cdum/www. cdum.ru/index.php www.cdum.ru/en/cdum/ www.cdum.ru/index.php.

25 Путин обсудил с соотечественниками «посткрымскую» миссию России," RBC, November 5, 2015, www.rbc.ru/politics/05/11/2015/563b51189a794702c003c7f7.

26 "Путин сирия одна не справится с терроризмом," December 24, 2017, www.youtube.com/watch?v=4gcsOwAiMHI—

27 Lawrence Wright, *The Looming Tower, Al-Qaeda and the Road to 9/11,* Vintage Books: New York, first edition, September, 2007, pp. 152–3.

28 Michael Rubin, "Who is Responsible for the Taliban?" *Middle East Review of International Affairs*, March 2002, www.washingtoninstitute.org/policy-analysis/view/who-is-responsible-for-the-taliban.

29 "Путин рассказал, как США поддерживали террористов в Чечне," June 13, 2017, https://ria.ru/20170613/1496357892.html.

30 "Макаренко Вадим Новая география древнего мира," reprinted from Moskovskiy Komsomolets,December 3, 2010, www.proza.ru/2010/12/03/836.

31 "Сирия—это наша земля," YouTube video excerpt of Bogdasarov's comment, October 2, 2015, www.youtube.com/watch?v=u25KbVSI53g.

32 larasdvatri123, "Сирия—земля наших предков," https://larasdvatri123.livejournal.com/27772.html 2016-02-06, February 6, 2016.

33 Anton Orekh, "Как же мы будем жить без Сирии?" Echo Moskvy, March 15, 2016, https://echo.msk.ru/programs/repl/1730222-echo/.

34 "Сирия сестра моя," Grani.ru, October 5, 2015, www.youtube.com/watch?v=Xjd77BKVZZg.

35 Lev Gudkov's Facebook page, ttps://www.facebook.com/photo.php?fbid=981217478586359&set=a.821288534579255.1073741826.100000943480007&type=1.

36 "Увязнем, братцы, в Сирии?" Echo Moskvy, September 7, 2015, https://echo.msk.ru/blog/kiselev/1617546-echo/.

37 "Олег Пономарь: Сирия станет для России вторым Афганистаном," NewsAder [no publication date] http://newsader.com/specialist/oleg-ponomar-siriya-stanet-dlya-rossii/.

38 Lyubov Chizhova, Mark Krutov, "Сирийская война Владимира Путина," September 30, 2015, www.svoboda.org/a/27279085.html.

39 "Russia's Military Gamble in Syria is Paying off Handsomely. But for How Long?" *The Economist,* May 16, 2019, www.economist.com/middle-east-and-africa/2019/05/16/russias-military-gamble-in-syria-is-paying-off-handsomely.

40 Natalia Kantovich, May 14, 2020.

41 Interview with Natalia, May 14, 2020.

42 Anna Borshchevskaya, "The Role of the Military in Russian Politics and Foreign Policy Over the Past 20 Years ," *Orbis*, July, 2020.

43 Alexander Golts, *Military Reform and Militarism in Russia*, Washington, DC: Jamestown Foundation, 2019, p. 5.

44 "Россияне о ситуации в Сирии," October 1, 2013, Levada www.levada.ru/2013/10/01/rossiyane-o-situatsii-v-sirii/.

45 "Общественное мнение о ситуации в Сирии." Levada, August 28, 2013, www.levada.ru/2013/08/28/obshhestvennoe-mnenie-o-situatsii-v-sirii/.

46 "Россияне выступают против ввода войск в Сирию," RBC, September 29, 2015, www.rbc.ru/politics/29/09/2015/560929559a794769d74d0ad2.

47 "Наши в Сирии: первый опрос," VTsIOM, October 9, 2015, https://wciom.ru/index.php?id=236&uid=151.

48 "Операция ВКС России в Сирии: подводя итоги," VTsIOM, March 18, 2016, https://wciom.ru/index.php?id=236&uid=268.

49 "Если завтра война . . ." VTsIOM, June 28, 2017, https://wciom.ru/index.php?id=236&uid=1918.

50 "Новая вспышка войны в Сирии: мнение россиян?" VTsIOM, February 27, 2018, https://wciom.ru/index.php?id=236&uid=8968.

51 Putin's approval ratings, Levada.ru, accessed in Russian and English, June 20, 2019, www.levada.ru/en/ratings/.

52 Ibid.

53 Natalia Galimova, "Это праздник с вопросами в глазах," Gazeta.ru, May 9, 2014, www.gazeta.ru/politics/2014/05/09_a_6024869.shtml.

54 Konstantin von Eggert, "Отказать в уважении. Как реагировать на то, что большинство россиян одобряет Сталина," Snob.ru, April 17, 2019, https://snob.ru/entry/175714/. Ivan Preobrazhenskiy, "Комментарий: Сталин вместо Путина," Deutsche Welle, April 16, 2019, www.dw.com/ru/комментарий-сталин-вместо-путина/a-48359779.

55 "Trust in Putin Doubles After Kremlin Criticizes Poll," The *Moscow Times* May 31, 2019, www.themoscowtimes.com/2019/05/31/trust-in-putin-doubles-after-kremlin-criticizes-poll-a65826.

56 "Russians Losing Interest in Foreign Policy, Poll Says," The *Moscow Times*, June 21, 2019, www.themoscowtimes.com/2019/06/21/russians-losing-interest-foreign-policy-poll-says-a66101.

57 "Большинство россиян выступили за окончание операции в Сирии," May 6, 2019, www.rbc.ru/politics/06/05/2019/5cc82ea09a794713911111669.

8 Diplomatic Efforts

1 "Маргелов: делегация Совфеда направится в Сирию в самое ближайшее время," RIA Novosti September 12, 2011, https://ria.ru/20110912/435727620.html.

2 Власти Сирии благодарят Москву за "взвешенную позицию" the BBC Russian Service, September 12, 2011, www.bbc.com/russian/russia/2011/09/110912_syria_official_moscow_visit.

3 Draft resolution on Syria, October 4, 2011, the United Nations Security Council, Available from: https://undocs.org/S/2011/612.

4 United Nations Security Council Sixty-sixth year, 6627th meeting Tuesday, October 4, 2011, 6 p.m. New York, p. 3, available from: https://undocs.org/S/PV.6627.

5 Associated Press, "Russia and China Veto UN Resolution against Syrian Regime," October 4, 2011, *The Guardian*, www.theguardian.com/world/2011/oct/05/russia-china-veto-syria-resolution.

6 "Syria: how it all began," PRI.org, April 23, 2011, www.pri.org/stories/2011-04-23/syria-how-it-all-began.

7 Sam Meredith, "Few countries are truly sovereign, and Russia is a target of systematic US interference, says Putin," CNBC, June 2, 2017, www.cnbc.com/2017/06/02/few-countries-are-truly-sovereign-and-russia-is-a-target-of-systematic-us-interference-says-putin.html.

8 Edward Cody, "From France, an Urge to Intervene in Syria," *The Washington Post*, September 10, 2012, www.washingtonpost.com/world/middle_east/from-france-an-urge-to-intervene-in-syria/2012/09/10/4c83c936-fb24-11e1-8adc-499661afe377_story.html?utm_term=.8478e10fb61f.

9 Neil MacFarquhar, "At UN, Pressure is on Russia for Refusal to Condemn Syria," *The New York Times*, January 31, 2012, www.nytimes.com/2012/02/01/world/middleeast/battle-over-possible-united-nations-resolution-on-syria-intensifies.html.

10 Letter dated February 14, 2012 from the Permanent Representative of the Russian Federation to the United Nations addressed to the Secretary-General, Annex to the letter dated February 14, 2012 from the Permanent Representative of the Russian Federation to the United Nations addressed to the Secretary-General State Duma of the Federal Assembly of the Russian Federation Declaration by the State Duma on the situation in Syria S. Y. Naryshkin President of the State Duma of the Federal Assembly of the Russian Federation Moscow February 10, 2012, https://undocs.org/S/2012/91.

11 Paul Harris, Martin Chulov, David Batty, Damien Pearse, "Syria Resolution Vetoed by Russia and China at United Nations," *The Guardian*, February 4, 2012, www.theguardian.com/world/2012/feb/04/assad-obama-resign-un-resolution.

12 Paul Harris, Martin Chulov, David Batty, Damien Pearse, "Syria Resolution Vetoed by Russia and China at United Nations," *The Guardian*, February 4, 2012, www.theguardian.com/world/2012/feb/04/assad-obama-resign-un-resolution.

13 Julian Borger and Bastien Inzaurralde "West 'ignored Russian offer in 2012 to have Syria's Assad step aside,'" *The Guardian*, September 15, 2015, www.theguardian.com/world/2015/sep/15/west-ignored-russian-offer-in-2012-to-have-syrias-assad-step-aside.

14 Based on private conversation with former senior UN official at a think tank in Washington, DC, May 2020.

15 Charlie Rose Show, "John Kerry: Russia's 'constructive role' Iran and Syria," show aired April 5, 2016, excerpt available from https://www.youtube.com/watch?v=9HvxduUv0cM https://charlierose.com/videos/25939.

16 Author interview with anonymous Western official, September 11, 2020.

17 Ibid.

18 John Irish, "France, Partners Planning Syria Crisis Group: Sarkozy," Reuters, February 4, 2012, www.reuters.com/article/us-syria-france/france-partners-planning-syria-crisis-group-sarkozy-idUSTRE8130QV20120204.

19 Aleem Maqbool ,"Friends of Syria group agree urgent support for rebels," BBC, June 22, 2013, www.bbc.com/news/av/world-middle-east-23016225/friends-of-syria-group-agree-urgent-support-for-rebels, "Group of Friends of the Syrian People: 1st Conference," Carnegie Endowment for Peace, Middle East, https://carnegie-mec.org/syriaincrisis/?fa=48418.

20 Lt. Col. J. Stewart Welch, CDR Kevin Bailey, *In Pursuit of Good Ideas: The Syrian Train-and-Equip program*, The Washington Institute for Near East Policy, Policy Note, September 12, 2016 https://www.washingtoninstitute.org/policy-analysis/pursuit-good-ideas-syria-train-and-equip-program. Tara McKelvey, "Arming Syrian rebels: Where the US went wrong," BBC October 10, 2015 https://www.bbc.com/news/magazine-33997408

21 United Nations Press Release, "In Presidential Statement, Security Council Gives Full Support to Efforts of Joint Special Envoy of United Nations, Arab League to End Violence in Syria," March 21, 2012, www.un.org/press/en/2012/sc10583.doc.htm. World News, "Text of Annan's six-point peace plan for Syria," Reuters, April 4, 2012, www.reuters.com/article/us-syria-ceasefire/text-of-annans-six-point-peace-plan-for-syria-idUSBRE8330HJ20120404.

22 "Замглавы МИД РФ: военная операция в Сирии приведет к катастрофе," RIA Novosti, June 8, 2012, https://ria.ru/20120608/668598840.html.

23 Chris Doyle, "Kofi Annan's Resignation is no Surprise, his Syria Peace Plan Undermined," *The Guardian*, August 2, 2012, www.theguardian.com/commentisfree/2012/aug/02/kofi-annan-resignation-syria-peace-plan.

24 United Nations Press Release, "Security Council Fails to Adopt Draft Resolution on Syria That Would Have Threatened Sanctions, Due to Negative Votes of China, Russian Federation," July 19, 2012, www.un.org/press/en/2012/sc10714.doc.htm.

25 United Nations Press Release, "Security Council Fails to Adopt Draft Resolution on Syria That Would Have Threatened Sanctions, Due to Negative Votes of China, Russian Federation," July 19, 2012, www.un.org/press/en/2012/sc10714.doc.htm.

26 Chris Doyle, "Kofi Annan's Resignation is no Surprise, his Syria Peace Plan Undermined," *The Guardian*, August 2, 2012.

27 Action Group for Syria Final Communiqué, June 30, 2012, www.un.org/News/dh/infocus/Syria/FinalCommuniqueActionGroupforSyria.pdf.

28 Karen DeYoung, "Syria Conference Fails to Specify Plan for Assad," *The Washington Post*, June 30, 2012, www.washingtonpost.com/world/national-security/syria-conference-fails-to-specify-plan-for-assad/2012/06/30/gJQAsPfeEW_story.

html?utm_term=.dc50dc502677. Nick Cumming, Bruce and Rob Nordland, "Talks Come Up With Plan for Syria, but Not for Assad's Exit," *The New York Times*, June 30, 2012, www.nytimes.com/2012/07/01/world/middleeast/future-of-syria-on-agenda-as-countries-gather-in-geneva.html?mtrref=undefined. Andrew J. Tabler, "Moscow's playbook in Syria, and how Washington is playing along," April 21, 2016 www.foreignaffairs.com/articles/russian-federation/2016-04-21/moscows-playbook-syria. Nick Cumming, Bruce and Rob Nordland, "Talks Come Up with Plan for Syria, but Not for Assad's Exit," *The New York Times*, June 30, 2012, www.nytimes.com/2012/07/01/world/middleeast/future-of-syria-on-agenda-as-countries-gather-in-geneva.html?mtrref=undefined. Anna Borshchevskaya, "Russia's Self-Serving Approach to Syrian Peace Talks," The Washington Institute for Near East Policy, August 18, 2015, www.washingtoninstitute.org/policy-analysis/view/russias-self-serving-approach-to-syrian-peace-talks.

29 Marcus George, "Iran Presents its own Cease-fire Proposal for Syria at Non-Aligned Summit," *The Christian Science Monitor*, August 29, 2012, www.csmonitor.com/World/Latest-News-Wires/2012/0829/Iran-presents-its-own-cease-fire-proposal-for-Syria-at-Non-Aligned-summit.

30 "UN envoy seeks Iranian help for Syria ceasefire," France 24, November 15, 2012, www.france24.com/en/20121015-syria-un-envoy-iran-brahimi-seeks-help-broker-ceasefire-bashar-assad-eid-al-adha.

31 President Barak Obama, "Remarks to reporters," August 20, 2012, https://obamawhitehouse.archives.gov/the-press-office/2012/08/20/remarks-president-white-house-press-corps.

32 Glenn Kessler, "President Obama and the 'red line' on Syria's chemical weapons," *The Washington Post*, September 6, 2013, www.washingtonpost.com/news/fact-checker/wp/2013/09/06/president-obama-and-the-red-line-on-syrias-chemical-weapons/?utm_term=.a7dfb2b8e70a.

33 J. K. Trotter, "Obama paints his red line on Syria," The Atlantic, March 30, 2013, www.theatlantic.com/politics/archive/2013/03/obama-red-line-syria-netanyahu-press-conference/317146/ chemical weapons are a "game changer."

34 Arms Control Association, *Timeline of Syrian Chemical Weapons Activity, 2012–2019*, www.armscontrol.org/factsheets/Timeline-of-Syrian-Chemical-Weapons-Activity.

35 Ibid.

36 Paul Lewis, "US strike on Syria could come within days as military assets 'ready to go,'" August 28, 2013, www.theguardian.com/world/2013/aug/27/syria-us-forces-ready-obama.

37 "Russia sends warships to Mediterranean as Syria tension rises," Reuters, August 29, 2013, www.reuters.com/article/us-syria-crisis-russia-navy/russia-sends-warships-to-mediterranean-as-syria-tension-rises-idUSBRE97S0AK20130829.

38 Rhodes also recalls that the House speaker John Boehner had written a letter to Obama, saying there was little support for getting dragged into wars—and this was ultimately the biggest domestic concern in the United States.

39 Ben Rhodes, "Inside the White House During the Syrian 'Red Line' Crisis," The Atlantic, June 3, 2018, www.theatlantic.com/international/archive/2018/06/inside-the-white-house-during-the-syrian-red-line-crisis/561887/.

40 "Remarks by President Obama and Prime Minister Reinfeldt of Sweden in Joint Press Conference," September 4, 2013, https://obamawhitehouse.archives.gov/the-press-office/2013/09/04/remarks-president-obama-and-prime-minister-reinfeldt-sweden-joint-press. Glenn Kessler, "President Obama and the 'Red Line' on Syria's Chemical Weapons," The Washington Post, September 6, 2013, www.washingtonpost.com/news/fact-checker/wp/2013/09/06/president-obama-and-the-red-line-on-syrias-chemical-weapons/?utm_term=.a7dfb2b8e70a.

41 Ben Rhodes, "Inside the White House During the Syrian 'Red Line' Crisis," The Atlantic, June 3, 2018, www.theatlantic.com/international/archive/2018/06/inside-the-white-house-during-the-syrian-red-line-crisis/561887.

42 Author telephone interview with Alexander Bick, May 4, 2020, Washington, DC.

43 Jeffrey Goldberg, "The Obama Doctrine. The US president talks through his hardest decisions about America's role in the world," The Atlantic, April 2016 issue, www.theatlantic.com/magazine/archive/2016/04/the-obama-doctrine/471525/#1.

44 UN Security Council Resolution 2118, www.securitycouncilreport.org/atf/cf/%7B65BFCF9B-6D27-4E9C-8CD3-CF6E4FF96FF9%7D/s_res_2118.pdf.

45 Marko Milanovic, A Few Thoughts on Resolution 2118 (2013) October 1, 2013 www.ejiltalk.org/a-few-thoughts-on-resolution-2118/.

46 Security Council Sixty-eighth year 7047th meeting, October 22, 2013, 10 a.m. New York, https://undocs.org/S/PV.7047.

47 Arshad Mohammed and Andrew Osborn, "Kerry: Syrian Surrender of Chemical Arms Could Stop US Attack," Reuters, September 9, 2013, www.reuters.com/article/us-syria-crisis-kerry/kerry-syrian-surrender-of-chemical-arms-could-stop-u-s-attack-idUSBRE9880BV20130909. Spetalnick, Arshad Mohammed, "Analysis: How Kerry's Off-hand Remark Put a Deal on Syria in Play," Reuters, September 9, 2013, www.reuters.com/article/us-syria-crisis-analysis/analysis-how-kerrys-off-hand-remark-put-a-deal-on-syria-in-play-idUSBRE98902D20130910.

48 "Obama asks Congress to Delay Vote on Syria Military Strike," Reuters, September 10, 2013, www.reuters.com/article/us-syria-crisis-delay/obama-asks-congress-to-delay-vote-on-syria-military-strike-idUSBRE98917420130910.

49 Vladimir V. Putin, "A Plea for Caution from Russia," The New York Times, September 11, 2012, www.nytimes.com/2013/09/12/opinion/putin-plea-for-caution-from-russia-on-syria.html.

50 "Framework for Elimination of Syrian Chemical Weapons," US Department of State, September 14, 2013, https://2009-2017.state.gov/r/pa/prs/ps/2013/09/214247.htm.

51 Author interview with anonymous Western official, September 11, 2020.

52 Ibid.

53 Security Council Sixty-eighth year 7038th meeting Friday, 27 September 2013, 8 p.m. New York, https://undocs.org/S/PV.7038, pp. 3–5.

54 Ibid.

55 Steve Gutterman, "Russia doubts mid-November date for Syria peace talks," October 1, 2013, www.reuters.com/article/us-syria-crisis-russia/russia-doubts-mid-november-date-for-syria-peace-talks-idUSBRE9900D220131001.

56 "Падение режима Асада сегодня может привести к тяжелым последствиям," Interview with Bogdanov, Interfax, December 19, 2013, www.interfax.ru/interview/347713.

57 Krishnadev Calamur, "Assad is Still Using Chemical Weapons in Syria. Neither the threat of US action nor an Obama-era agreement appears to deter Bashar al-Assad," The Atlantic, February 6, 2018, www.theatlantic.com/international/archive/2018/02/syria-chemical-weapons/552428/.

58 Alicia Sanders-Zakre, "What You Need to Know About Chemical Weapons Use in Syria," Arms Control Association, September 23, 2018, then updated March 14, 2019, www.armscontrol.org/blog/2018-09-23/what-you-need-know-about-chemical-weapons-use-syria.

59 Oren Dorell, "Canceled Syria talks may get new start in Moscow," USA Today, November 7, 2013, www.usatoday.com/story/news/world/2013/11/07/syria-peace-talks-chemical-weapons/3464091/.

60 "Syria Geneva II peace talks witness bitter exchanges," BBC, January 22, 2014, www.bbc.com/news/world-middle-east-25836827.

61 Anna Borshchevskaya, "What to Expect from Syria Peace Talks in Moscow," The Washington Institute for Near East Policy, January 23, 2015, www.washingtoninstitute.org/policy-analysis/view/what-to-expect-from-syria-peace-talks-in-moscow. Anna Borshchevskaya, "Russia's Self-Serving Approach to Syrian Peace Talks," The Washington Institute for Near East Policy, August 18, 2015, www.washingtoninstitute.org/policy-analysis/view/russias-self-serving-approach-to-syrian-peace-talks.

62 Jeffrey Goldberg, "The Obama Doctrine. The US president talks through his hardest decisions about America's role in the world," The Atlantic, April 2016 issue, www.theatlantic.com/magazine/archive/2016/04/the-obama-doctrine/471525/#1.

9 Diplomacy with Military Action

1 Interview with Alexander Bick, May 4, 2020.

2 Ibid.

3 Ali Watkins, "Obama team was warned in 2014 about Russian interference," Politico, August 14, 2017, www.politico.com/story/2017/08/14/obama-russia-election-interference-241547.

4   John W. Parker, *Putin's Syrian Gambit: Sharper Elbows, Bigger Footprint, Stickier Wicket*, Institute For National Strategic Studies, National Defense University Press, Washington, DC, July 2017 p. 84, https://inss.ndu.edu/Portals/68/Documents/ stratperspective/inss/Strategic-Perspectives-25.pdf.

5   "Лавров: Никто не знает, где находится 'умеренная сирийская оппозиция,'" Regnum, October 5, 2015, https://regnum.ru/news/polit/1984719.html.

6   Thomas Erdbrink, Sewell Chan and David E. Sanger, "After a US Shift, Iran Has a Seat at Talks on War in Syria," *The New York Times*, October 28, 2015 www.nytimes. com/2015/10/29/world/middleeast/syria-talks-vienna-iran.html.

7   "Exclusive: Russia to propose Syrians launch 18-month reform process—document," Reuters, November 10, 2015 www.reuters.com/article/us-mideast-crisis-syria-draft-idUSKCN0SZ2F720151110.

8   Andrew J. Tabler "Beyond Deconfliction in Syria," The Washington Institute for Near East Policy, November 16, 2017 www.washingtoninstitute.org/policy-analysis/view/ beyond-deconfliction-in-syria.

9   Julian Borger, "UN Resolution on Syria Creates a Framework—But One with Yawning Gaps," *The Guardian*, December 19, 2015 www.theguardian.com/ world/2015/dec/19/un-resolution-syria-creates-framework-yawning-gaps-assad.

10 Press release, "Security Council Unanimously Adopts Resolution 2254 (2015), Endorsing Road Map for Peace Process in Syria, Setting Timetable for Talks," December 18, 2015 www.un.org/press/en/2015/sc12171.doc.htm.

11 Ben Mathis-Lilley, "Trump Jr. Was Apparently Paid at Least $50,000 by Kremlin-Connected Foreign Policy Group," Slate, March 2, 2017 https://slate.com/news-and-politics/2017/03/donald-trump-jr-possibly-paid-50000-by-russia-connected-group. html.

12 Brian Ross, Matthew Mosk, Rym Momtaz, "For Donald Trump Jr., lingering questions about meeting with pro-Russia group," ABC News, March 2, 2017 https:// abcnews.go.com/Politics/trump-jr-lingering-questions-meeting-pro-russia-group/ story?id=45858839.

13 "Syria crisis plan: Cessation of hostilities, humanitarian airdrops, peace talks laid out in Munich," RT, February 12, 2016 www.rt.com/news/332211-munich-lavrov-kerry-un-syria/.

14 "Syria needs new constitution, says Russia's Putin," Reuters, January 11, 2016 www. reuters.com/article/us-mideast-crisis-syria-putin-idUSKCN0UQ09H20160112.

15 Sammer Abboud, "Russia's draft constitution: End of Syria's Baath era?" May 29, 2016 www.aljazeera.com/news/2016/05/russia-draft-constitution-syria-baath-era-160529064231915.html.

16 Ricardo Giucci, Anne Mdinaradze, *The Eurasian Economic Union. Analysis From a Trade Policy Perspective-Financed by the Federal Ministry for Economic Affairs and Energy*—Second version: September 8, 2017, p. 5, https://berlin-economics.com/ wp-content/uploads/Eurasian-Economic-Union-trade-policy-perspective.pdf.

17 Lyse Doucet, "Syria peace talks: Armed groups come in from the cold," BBC, January 23, 2017 www.bbc.com/news/world-38712444.

18 Ibid.

19 Aron Lund, "The Qadri Jamil Affair," Carnegie Middle East Center, Carnegie Middle East, November 1, 2013 https://carnegie-mec.org/diwan/53486.

20 Anne Barnard, "Syrian Peace Talks in Russia: 1,500 Delegates, Mostly Pro-Assad," January 30, 2018 www.nytimes.com/2018/01/30/world/middleeast/syria-russia-sochi-talks.html.

21 Author telephone interview with Ilyas Akhmadov, May 25, 2020.

22 Interview with Ilyas Akhmadov.

23 John W. Parker, *Putin's Syrian Gambit: Sharper Elbows, Bigger Footprint, Stickier Wicket* Institute or National Strategic Studies, National Defense University Press Washington, DC, July 2017 p. 23, https://inss.ndu.edu/Portals/68/Documents/stratperspective/inss/Strategic-Perspectives-25.pdf.

24 Reuters, "Syria Constitution Body Could Be Agreed on Soon—Russian Official," *The Moscow Times*, April 26, 2019 www.themoscowtimes.com/2019/04/26/syria-constitution-body-could-be-agreed-on-soon-russian-official-a65407. Stephanie Nebehay, Ali Kucukgocmen, "Russia, Iran, Turkey Back New Syria Constitution Body but Fail to Agree Makeup," Reuters, December 17, 2018 www.reuters.com/article/us-mideast-crisis-syria-un/russia-iran-turkey-back-new-syria-constitution-body-but-fail-to-agree-makeup-idUSKBN1OG2D8.

25 George Baghdadi, "What to expect as Syria peace talks resume," CBS News, February 23, 2017 www.cbsnews.com/news/syria-peace-talks-geneva-4-assad-rebels-opposition-little-hope-breakthrough/.

26 James Dobbins, Philip Gordon, and Jeffrey Martini, *A Peace Plan for Syria IV, a Bottom up Approach Linking Reconstruction to Government Formation*, RAND Corporation, 2017, p. 4 www.rand.org/content/dam/rand/pubs/perspectives/PE200/PE276/RAND_PE276.pdf.

27 Hashem Osseiran, "How De-Escalation Zones in Syria Became a War Management Strategy," Syria Deeply, February 6, 2018 www.newsdeeply.com/syria/articles/2018/02/06/how-de-escalation-zones-in-syria-became-a-war-management-strategy.

28 Foreign Minister Sergey Lavrov's statement and answers to media questions at a news conference on Russian diplomacy in 2017, Moscow, January 15, 2018 www.mid.ru/en/foreign_policy/news/-/asset_publisher/cKNonkJE02Bw/content/id/3018203.

29 Syrian Democratic Council ready for "unconditional talks" with Assad regime www.rudaw.net/english/middleeast/syria/100620182.

30 Kirill Semenov, "New name, same old problems: Syria talks kick off in Kazakh capital," Al Monitor, April 30, 2019, www.al-monitor.com/pulse/originals/2019/04/russia-turkey-iran-nursultan-astana-talks.html.

31 Из выступления и ответов на вопросы СМИ Министра иностранных дел России С.В.Лаврова в ходе пресс-конференции по итогам деятельности российской дипломатии в 2018 году, Москва, 16 января 2019 года www.mid.ru/obstanovka-v-sirii-i-perspektivy-vnutrisirijskogo-dialoga/-/asset_publisher/uFvfWVmCb4Rl/content/id/3296770.

32 Tom Miles, "UN Looks for US-Russia Understanding to Spur Syria Peace Process," Reuters, June 27, 2019, www.reuters.com/article/us-syria-security-un/un-looks-for-us-russia-understanding-to-spur-syria-peace-process-idUSKCN1TS13S.

10 Moscow's Relationships with Regional Actors: Israel

1 Mark N. Katz, "Putin's Pro-Israel Policy," *Middle East Quarterly*, Winter 2005, pp. 51–9, www.meforum.org/690/putins-pro-israel-policy.

2 It is currently down to approximately 700,000.

3 Stuart Winer, "Israel's Population Nears 9 million of Eve of 2019," *Times of Israel*, December 31, 2018, www.timesofisrael.com/israels-population-nears-9-million-on-eve-of-2019/.

4 It is noteworthy that Putin exaggerated the number of Israeli citizens who came from the former Soviet Union and added that the number of Russian pilgrims going to Jerusalem to visit holy sites is growing. "Putin Says He Plans to Meet Israeli Prime Minister Soon," TASS, March 16, 2016, http://tass.com/politics/862850.

5 Mark N. Katz, "Putin's Pro-Israel Policy," *Middle East Quarterly*, winter 2005, pp. 51–9.

6 "Визиты в Государство Израиль и на территории Палестинской национальной администрации," Kremlin.ru, 27–29 April 2005, www.kremlin.ru/catalog/countries/IL/events/45556.

7 "Совместное российско-израильское заявление," Kremlin.ru, April 27, 2005, www.kremlin.ru/supplement/3633.

8 Sophia Kishkovsky, "Anti-Semitic Letter Embroils Duma," *The New York Times*, February 5, 2005, www.nytimes.com/2005/02/05/world/antisemitic-letter-embroils-duma.html.

9 Carl Schreck, "Russian Government Spokeswoman Suggests Trump Won Thanks To 'The Jews,'" RFE/RL, November 16, 2016, www.rferl.org/a/russian-government-spokeswoman-trump-won-thanks-to-jews/28124518.html. Petr Tolstoy, vice Duma speaker had made widely condemned anti-semitic comments in January 2017. See "Вице-спикер Госдумы Петр Толстой выступил с антисемитским заявлением. И сам обвинил журналистов в антисемитизме," Meduza, January 7, 2017, https://meduza.io/feature/2017/01/24/vitse-spiker-gosdumy-petr-tolstoy-vystupil-s-antisemitskim-zayavleniem-i-sam-obvinil-zhurnalistov-v-antisemitizme.

10 Carl Schreck, "Russian Government Spokeswoman Suggests Trump Won Thanks to 'The Jews,'" RFE/RL November 17, 2016, www.rferl.org/a/russian-government-spokeswoman-trump-won-thanks-to-jews/28124518.html.

11 "Meeting with Israeli President Shimon Peres," transcript, Kremlin, June 25, 2012, http://kremlin.ru/events/president/news/15731.

12 See Martin Kramer, "Who saved Israel in 1947?" Mosaic Magazine, November 6, 2017, https://mosaicmagazine.com/essay/israel-zionism/2017/11/who-saved-israel-in-1947/.

13 Jonathan Lis, "Putin Arrives in Israel to Discuss West's Standoff with Iran," Haaretz, June 25, 2012, www.haaretz.com/putin-arrives-in-israel-1.5186629.

14 Richard Pipes, *The Russian Revolution*. Chapter 18, "The Red Terror, Bolsheviks Create Concentration Camps," Vintage Books, New York: December 1991, first edition.

15 Amotz Asa-El, "Can Israel be neutral on Ukraine?" *Jerusalem Post*, April 17, 2014, www.jpost.com/Features/Front-Lines/Can-Israel-be-neutral-on-Ukraine-349814.

16 Ibid.

17 Raphael Ahren, TOI Staff, "After 'historic' Russia visit, Netanyahu says US remains top ally," *Times of Israel*, June 8, 2016, www.timesofisrael.com/after-historic-russian-visit-netanyahu-says-us-remains-top-ally/.

18 "Встреча с Премьер-министром Израиля Биньямином Нетаньяху," Kremlin.ru, September 21 2015, www.kremlin.ru/events/president/news/50335.

19 "Встреча с Премьер-министром Израиля Биньямином Нетаньяху," Kremlin.ru, November 30, 2015, www.kremlin.ru/events/president/news/50847.

20 Maria Tsvetkova, "Israel, Russia to Coordinate Military Action on Syria: Netanyahu," Reuters, November 21, 2015, www.reuters.com/article/us-mideast-crisis-russia-israel/israel-russia-to-coordinate-military-action-on-syria-netanyahu-idUSKCN0RL10K20150921.

21 Ibid.

22 Ibid.

23 "Встреча с Премьер-министром Израиля Биньямином Нетаньяху," Kremlin.ru, July 11, 2018, www.kremlin.ru/events/president/news/57983.

24 "Встреча с Премьер-министром Израиля Биньямином Нетаньяху," Kremlin.ru, February 27, 2019, www.kremlin.ru/events/president/news/59902.

25 "Встреча с Премьер-министром Израиля Биньямином Нетаньяху," Kremlin.ru, November 30, 2015, www.kremlin.ru/events/president/news/50847.

26 "Встреча с Премьер-министром Израиля Биньямином Нетаньяху," Kremlin.ru, March 9, 2017, www.kremlin.ru/events/president/news/54016.

27 Andrei Kolesnikov, "Один в боли не воин. Биньямин Нетаньяху приехал к Владимиру Путину искать защиты от Ирана," Kommersant August 24, 2017, www.kommersant.ru/doc/3391322.

28 Aydyn Mekhtiyev, Провал Нетаньяху в Сочи: что творится в треугольнике Россия—Иран—Израиль" August 30 2018, www.pravda.ru/authored/1346489-netanyahu/.

29 David Makovsky, "Putin's Golan Comments: Implications for Israeli Security," The Washington Institute for Near East Policy, July 19, 2018, www.washingtoninstitute. org/policy-analysis/view/putins-golan-comments-implications-for-israeli-security.

30 Alex Fishman, "'Hezbollah Evades Israeli bombs in Syria by flying Russian flag,'" Ynet, December 12, 2018, www.ynetnews.com/articles/0,7340,L-5425367,00.html. Marianna Belen'kaya, Ivan Safronov "Израиль и Россия поспорят об Иране. Возобновление военных контактов двух стран будет непростым," Kommersant, December 12, 2018, www.kommersant.ru/doc/3827707. Raja Abdulrahim, "Iran-Backed Fighters Switch to Syrian Uniforms to Avoid Israeli Strikes, Rebels Say," The Wall Street Journal, June 8, 2018, www.wsj.com/articles/iran-backed-fighters-switch-to-syrian-uniforms-to-avoid-israeli-strikes-rebels-say-1528478351.

31 Dmitry (Dima) Adamsky, "Russia and the Next Lebanon War. How Moscow Could Benefit from A Conflict Between Israel and Hezbollah," Foreign Affairs, October 6, 2017, www.foreignaffairs.com/articles/israel/2017-10-06/russia-and-next-lebanon-war.

32 Aleksandra Arsentyeva, "'Россия—не пожарная команда и не может спасать все': Путин о ядерной сделке с Ираном," TV Zvezda, May 15, 2019, https://tvzvezda.ru/news/vstrane_i_mire/content/20195151811-RKcI5.html.

33 Official Statement by Patrushev, "Israel: 'Iran remains our ally and partner'—Russia's Patrushev after trilateral security talks," RT, Video, June 25, 2019, www.youtube.com/watch?v=xfrGxk9Oi7M.

34 Petr Akopov, "Россия выбрала союзника на Ближнем Востоке," Vzglyad, June 25, 2019, https://vz.ru/world/2019/6/25/984190.html.

35 The quote in Russian is "У нас действительно выстроились очень добрые, деловые, партнёрские, а во многом даже с элементами союзничества отношения со многими странами региона, включая не только Иран и Турцию, но и другие страны." The full transcript of the interview is available from: "Интервью газете The Financial Times," Kremlin.ru, June 27, 2019, http://kremlin.ru/events/president/news/60836. The FT has published an article with interview excerpts, which does not include the comment about Iran, Lionel Barber and Henry Foy in Moscow and Alex Barker in Osaka "Vladimir Putin says Liberalism has 'Become Obsolete,'" FT.com, June 27, 2019, www.ft.com/content/670039ec-98f3-11e9-9573-ee5cbb98ed36.

36 "Соболезнования Премьер-министру Израиля Биньямину Нетаньяху," Kremlin. ru, January 8, 2017, www.kremlin.ru/events/president/news/53709.

37 For example, "Russia offers Israel help in fighting wildfires," TASS, May 24, 2019, https://tass.com/emergencies/1059985.

38 Svetlana Bolotnikova "In Russia, some men want to watch the world burn," Open Democracy, September 21, 2016, www.opendemocracy.net/en/odr/kuban-some-men-want-to-watch-world-burn/. See also Miriam Laskoy's presentation, Atlantic Council public event, Vladimir Putin's Anti-Terrorism Strategy, September 16, 2016, www.c-span.org/video/?415378-1/atlantic-council-examines-vladimir-putins-antiterrorism-strategy.

39 "Medvedev's Awkward Crimea Moment: 'There's Just No Money. But You Take Care!'" RFE/RL, May 24, 2016, www.rferl.org/a/russia-medvedev-crimea-visit-no-money-social-media-pensioner/27754644.html.

40 Joshua Krasna, *Moscow on the Mediterranean: Russia and Israel's Relationship*, Foreign Policy Research Institute (FPRI), Russia foreign policy papers, June 2018, www.fpri.org/wp-content/uploads/2018/06/krasna2018.pdf p. 10.

41 Judah Ari Gross and TOI staff, "Putin: Syria Helped Russian Army find Remains of IDF Soldier Missing since 1982," *Times of Israel*, April 4, 2019, www.timesofisrael.com/putin-syria-helped-russian-army-find-remains-of-idf-soldier-missing-since-1982/.

42 "Putin accepts Israeli PM's invite to unveiling of monument to Siege of Leningrad victims," TASS, February 27, 2019, https://tass.com/society/1046677.

43 Cnaan Liphshiz, "Most Gets First Major Holocaust Monument," *Jerusalem Post*, www.jpost.com/Diaspora/Antisemitism/Moscow-gets-1st-major-Holocaust-monument-591614.

44 Itamar Eichner, "Israel–Russia relations sour over Sobibór memorial exclusion," Ynet, August 20, 2017, www.ynetnews.com/articles/0,7340,L-5005138,00.html, Rafael Fakhrutdinov, "Захарова обрушилась на Израиль," Gazeta. ru, August 19, 2017, www.gazeta.ru/politics/2017/08/19_a_10838120.shtml.

45 Andrew Roth, "How an Unlikely PR Campaign Made a Ribbon the Symbol of Russian Patriotism," *The Washington Post*, May 9, 2017, www.washingtonpost.com/news/worldviews/wp/2017/05/09/how-an-unlikely-pr-campaign-made-a-ribbon-the-symbol-of-russian-patriotism/?utm_term=.40251563169f.

46 Yaroslav Trofimov, "At Putin's Parade, Netanyahu Seeks Understanding on Iran. Israeli Leader Wants to Make sure that the Russians Consider his Security Concerns," *The Wall Street Journal*, May 9, 2018, www.wsj.com/articles/at-putins-parade-netanyahu-seeks-understanding-on-iran-1525876793.

47 Vladimir Putin, speech at the Congess of the United Israel Appeal (Keren Hayesod) in Moscow, "Путин: 'Считаем Израиль русскоязычным государством,'" September 17, 2019, www.youtube.com/watch?v=TmNGT1MxwG4.

48 "Lavrov comments on Israel's recent air raids against targets in Syria," TASS, March 22, 2017, https://tass.com/politics/936846.

49 "Враждебные действия» и «адекватный ответ»: главное о сбитом в Сирии самолете Минобороны," TV Dozhd (Rain), September 18, 2018, https://tvrain.ru/articles/glavnoe_o_sbitom_v_sirii_samolete_minoborony-471674/.

50 "Russia's Reactions to the Russian Plane Crash in The Mediterranean," The Middle East Media Research Institute (MEMRI), September 23, 2018, www.memri.org/reports/russias-reactions-russian-plane-crash-mediterranean#_edn3.

51 "После уничтожения Ил-20 в Думе предложили сбивать израильские самолеты," Vesti.ru, 23 September, 2018, www.vesti.ru/doc.html?id=3063568.

52 "В комитете Госдумы по обороне призвали нанести удар по Израилю," Govorit Moskva, September 18, 2018, https://govoritmoskva.ru/news/173702/.

53 "Пресс-конференция по итогам российско-венгерских переговоров," transcript, Kremlin.ru, September 18, 2018, http://kremlin.ru/events/president/transcripts/58586.

54 Tom O'Connor, "Russia Calls Israel 'the Problem' in the Middle East, Defends Iran and Its Allies," Newsweek, December 8, 2020 https://www.newsweek.com/russia-israel-problem-mideast-defends-iran-allies-1553259.

11 Moscow's Relationships with Sunni Actors, Iran, and Assad

1 Robert O. Freedman, "Russia and the Middle East under Putin," Ortadogu Etutleri 2, No. 3, p. 26, July 2010, www.orsam.org.tr/en/enUploads/Article/Files/201082_robertfeedman.orsam.etutler.pdf; "Russia Offers Gas to Turks," Kommersant, November 24, 2000, www.kommersant.ru/doc/161412; Turkish Ministry of Foreign Affairs. "Turkey's Political Relations with Russian Federation," www.mfa.gov.tr/turkey_s-political-relations-with-russian-federation.en.mfa.

2 Robert O. Freedman, "Russia and the Middle East under Putin," p. 26.

3 "Turkey," Wilson Center, July 7, 2011, www.wilsoncenter.org/pub-lication/turkey#sthash.gpdUdBIQ.dpuf.

4 "President Vladimir Putin Met with Turkish Prime Minister Recep Tayyip Erdogan," press release, Kremlin, January 10, 2005, http://en.kremlin.ru/events/president/news/32567.

5 "Press Statements and Answers to Questions following Russian-Turkish Talks," Kremlin.ru, July 18, 2005, http://en.kremlin.ru/events/president/transcripts/23093.

6 Andrei Terekhov, "Путин создаст напряжение в Ираке," Nezavisimaya Gazeta, July 19, 2005, www.ng.ru/politics/2005-07-19/2_putin.html.

7 Bulent Aras, "Turkey and the Russian Federation: An Emerging Multidimensional Partnership," Today's Zaman, August 11, 2009, www.to-dayszaman.com/todays-think-tanks_turkey-and-the-russian-federation-an-emerging-multidimensional-partnership_183695.html.

8 "Turkey, Russia to Seek New Ways to Deepen Economic Ties despite Dis-agreements in Syria, Ukraine," Hurriyet Daily News, December 1, 2014, www.hurriyetdailynews.com/turkey-russia-to-seek-new-ways-to-deepen-economic-ties-despite-disagreements-in-syria-ukraine.aspx?pageID=238&nID=75027&NewsCatID=510.

9 "Turkey becomes Russia's 5th Biggest Trading Partner in H1 2018," *Daily Sabah*, August 8, 2018, www.dailysabah.com/economy/2018/08/08/turkey-becomes-russias-5th-biggest-trading-partner-in-h1-2018.

10 International Monetary Fund Direction of Trade database, accessed August 5–6, 2019.

11 Ibid.

12 For years, Turkey ranked below Russia according to Reporters without Borders. See official rankings at: https://rsf.org/en/ranking.

13 "Factbox: Russia–Turkey Economic and Trade Relations," Reuters, November 24, 2015, www.reuters.com/article/us-mideast-crisis-russia-turkey-ties-fac/factbox-russia-turkey-economic-and-trade-relations-idUSKBN0TD26K20151124.

14 Jeffrey Mankoff, "Russia and Turkey's Rapprochement. Don't Expect an Equal Partnership," Foreign Affairs, July 20, 2016, www.foreignaffairs.com/articles/turkey/2016-07-20/russia-and-turkeys-rapprochement. Holly Ellyatt, "This is how Russia could hurt Turkey's economy," CNBC November 26, 2015, www.cnbc.com/2015/11/26/this-is-how-russia-could-hurt-turkeys-economy.html. Keith Johnson, "Russia, Turkey Fight Spreads to Energy Sector Tensions between Moscow and Ankara keep heating up after the downing of a Russian jet. Now, multibillion-dollar energy projects like pipelines and nuclear reactors could be axed," December 9, 2015, https://foreignpolicy.com/2015/12/09/russia-turkey-fight-spreads-to-energy-sector-putin-erdogan-turkish-stream-akkuyu/. Berivan Orucoglu, "The Tsar Meets the Sultan. These days, Turkey's Erdogan looks more and more like Putin. Now, the two are teaming up to lash out at Europe," Foreign Policy, December 4, 2014, https://foreignpolicy.com/2014/12/04/the-tsar-meets-the-sultan-turkey-russia/.

15 Natasha Ezro, "Will Russian Airstrikes in Syria Derail Turkey Relationship?" CNN, October 8, 2015, www.cnn.com/2015/10/08/opinions/syria-airstrikes-russia-turkey-opinion/. Robin Emmott and Laila Bassam, "NATO Rejects Russia Explanation on Turkish Air Space," Reuters, October 6, 2015, www.reuters.com/article/2015/10/07/us-mideast-crisis-syria-idUSKCN0S01DS20151007.

16 James F. Jeffrey, "Russian Overflight of Turkey: More than Meets the Eye?" Policy Alert Washington Institute for Near East Policy, October 6, 2015, www.washingtoninstitute.org/policy-analysis/view/russian-over-flight-of-turkey-more-than-meets-the-eye.

17 "Turkey Summons Russian Envoy over Bombing of Turkmens in Syria: PM," Reuters, November 20, 2015, www.reuters.com/article/us-mid-east-crisis-syria-turkey-russia-idUSKCN0T91MO20151120.

18 Don Melvin, Michael Martinez, and Zeynep Bilginsoy, "Putin Calls Jet's Downing 'Stab in the Back'; Turkey Says Warning Ignored," CNN, November 24, 2015, www.cnn.com/2015/11/24/middleeast/warplane-crashes-near-syria-turkey-border/.

19 "Внесены изменения в Указ о мерах по обеспечению национальной безопасности и защите граждан России от противоправных действий

и о применении специальных экономических мер в отношении Турции. Kremlin.ru, December 28, 2015, http://kremlin.ru/acts/news/51027.

20 Anna Borshchevskaya, "Russia, Syrian Kurds, and the Assad regime," in Patrick Clawson, editor, Syrian Kurds as a US Ally, Policy Focus, The Washington Institute for Near East Policy, November 18, 2016, www.washingtoninstitute.org/uploads/Documents/pubs/PolicyFocus150_Clawson-2.pdf. Michael A. Reynolds "Vladimir Putin, Godfather of Kurdistan?" The National Interest, March 1, 2016, https://nationalinterest.org/feature/vladimir-putin-godfather-kurdistan-15358.

21 For more details on this history, see Michael Rubin, *Kurdistan Rising? Considerations for Kurds, Their Neighbors, and the Region*, American Enterprise Institute, July 2016. Anna Borshchevskaya, "Russia, Syrian Kurds, and the Assad regime," in Patrick Clawson, editor, Syrian Kurds as a US Ally, Policy Focus, The Washington Institute for Near East Policy, November 18, 2016.

22 "Syrian Kurdish PYD committee on visit to Russia, Salih Muslim to give address in the Duma," EKurd Daily, December 18, 2013, https://ekurd.net/mismas/articles/misc2013/12/syriakurd974.htm.

23 Roland Oliphant, "Syrian Kurds open diplomatic mission in Moscow," *The Telegraph*, February 10, 2016, www.telegraph.co.uk/news/worldnews/europe/russia/12150692/Syrian-Kurds-open-diplomatic-mission-in-Moscow.html.

24 John Parker, *Putin's Syrian Gambit.*

25 "Юрий Шафраник: Россия возвращает лидерские позиции на Ближнем Востоке," NIA Krasnoyarsk, June 1, 2010, https://24rus.ru/more.php?UID=55237

26 "Meeting with the Successor to the Crown Prince, Minister of Defense of Saudi Arabia, Muhammad bin Salman," press release, Kremlin, June 18, 2015, http://kremlin.ru/events/president/news/49724.

27 "Syria conflict: Turkey Shells Kurdish Militia," BBC, February 13, 2016, www.bbc.com/news/world-middle-east-35571663.

28 "'Crimes of historic proportions' being committed in Aleppo, UN rights chief warns," UN News, October 21, 2016, https://www.bloomberg.com/opinion/articles/2015-06-09/iran-spends-billions-to-prop-up-assad.

29 Natasha Bertrand, "Russian embassy trolls US and Britain: Grozny today is 'solution we're all looking for,'" Business Insider, October 17, 2016, www.businessinsider.com/russian-embassy-us-grozny-aleppo-syria-2016-10.

30 Soner Cagaptay, Anna Borshchevskaya, and Nader Uskowi, "Turkish-Russian-Iranian Summit: Limits to a Tripartite Entente," The Washington Institute for Near East Policy, April 3, 2018, www.washingtoninstitute.org/policy-analysis/view/turkish-russian-iranian-summit-limits-to-a-tripartite-entente.

31 Roy Gutman, "Syria Ceasefire Brings Turkey Closer to War," *Foreign Policy*, February 16, 2016, https://foreignpolicy.com/2016/02/16/syria-ceasefire-brings-turkey-closer-to-war/February 16, 2016.

32 Liz Sly and Suzan Haidamous, "Syria Deal Draws Iran into Alliance with Russia and Turkey," *The Washington Post*, January 24, 2017, www.washingtonpost.com/world/middle_east/syria-deal-draws-iran-into-alliance-with-russia-and-turkey/2017/01/24/5336057c-e199-11e6-a419-eefe8eff0835_story.html?noredirect=on&utm_term=.80ec95e64535.

33 John Parker, *Putin's Syrian Gambit.*

34 Michael Rubin, "It's Time to Designate Turkey as a Sponsor of Terrorism," *The Washington Examiner*, January 18, 2019, www.washingtonexaminer.com/opinion/its-time-to-designate-turkey-as-a-sponsor-of-terrorism. Michael Rubin, "It's Impossible to Beat ISIS with Erdogan in Power," Newsweek, March 31, 2016, www.newsweek.com/impossible-beat-isis-erdogan-power-442767.

35 H. Akin Unver, "Russia Has Won the Information War in Turkey," *Foreign Policy*, April 21, 2019, https://foreignpolicy.com/2019/04/21/russia-has-won-the-information-war-in-turkey-rt-sputnik-putin-erdogan-disinformation/.

36 Khaled Yacoub Oweis, "Saudi-Qatar Rivalry Divides Syrian Opposition," Reuters, January 15, 2014, www.reuters.com/article/us-syria-crisis-qatar/saudi-qatar-rivalry-divides-syrian-opposition-idUSBREA0E1G720140115.

37 Jonathan Schanzer, "Saudi Arabia Is Arming the Syrian Opposition What Could Possibly go Wrong?" *Foreign Policy*, February 27, 2012, https://foreignpolicy.com/2012/02/27/saudi-arabia-is-arming-the-syrian-opposition/. "Who is supplying weapons to the warring sides in Syria?" BBC June 14, 2013, www.bbc.com/news/world-middle-east-22906965. Karen J. DeYoung, "Syrian Rebels' Backers, Meeting in Qatar, Agree to Send Weapons," *The Washington Post*, June 22, 2013, www.washingtonpost.com/world/middle_east/syrian-rebels-backers-meeting-in-qatar-agree-to-send-weapons/2013/06/22/a7707274-db50-11e2-b418-9dfa095e125d_story.html?utm_term=.161a5288c9e3. Martin Chulov, "Qatar Crosses the Syrian Rubicon: £63m to Buy Weapons for the Rebels," *The Guardian*, March 1, 2012, www.theguardian.com/world/2012/mar/01/syria-conflict-rebels-qatar-weapons.

38 See for example Richard Spencer, "Who are the Syrian Rebels Holding Talks in Saudi Arabia?" *The Telegraph*, December 8, 2015, www.telegraph.co.uk/news/worldnews/middleeast/syria/12040147/Who-are-the-Syrian-rebels-holding-talks-in-Saudi-Arabia.html.

39 Roula Khalaf and Abigail Fielding Smith, "Qatar Bankrolls Syrian Revolt with Cash and Arms," *Financial Times*, May 16, 2013, http://ig-legacy.ft.com/content/86e3f28e-be3a-11e2-bb35-00144feab7de#axzz5uhsw7Tou.

40 Ivan Denezhkin, "ТЭК, автомобили, банки: российские компании готовы работать в Сирии," Rueconomics.ru, February 16, 2017 https://rueconomics.ru/227744-tek-mashiny-banki-rossiiskie-kompanii-gotovy-rabotat-v-sirii Reposted on Shafranik's page with title "Готовы работать в Сирии," https://shafranik.ru/node/16177.

41 Bruce Riedel, "Saudi's star prince keeps rising, visits Putin in St. Petersburg," June 19, 2015, www.brookings.edu/blog/markaz/2015/06/19/saudis-star-prince-keeps-rising-visits-putin-in-st-petersburg/. Bruce Riedel, "Saudi deputy crown prince seeks Russia deals," Al Monitor, June 21, 2015, www.al-monitor.com/pulse/originals/2015/06/saudi-crown-prince-russia-deals.html.

42 "Saudi Sovereign Fund to Invest $10bn in Russia," *Financial Times*, July 6, 2015, www.ft.com/content/0205a0d6-2412-11e5-bd83-71cb60e8f08c?mhq5j=e7.

43 Leonid Issaev and Nikolay Kozhanov, "Russian delegation in Syria to talk reconstruction," France 24, December 18, 2017 https://www.france24.com/en/20171218-russian-delegation-syria-talk-reconstruction.

44 Benoit Faucon, Summer Said, Christopher Alessi, "OPEC, Russia Strike Deal to Cut Oil Production. The Cartel along with Russia and its Allies will Curb Oil Output by a Collective 1.2 million Barrels a Day," *The Wall Street Journal*, December 7, 2018, www.wsj.com/articles/saudis-still-skeptical-of-opec-coalition-cuts-1544178705.

45 Henry Meyer and Glen Carey, "Even the Saudis are Turning to Russia as Assad's Foes Lose Heart," Bloomberg, September 8, 2017, www.bloomberg.com/news/articles/2017-09-08/even-the-saudis-are-turning-to-russia-as-assad-s-foes-lose-heart.

46 "Документы, подписанные по итогам российско-саудовских переговоров," October 5, 2017, http://kremlin.ru/supplement/5236.

47 "Saudi Arabia agrees to buy Russian S-400 air defense system: Arabiya TV," Reuters, October 5, 2017, www.reuters.com/article/us-saudi-russia-missiles/saudi-arabia-agrees-to-buy-russian-s-400-air-defense-system-arabiya-tv-idUSKBN1CA1OD.

48 Moscow also had one in Iraq, though it did little in terms of actual counter-terrorism.

49 Suleiman Al-Khalidi, "Russia, Jordan Agree to Speed De-escalation Zone in South Syria," Reuters, September 11, 2017, www.reuters.com/article/us-mideast-crisis-jordan-russia/russia-jordan-agree-to-speed-de-escalation-zone-in-south-syria-idUSKCN1BM2A5. Yury Barmin, "Russia calls on Jordan to help stabilize Syrian 'safe' zones," Al Monitor, February 20 2018, www.al-monitor.com/pulse/originals/2018/02/putin-abdullah-russia-jordan-meeting.html.

50 Kira Latukhina, "Путин призвал принять Иран в ШОС," Rossiyskaya Gazeta, June 25, 2016, https://rg.ru/2016/06/24/putin-prizval-priniat-iran-v-shos.html.

51 Official site of the Qingsao summit, June 9–10, 2018, www.xinhuanet.com/english/cnleaders/2018SCOSummit/index.htm. Fars News Agency, "Iran, SCO Negotiating Tehran's Membership," March 23, 2019, www.msn.com/en-xl/middleeast/top-stories/iran-sco-negotiating-tehrans-membership/ar-BBV4GcE.

52 Ibid.

53 Reporting by Ben Blanchard; editing by Michael Perry, "China Says Iran Membership of Shanghai Security Bloc to be Discussed at Summit," Reuters, June 4,

2017, www.reuters.com/article/us-china-sco-iran/china-says-iran-membership-of-shanghai-security-bloc-to-be-discussed-at-summit-idUSKBN18W0CD.

54 Anne Barnard and Andrew E. Kramer "Iran Revokes Russia's Use of Air Base, Saying Moscow 'Betrayed Trust,'" *The New York Times*, August 22, 2016, www.nytimes.com/2016/08/23/world/middleeast/iran-russia-syria.html?_r=0.

55 Allen Cone, "Russia gets permission to use Iran's Hamadan air base for Syria airstrikes," UPI.com, November 30, 2016, www.upi.com/Top_News/World-News/2016/11/30/Russia-gets-permission-to-use-Irans-Hamadan-air-base-for-Syria-airstrikes/8251480520159/.

56 Heshmat Alavi, "Astana Talks: Why Iran and Russia differ on Syria?" Al Arabiya, January 23, 2017, https://english.alarabiya.net/en/features/2017/01/23/Astana-Talks-Why-Iran-Russia-differ-on-Syria-.html.

57 Jaime Dettmer, "Россия и Иран конкурируют за влияние в Сирии," Voice of America (VOA), May 2, 2019, www.golos-ameriki.ru/a/syria-russia-iran/4900974.html.

58 "Top Kremlin official: We are not that threatening," Ryabkov's interview with Frederik Pleitgen, January 25, 2019, https://edition.cnn.com/videos/world/2019/01/25/sergei-ryabkov-russian-deputy-foreign-minister-pleitgn-dnt-tsr-vpx.cnn/video/playlists/around-the-world/.

59 "Иран России больше не союзник," Rosbalt, January 31, 2019, www.rosbalt.ru/world/2019/01/31/1761370.html.

60 Reuters and Haaretz, "Israel's 'Arbitrary' Airstrikes on Syria Must Stop, Russia Warns," Haaretz, January 23, 2019, www.haaretz.com/middle-east-news/syria/israel-s-arbitrary-airstrikes-on-syria-must-stop-russia-warns-1.6869172.

61 Christopher Woolf and Joyce Hackel, "Putin makes Assad an offer he can't refuse," PRI, October 21, 2015, www.pri.org/stories/2015-10-21/putin-makes-assad-offer-he-cant-refuse.

62 Sam Dagher, *Assad or We Burn the Country. How One Family's Lust for Power Destroyed Syria*, Little, Brown and Company: New York, 201, p. 363.

63 BBC Monitoring Service, "Russian military launches webpage to 'combat fakes' on Syria" August 1, 2019.

64 Anne Barnard, "Stubbornly Confident, Assad Emerges as a Survivor Adept at Juggling Allies," *The New York Times*, March 26, 2016, available at www.nytimes.com/2016/03/23/world/middleeast/ bashar-al-assad-syria-russia-west.html.

65 Muhammed Shekh Yusuf, "Режим Асада является марионеткой в руках Ирана и России," Anadolu Agency, November 21, 2015, www.aa.com.tr/ru/мир/режим-асада-является-марионеткой-в-руках-ирана-и-россии/449219.

66 "The Scorpion's Tale: Did Assad Take Putin for a Ride?" March 22, 2016, www.nytimes.com/2016/03/23/world/middleeast/bashar-al-assad-syria-russia-west.html.

67 Anne Barnard, "Stubbornly Confident, Assad Emerges as a Survivor Adept at Juggling Allies."

68 Sinan Hatahet, "Russia and Iran: Economic Influence in Syria," Chatham House, March 8, 2019, www.chathamhouse.org/publication/russia-and-iran-economic-influence-syria.

69 "Syria parliament okays Russian lease of Tartus port: state media," France 24, June 12, 2019 https://www.france24.com/en/20190612-syria-parliament-okays-russian-lease-tartus-port-state-media artus port: state media - France 24.

70 "Россия применяет свое влияние на Асада, но не на благо—Ельченко," Ukrinform, 12.4.17 www.ukrinform.ru/rubric-polytics/2210707-rossia-primenaet-svoe-vlianie-na-asada-no-ne-na-blago-elcenko.html.

12 Russia and Syria's Resources

1 "Factsheet: Syria–Russia Economic Relations," The Syria Report, May 2, 2017, accessed August 9, 2019.

2 Ibid.

3 Ibid.

4 Ibid.

5 Theodore Karasik, "Russia's Financial Tactics in the Middle East," December 20, 2017, *The Jamestown Foundation*, https://jamestown.org/program/russias-financial-tactics-middle-east/.

6 Suleiman Al Khalidi, "Exclusive: Syria prints new money as deficit grows: bankers," *Reuters*, June 13, 2012, www.reuters.com/article/us-syria-economy-money-idUSBRE85C0CL20120613.

7 "Syria's Assad Regime Wants to Join Russia, Kazakhstan, Belarus in Customs Union," Sofia News Agency, August 3, 2012, www.novinite.com/articles/141992/Syria%27s+Assad+Regime+Wants+to+Join+Russia%2C+Kazakhstan%2C+Belarus+in+Customs+Union.

8 "Сирия хочет вступить в Таможенный союз России, Казахстана и Белоруссии," Regnum, February 4, 2013, https://regnum.ru/news/polit/1621001.html. "Сирия согласовала с Россией вступление в Таможенный союз," the Insider.ua, October 21, 2012, www.theinsider.ua/rus/business/526540b53814c/.

9 "Реально ли вступление Сирии в Таможенный союз: мнения," REX news agency, February 7, 2013, www.iarex.ru/interviews/33761.html.

10 "Syria," Country analysis brief, Energy Information Administration, updated August 2011, www.eia.gov/beta/international/analysis_includes/countries_long/Syria/archive/pdf/syria_2011.pdf.

11 Ibid.

12 *Syria's Oil and Gas Industry—A Sector Profile, Executive Summary*, www.syria-report.com/library/reports-surveys/syrias-oil-and-gas-industry-sector-profile.

13 Global oil production up in 2012 as reserves estimates rise again, anonymous, *Oil & Gas Journal*; Dec. 3, 2012; 110, 12; ProQuest pp. 28–31.

14 BP (The British Petroleum Company), *Statistical Review of World Energy, All Data, 1965–2018*, available for download from: www.bp.com/en/global/corporate/ energy-economics/statistical-review-of-world-energy.html.

15 "Syria—Oil Reserves," March 12, 2018, *APS Review Gas Market Trends*, APSG, Volume 90; Issue 10, 2018.

16 Alex Lawler, "Venezuela Tops Oil Reserves League in OPEC Table," Reuters, July 9, 2011, www.reuters.com/article/businesspro-us-opec-oil-reserves/venezuela-tops-oil-reserves-league-in-opec-table-idUSTRE76I3SZ20110719.

17 "Iran oil Exports: Where do They Go?" Datablog, *The Guardian*, February 6, 2012, www.theguardian.com/news/datablog/2012/feb/06/iran-oil-exports-destination.

18 Vanand Meliksetian, "What Happens to Syrian Oil Post-Civil War?" Oilprice.com, August 11, 2018, https://oilprice.com/Energy/Energy-General/What-Happens-To-Syrian-Oil-Post-Civil-War.html.

19 The World Bank, "Syria's Economic Outlook—Spring 2016," www.worldbank.org/en/ country/syria/publication/economic-outlook-spring-2016.

20 Iran, country profile, OPEC, www.opec.org/opec_web/en/about_us/163.htm.

21 "Syria," Country analysis brief, Energy Information Administration, updated August 2011, www.eia.gov/beta/international/analysis_includes/countries_long/Syria/ archive/pdf/syria_2011.pdf.

22 "Syria," Country analysis brief, Energy Information Administration, updated August 2011, www.eia.gov/beta/international/analysis_includes/countries_long/Syria/ archive/pdf/syria_2011.pdf.

23 Vanand Meliksetian, "What Happens to Syrian Oil Post-Civil War?" Oilprice.com, August 11, 2018, https://oilprice.com/Energy/Energy-General/What-Happens-To-Syrian-Oil-Post-Civil-War.html.

24 *Syrian Arab Republic: 2009 Article IV Consultation—Staff Report; and Public Information Notice,* IMF Country Report No. 10/86 March 2010 p. 18, www.imf.org/ external/pubs/ft/scr/2010/cr1086.pdf.

25 "Юрий Шафраник: Россия возвращает лидерские позиции на Ближнем Востоке," NIA Krasnoyarsk, June 1, 2010, https://24rus.ru/more.php?UID=55237.

26 Dafna Linzer, Jeff Larson and Michael Grabell, "Flight Records Say Russia Sent Syria Tons of Cash," ProPublica, November 26, 2012, www.propublica.org/article/ flight-records-list-russia-sending-tons-of-cash-to-syria.

27 "Factsheet: Syria–Russia Economic Relations," The Syria Report, May 2, 2017, accessed August 9, 2019.

28 Eli Lake, "Iran Spends Billions to Prop Up Assad. Yet Obama insists Iran support is a relative pittance," Bloomberg, June 9, 2015. https://www.bloomberg.com/opinion/ articles/2015-06-09/iran-spends-billions-to-prop-up-assad

29 "List of Russian companies involved in the Syrian market," The Syria Report, October 9, 2018, accessed August 9, 2019.

30 "Russian firms to rebuild war-torn Syria," RT, October 28, 2015, www.rt.com/business/319974-russia-syria-contracts-construction/.

31 Author Interview with Nikolay Kozhanov, May 14, 2020.

32 Patrick Wintour "Russia should foot Syria reconstruction bill, European leaders say," November 29, 2016, www.theguardian.com/world/2016/nov/29/russia-should-foot-syria-reconstruction-bill-european-leaders-say.

33 Home page of the company: Адыг-Юрак, АО, https://sbis.ru/contragents/0105005310/010501001.

34 Valery Dzutsati, "Adygea Can Accommodate Hundreds of Circassian Refugees from Syria," Eurasia Daily Monitor, Jamestown, Volume 10, Issue 40, March 4, 2013, https://jamestown.org/program/adygea-can-accommodate-hundreds-of-circassian-refugees-from-syria-2/.

35 "Сирия с помощью России начала реконструкцию НПЗ в г Хомс. Почему?" Neftegaz.ru, June 6, 2018, https://neftegaz.ru/news/neftechim/200944-siriya-s-pomoshchyu-rossii-nachala-rekonstruktsiyu-npz-v-g-khoms-pochemu/.

36 "Russia to build Syrian electronic government," The Syria Report, December 13, 2017, accessed August 9, 2019.

37 Ilya Khrennikov, "Made in Syria: Putin Hotspots Spur Shoe Sales for Russian Chain," Bloomberg, May 22, 2017, see www.bloomberg.com/news/articles/2017-05-23/made-in-syria-putin-hotspots-spur-shoe-sales-for-russian-chain.

38 Ilya Khrennikov, "Made in Syria: Putin Hotspots Spur Shoe Sales for Russian Chain," Bloomberg, May 22, 2017, See www.bloomberg.com/news/articles/2017-05-23/made-in-syria-putin-hotspots-spur-shoe-sales-for-russian-chain.

39 "ТЭК, автомобили, банки: российские компании готовы работать в Сирии," https://rueconomics.ru/227744-tek-mashiny-banki-rossiiskie-kompanii-gotovy-rabotat-v-sirii.

40 Ivan Denezhkin, "ТЭК, автомобили, банки: российские компании готовы работать в Сирии," Rueconomics.ru, February 16, 2017 https://rueconomics.ru/227744-tek-mashiny-banki-rossiiskiekompanii- gotovy-rabotat-v-sirii Reposted on Shafranik's page with title "Готовы работать в Сирии," https://shafranik.ru/node/16177.

41 "Syria cedes oil and gas assets to 'Putin's cook'—report" The Syria Report, December 12, 2017, accessed August 9, 2019.

42 "Немного бизнеса в сирийской войне," Fontanka.ru, June 26, 2018, www.fontanka.ru/2017/06/26/084/. Irina Malkova, Anastasia Stogney, Anastasia Yakoreva, "Russian mercenary army financier made an oil deal with Syria just before clash with US troops," February 27, 2018, https://thebell.io/en/russian-mercenary-army-financier-made-oil-deal-syria-just-clash-u-s-troops/.

43 "Russian delegation in Syria to talk reconstruction," France 24, December 18, 2017 https://www.france24.com/en/20171218-russian-delegation-syria-talk-reconstruction.

44 Annia Ciezadlo "The most unconventional weapon in Syria: Wheat," *The Washington Post*, December 18, 2015, www.washingtonpost.com/opinions/the-most-unconventional-weapon-in-syria-wheat/2015/12/18/781a0ae0-9cf4-11e5-bce4-708fe33e3288_story.html.

45 Kinda Makieh, "Exclusive: Syria signs 3 million ton wheat contract with Russia," September 29, 2017, www.reuters.com/article/us-syria-russia-wheat-exclusive/exclusive-syria-signs-3-million-ton-wheat-contract-with-russia-idUSKCN1C420B.

46 "Russian trading house becomes key player in Syrian–Russian economic relationship," June 13, 2017, The Syria Report, accessed August 9, 2019.

47 "Exclusive: Syria Calls off Mysterious Million Tonne Russian Wheat Deal," Reuters, December 13, 2017, www.reuters.com/article/us-syria-russia-wheat/exclusive-syria-calls-off-mysterious-million-tonne-russian-wheat-deal-idUSKCN1BO10S.

48 "Две российские компании получили право нефтедобычи в Сирии," Regnum, December 16, 2019, https://regnum.ru/news/economy/2809290.html.

49 "Сирия стучится в Таможенный союз," July 27, 2010, Neftegaz.ru, https://neftegaz.ru/news/politics/268535-siriya-stuchitsya-v-tamozhennyy-soyuz/, https://pronedra.ru/kto-vxodit-v-spisok-stran-eaes-v-2019-godu-383793-pid-dj.html.

50 Angus McDowall, Kinda Makiehm "Syrian Trade Fair Shows Road to Recovery Still Strewn with Debris of War," Reuters, September 7, 2018, www.reuters.com/article/us-mideast-crisis-syria-international-fa/syrian-trade-fair-shows-road-to-recovery-still-strewn-with-debris-of-war-idUSKCN1LN13H.

51 "Russia, Syria Ink Energy Cooperation Agreement—Ministry," Reuters, January 31, 2018, https://af.reuters.com/article/energyOilNews/idAFL8N1PQ7GE.

52 Jaime Dettmer, "Россия и Иран конкурируют за влияние в Сирии," Voice of America (VOA), May 2, 2019, www.golos-ameriki.ru/a/syria-russia-iran/4900974.html.

53 Vanand Meliksetian, "What Happens to Syrian Oil Post-Civil War?" Oilprice.com, August 11, 2018, https://oilprice.com/Energy/Energy-General/What-Happens-To-Syrian-Oil-Post-Civil-War.html.

54 Pavel Kazarin, "Нефть в обмен на наемников: зачем России война в Сирии," Krym Realii, RFE/RL, https://ru.krymr.com/a/29194217.html.

55 Vladimir Vasiliev, "Война в Сирии: всё-таки из-за нефти," Regnum, August 30, 2018, https://regnum.ru/news/polit/2472991.html.

56 Ibid.

57 "Россия и Сирия обсудили сотрудничество в сфере телекоммуникаций," January 19, 2018, https://digital.gov.ru/ru/events/37803/. "Россия поможет Сирии восстановить телекоммуникации," TVC, January 19, 2018, www.tvc.ru/news/show/id/131128.

58 Kathrin Hille, Henry Foy and Max Seddon "Russian Business First in Line for Spoils of Syrian War," March 2, 2018, *Financial Times*, www.ft.com/content/c767cfba-1c9a-11e8-aaca-4574d7dabfb6.

59 Author interview with Nikolai Kozhanov, May 14, 2020.

60 "Russian Ambitions for Syrian Phosphates," *The Syrian Observer*, August 3, 2018, https://syrianobserver.com/EN/features/19755/russian_ambitions_syrian_phosphates.html.

61 Anastasia Lyalikova,"Герой Сирии: заработает ли Тимченко на добыче фосфатов под Пальмирой," Forbes, April 21, 2018, www.forbes.ru/milliardery/360473-geroy-sirii-zarabotaet-li-timchenko-na-dobyche-fosfatov-pod-palmiroy.

62 "Russian Ambitions for Syrian Phosphates," The Syrian Observer, August 3, 2018, https://syrianobserver.com/EN/features/19755/russian_ambitions_syrian_phosphates.html.

63 "Сирия готова начать поставку фосфатов в Крым," RIA Novosti, December 28, 2018, https://ria.ru/20181228/1548862364.html. "Александр Новак и Министр электроэнергетики Сирийской Арабской Республики Мухаммед Зухейр Харбутли подписали Дорожную карту сотрудничества в сфере энергетики," Russian Ministry of Energy announcement, January 31 2018, https://minenergo.gov.ru/node/10442.

64 "From Crimea, Syria and Russian Sign New Economic Deals", The Syria Report, April 24, 2018, accessed August 9, 2019.

65 Ibid.

66 "В промышленную "дорожную карту" России и Сирии вошли 30 проектов," RIA Novosti, December 14, 2018, https://ria.ru/20181214/1547993370.html.

67 "Lavrov blasts West's refusal to participate in Syria's reconstruction," TASS, December 28, 2018, https://tass.com/politics/1038332.

68 Igor A. Matveev, "Russia, Lebanon seek synergy in projects to rebuild Syria," Al Monitor, August 8, 2019, www.al-monitor.com/pulse/originals/2019/08/russia-seek-embrace-lebanon-syria-reconstruction-plan.html.

69 "Syria parliament okays Russian lease of Tartus port: state media," France 24, June 12, 2019 https://www.france24.com/en/20190612-syria-parliament-okays-russian-lease-tartus-port-statemedia artus port: state media - France 24.

70 "Syria, Crimea sign agreement on enhancing economic, trade cooperation," Syrian Arab News Agency (SANA), August 29, 2019, www.sana.sy/en/?p=172282.

71 "Ministry of Oil Signs Three Contracts With Russian Companies", The Syrian Observer, September 5, 2019, https://syrianobserver.com/EN/news/52756/ministry-of-oil-signs-three-contracts-with-russian-companies.html.

72 Andrei Ontikov,"Снова за нефтью: США усиливают присутствие на месторождениях Сирии," August 1, 2019, https://iz.ru/904635/andrei-ontikov/snova-za-neftiu-ssha-usilivaiut-prisutstvie-na-mestorozhdeniiakh-sirii.

73 "Assad must take control of northern Syria: Russian FM," Rudaw, January 16, 2019, www.rudaw.net/english/middleeast/syria/16012019.

74 "США крадут нефть Сирии: ФАН публикует маршрут американских нефтевозов," Federal News Agency, February 14, 2019, https://riafan.ru/1150747-ssha-kradut-neft-sirii-fan-publikuet-marshrut-amerikanskikh-neftevozov.

75 *Rebuilding Syria: The Middle East's Next Power Game?* Edited by Eugenio Dacrema and Valeria Talbot, Kindle edition, First edition: September 2019, Locations-830.

76 "Вот и всё: Россия приготовилась качать нефть из Сирии, США остались ни с чем." Livejournal blog, https://matveychev-oleg.livejournal.com/7306321.html.

77 Nikolay Kozhanov, May 14, 2020.

78 "Caesar Syria Civilian Protection Act," Fact Sheet, office of the Spokesperson, June 17, 2020, www.state.gov/caesar-syria-civilian-protection-act/.

Conclusion

1 Sirwan Kajjo, "Russia Seeks to Build Local Force in Northeast Syria," Voice of America (VOA) December 19, 2019, https://www.voanews.com/extremism-watch/russia-seeks-build-local-force-northeast-syria.

2 Josie Ensor, "Three million in rebel Syria seek shelter in area size of Somerset as Idlib turns into open air refugee camp," The Telegraph, February 11, 2020, https://www.telegraph.co.uk/news/2020/02/11/three-million-rebel-syria-seek-shelter-area-size-somerset-idlib/.

3 Fabrice Balanche, "Idlib May Become the Next Gaza Strip," The Washington Institute for Near East Policy, Policywatch, March 26, 2020, https://www.washingtoninstitute.org/policy-analysis/idlib-may-become-next-gaza-strip.

4 Stephen R. Covington, The Culture of Strategic Thought Behind Russia's Modern Approaches to Warfare, Defense and Intelligence Projects Belfer Center for Science and International Affairs Harvard Kennedy School, pp. 39–40 https://www.belfercenter.org/sites/default/files/legacy/files/Culture%20of%20Strategic%20Thought%203.pdf.

5 Fouad Ajami, *The Foreigner's Gift: The Americans, the Arabs, and the Iraqis in Iraq*, Free Press: New York, 2006.

6 Sarah Dadouch and Asser Khattab "UN Announces Formation of Syrian Constitutional Committee," September 23, 2019, *The Washington Post*, www.washingtonpost.com/world/middle_east/un-announces-formation-of-syrian-constitutional-committee/2019/09/23/73c1b5c0-de0d-11e9-be7f-4cc85017c36f_story.html.

7 Andrew Osborn and Alexander Marrow, "Russia sets up helicopter base in northern Syria after US exit," Reuters, November 14, 2019, https://uk.reuters.com/article/

uk-syria-security-russia/russia-sets-up-helicopter-base-in-northern-syria-after-u-s-exit-idUKKBN1XO0Y3.

8 Transcript: Maximum Pressure on the Assad Regime for its Chemical Weapons Use and Other Atrocities, online event with Michael Doran and David Asher, The Hudson Institute, May 12, 2020, www.hudson.org/research/16032-transcript-maximum-pressure-on-the-assad-regime-for-its-chemical-weapons-use-and-other-atrocities.

9 See for example Rose Gottemoeller, Thomas Graham, Fiona Hill, Jon Huntsman Jr., Robert Levgold and Thomas R. Pickering, "It's Time to Rethink Our Russia Policy," Politico, August 5, 2020, https://www.politico.com/news/magazine/2020/08/05/open-letter-russia-policy-391434.

Index

Graphs are given in italics.